GOD'S LITTLE DEVOTIONAL BOOK

FOR MOMS

RACINE, WI

God's Little Devotional Book for Moms
ISBN: 979-8-88898-091-0 - *Paperback*
ISBN: 979-8-88898-092-7 - *Hardcover*
ISBN: 979-8-88898-093-4 - *Ebook*
Copyright © 2023 by Honor Books, Racine, WI

INTRODUCTION

Today's busy moms often have a problem: not enough time to read. *God's Little Devotional Book for Moms* provides a good solution!

Each of the devotionals presented on the following pages can be read within a matter of a few minutes, yet each gives to the reader truth and inspiration to last all day. Each is based not only upon a positive and beneficial quotation, but also on a passage from God's Word. As such, these devotionals are not only timely, but timeless. Indeed, they each have an *eternal* spiritual truth embedded in them.

With moral training lacking in so many areas of our culture today, the stories and illustrations presented here provide a means for a woman to reinforce within herself what she knows to be good, right and just. Many of the illustrations are ones a mother might share with her children, regardless of their ages.

The Word of God gives us the principle for acquiring God's truth in our lives: "For precept must be upon precept, precept upon precept; line upon line, line upon line; here a little, and there a little" (Isaiah 28:10). *God's Little Devotional Book for Moms*— guaranteed to provide insight and inspiration to mothers everywhere!

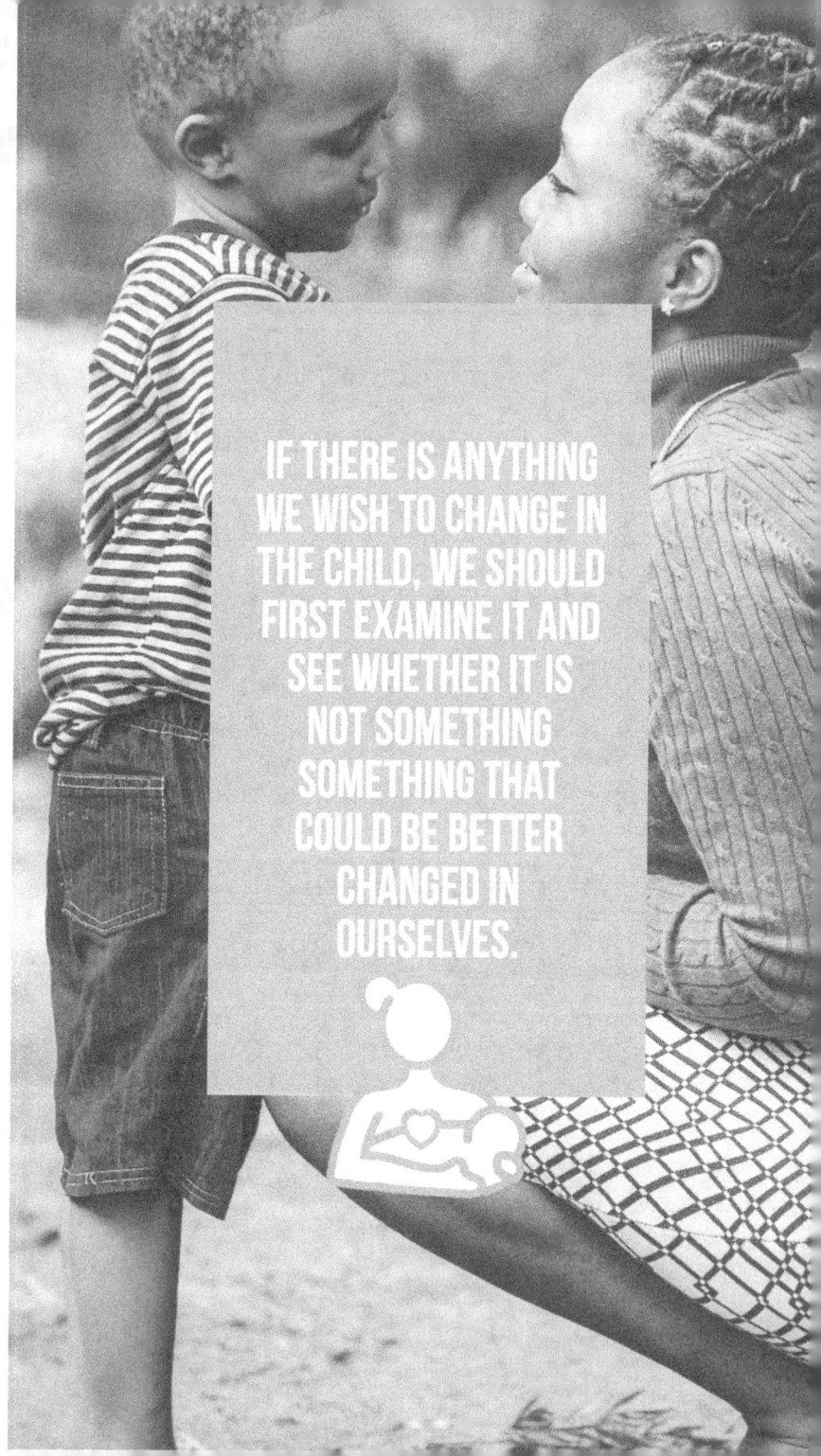

IF THERE IS ANYTHING WE WISH TO CHANGE IN THE CHILD, WE SHOULD FIRST EXAMINE IT AND SEE WHETHER IT IS NOT SOMETHING SOMETHING THAT COULD BE BETTER CHANGED IN OURSELVES.

Coming down the main walk from the capitol in Washington, DC, toward Pennsylvania Avenue, one encounters a group of steps. In watching the crowds go up and down those steps, a man once observed that people were continually stumbling on them, while they didn't seem to stumble on any other flights of stairs in the city.

He called the attention to the capitol architect to the matter. The architect couldn't believe this was so until he observed the people for himself. He was was amazed at the number of people who stumbled in going up the steps. "I cannot account for it," he said, "I spent weeks in arranging this steps. I had wooden models of them put down at my own place, and I walked over them day after day until I felt sure they were perfect."

A person hearing him speak asked, "Isn't one of your legs shorter than the other, Mr. Olmstead?" Sure enough . . . the architect had designed the steps of the capitol based on his own inequality of limbs, and had thus made the stairs truly suitable only for those with a similar condition!

First take the beam out of your own eye, and then you will see clearly to take out the speck that is in your brother's eye.

LUKE 6:42C AMP

THE DARN TROUBLE WITH CLEANING THE HOUSE IS IT GETS DIRTY THE NEXT DAY ANYWAY, SO SKIP A WEEK IF YOU HAVE TO. THE CHILDREN ARE THE MOST IMPORTANT THING.

During the Christmas season, a bubbly four-year-old girl became caught up in the excitement of the season, especially as she saw the number of presents under the tree slowly increasing as Christmas Day approached. Several times during a day, she would pick up various gifts, examine the box closely—shaking it and looking at it from all angles—and then try to guess what was inside the package.

One evening as she picked up a box, its big red bow fell from it. In a burst of inspiration, she picked up the bow and stuck it on top of her head. With a twinkle in her eyes and a smile as bright as the star atop the Christmas tree, she twirled and announced to her parents, "Mommy and Daddy, look at me! I'm a present!"

This little girl's words were more true than she realized. Our children are the most wonderful gifts God has ever given to us. Take time today not only to admire your child's talents and achievements . . . not only to enjoy your child's personality . . . but to truly delight in the fact that your child is a present from the Creator to you and your family!

Lo, children are an heritage of the Lord: and the fruit of the womb is his reward.

PSALM 127:3

MAN HAS HIS WILL— BUT WOMAN HAS HER WAY.

A man listened with great admiration to a well-known and very popular leader make a speech at a banquet. He not only hung on every word the speaker said, but studied his appearance. He felt honored to be seated next to the speaker's wife and he candidly told her that her husband was one of his heroes.

During the speech, the man noticed that the speaker had monogrammed socks. Intrigued by this, he looked closer and saw that the monogram had four letters, rather than the usual two or three initials. Furthermore, the letters didn't seem to have any relationship to the man's name—they were "TGIF."

After the speech was over and the man had complimented the speaker, he turned to the wife and said, "I couldn't help but notice the monogram on your husband's socks. Is there some reason he has chosen 'Thank Goodness It's Friday' for a monogram?"

She shook her head and said, "Oh, that's not what the letters mean. The monograms are there to help him get dressed. They stand for 'Toes Go In First!'"

A merry heart doeth good like a medicine.

PROVERBS 17:22

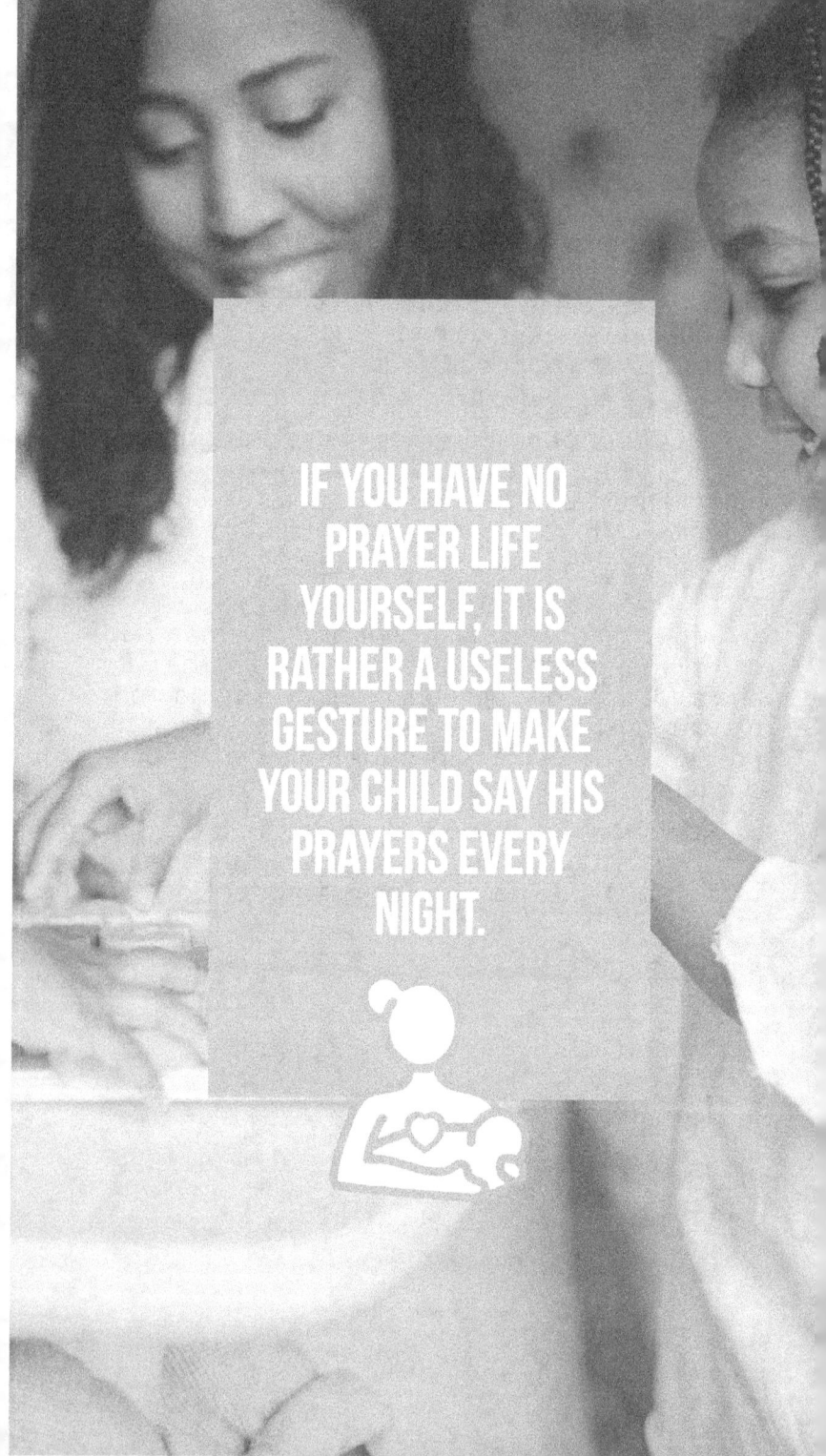

IF YOU HAVE NO PRAYER LIFE YOURSELF, IT IS RATHER A USELESS GESTURE TO MAKE YOUR CHILD SAY HIS PRAYERS EVERY NIGHT.

The actor known as Mr. T. gave an unusual tribute to his mother. He said that he wanted to recognize "her hands, her feet, and her knees."

He called attention to his mother's feet because they had taken her across town to do domestic work—her hands and knees used to scrub floors and toilets. He also said, "She used her feet to walk against my sickness when my body was ill and racked with pain. It was my mother who walked the floor with me, on her feet all night long, talking to God; then she would get down on her knees to pray some more, still holding me in her hands." He adds, "I guess the only payment she ever wanted was for me to grow up and carry on her teachings . . . to share, to love, to be kind and always take God with me wherever I go . . . She always said, 'Don't be bitter, don't hate, don't hold grudges, and never forget to pray.'

"It's so hard to try to describe my mother's endurance, her patience, her love, her feelings for her family, her spiritual convictions, her right to be, her loyalty and her pride in parenthood. I will just say that my mother was God-sent."

Feet to walk, hands to carry, knees to bend in prayer. What a legacy for any mother to give a child!

Pray without ceasing.

1 THESSALONIANS 5:17

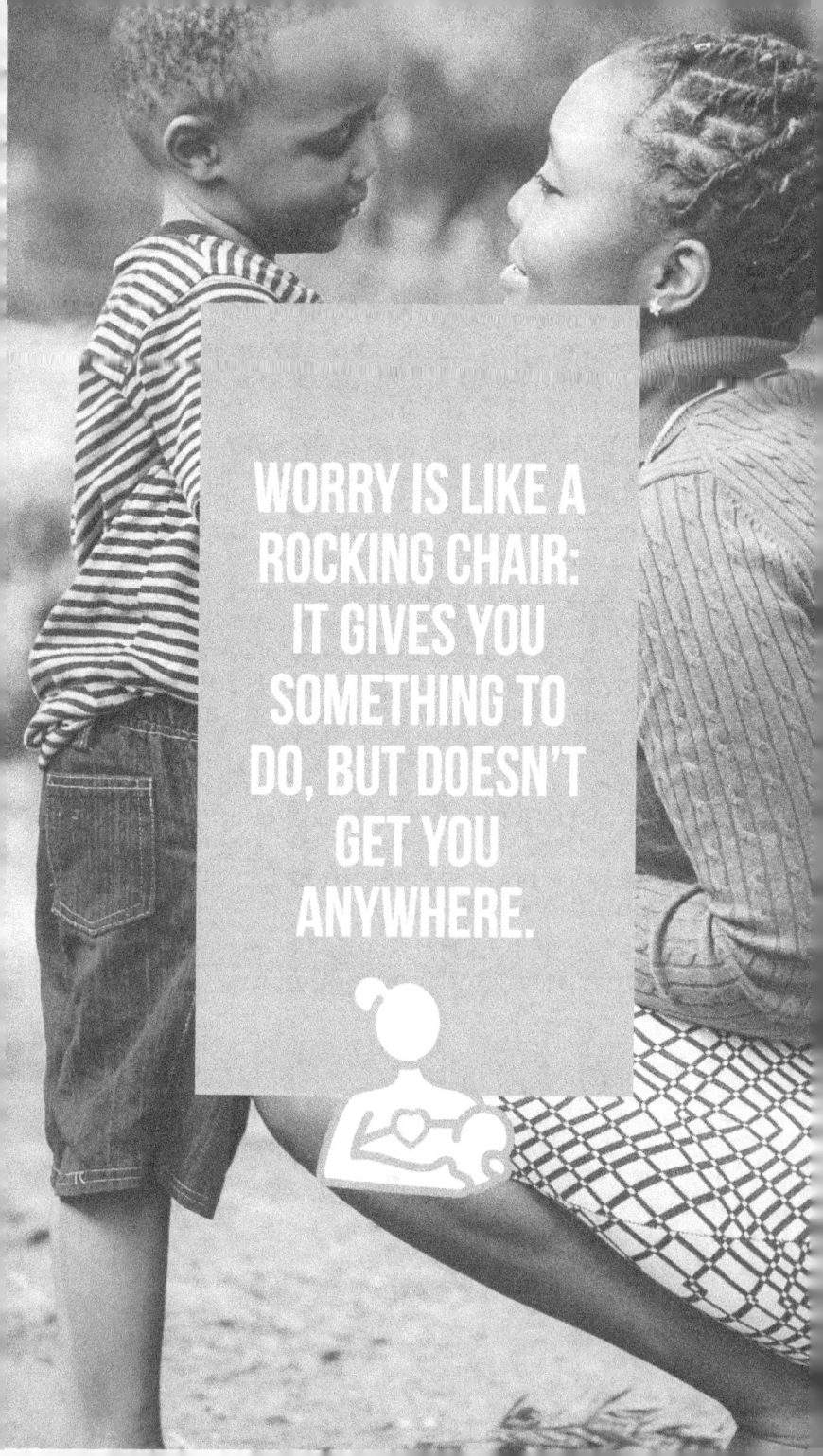

WORRY IS LIKE A ROCKING CHAIR: IT GIVES YOU SOMETHING TO DO, BUT DOESN'T GET YOU ANYWHERE.

A philosophical clock—one capable of deep pondering and meditation—once spent a great deal of time thinking about its own future. It reasoned that it had to tick twice each second. *How much ticking might that be?* the clock questioned.

The clock calculated that it would tick 120 times each minute ... which was 7,200 times every hour. In the twenty-four hours of a day it would tick 172,800 times. This meant 63,072,000 times every year. By this time, the clock had come to perspire profusely at the very' thought.

Finally the clock calculated that in a ten- year period it would have to tick 630,720,000 times—and at that point the clock collapsed from nervous exhaustion!

An equally scientific and philosophical person has concluded that ninety-five percent of all that we worry about happening ... doesn't. Of the five percent that does happen ... four out of five times, things turn out much better than anticipated, including a few outright blessings! In the end, only one percent of all the bad that we think *might happen* actually does, and of this it's rarely *as bad* as feared. So, in the words of a Bobby McFarrin song, "Don't worry! Be happy!"

Casting the whole of your care—all your anxieties, all your worries, all your concerns, once and for all—on Him; for he cares for you affectionately, and cares for you watchfully.

1 PETER 5:7 AMP

A MAN'S WORK IS FROM SUN TO SUN, BUT A MOTHER'S WORK IS NEVER DONE.

A businessman called his wife one clay to get her permission for him to bring home a visiting foreigner as a dinner guest that night. At the time, the wife had three children in school and one preschooler at home, so she had a full workload on any given day, apart from entertaining strangers. Still, she consented and the meal she prepared was both delicious and graciously served. The foreigner, an important official in Spain, had a delightful time and thanked the couple repeatedly for inviting him into their home and treating him to a home-cooked meal and an evening of family warmth and fellowship.

Years later, friends of this family went to Spain as missionaries. Their work was brought to a standstill, however, by government regulations. This particular Spanish official got word that the missionaries were friends of the couple who had hosted him in such a loving manner, and he used his influence to clear away the restrictions on their behalf. A church exists today in that province of Spain, due in part to the setting of one extra place at one dinner table!

As busy as you may be today, take time for the people God may bring across your path. Who knows what plan God may have for both of your futures.

... her candle goeth not out by night.

PROVERBS 31:18

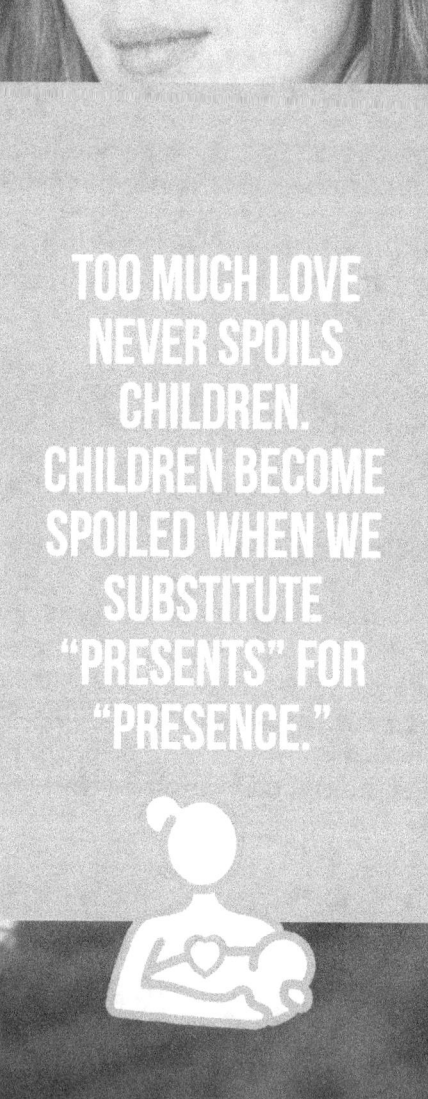

TOO MUCH LOVE NEVER SPOILS CHILDREN. CHILDREN BECOME SPOILED WHEN WE SUBSTITUTE "PRESENTS" FOR "PRESENCE."

n 1971, child-care expert Penelope Leach had a crisis that changed her life, and also many of her opinions about the needs and growth of children. Leach was well launched into a promising career as a child-development researcher when her two-year-old son, Matthew, nearly died of viral meningitis. While allowing her time to care for her sick child, Leach's employer also pressed her to return to work as quickly as possible. So as soon as Matthew was out of danger, Leach left him with a babysitter and returned to her job. She says, "I just took it for granted that's what I had to do."

Physically, Matthew was well, but Leach found that "you could reduce him to tears playing peek-aboo. The only person he was okay with was me." So, two months later, Leach made another decision—this time to quit her job and devote herself to the "total health" of her child. Today, she looks back with embarrassment that she ever allowed her son to reach such a low point in his emotional growth. She recalls, "Quitting was tough, but it wasn't as if we were going to starve." What *didn't* happen as the result of her quitting was that Matthew didn't starve ... for the assurance, comfort, attention, and love he needed.

We loved you so much that we were delighted to share with you not only the gospel of God but our lives as well, because you had become so dear to us.

1 THESSALONIANS 2:8 NIV

Humorist Erma Bombeck once wrote: "Every mother has a favorite child. She cannot help it. She is only human. I have mine—the child for whom I feel a special closeness, with whom I share a love that no one else could possibly understand. My favorite child is the one who was too sick to eat ice cream at his birthday party . . . who had measles at Christmas . . . who wore leg braces to bed because he toed in . . . who had a fever in the middle of the night, the asthma attack, the child in my arms at the emergency ward.

"My favorite child is the one who messed up the piano recital, misspelled committee in a spelling bee, ran the wrong way with the football, and had his bike stolen because he was careless.

"My favorite child was selfish, immature, bad-tempered and self-centered. He was vulnerable, lonely, unsure of what he was doing in this world—and quite wonderful.

"All mothers have their favorite child. It is always the same one: the one who needs you at the moment. Who needs you for whatever reason—to cling to, to shout at, to hurt, to hug, to flatter, to reverse charges to, to unload on—but mostly just to be there."

Be ye therefore merciful, as your Father also is merciful.

LUKE 6:36

Every morning a mother announced, "This is not a restaurant; there are no menus." She still got orders as she packed school lunches for all her children.

"Peanut butter and jelly?" one would cry. "Oh no! Why can't we ever have cheese."

That child seemed to have totally forgotten that yesterday's sandwich was cheese and he had complained it wasn't peanut butter.

"Grape jelly?" another asked. "Can't we ever get strawberry?"

Yet, another would say, "Leave the jelly off mine, but can I have two sandwiches?"

Over the years, the mother felt confident that she had finally learned what each child liked. Her youngest, Jim, always seemed to return home with an empty sack, a fact she took as a high compliment. Until one day . . . when she handed Jim his sack and said, "Enjoy your lunch." He replied, "Oh, I'm not gonna eat this, Mom. I'm trading with Josh. His Mom bakes cookies and he told me he'd trade lunches today if I let him play with my football. Isn't that great? I can hardly wait!"

"Does anybody ever want to trade for your lunch?" the mother asked hopefully.

"Naw," the boy replied. "But don't worry about me. I still eat well. Nobody else in my class has a football."

A merry heart doeth good like a medicine.

PROVERBS 17:22

MOTHERHOOD
IS A
PARTNERSHIP
WITH GOD.

Wesley L. Gustafson once related that when he was a boy—and as long as he was living at home as a young man—his mother would never go to bed until he was safely in the house. Even if he was traveling and didn't get home until near dawn, he would creep up the stairs to his room, only to find that the light was still on in his mother's room. Putting his head against the door of her room, he would hear her praying for him. Then, after he was in bed, she would come into his room. "Wes," she would call his name softly again and again.

He would pretend to be asleep and would not respond. Feeling assured that her son was asleep, she would stand by the window and pray audibly, "O God, save my boy." Gustafson said about this, "I myself am quite sure that the prayers of a good mother never die."

Another mother, Susanna Wesley, spent one hour each day praying for her children—even though she had seventeen children for whom to care! Two of her sons are credited with bringing revival to England.

Perhaps the most beneficial thing you can do for your child is to pray for your child diligently, faithfully, daily, and with detail.

For this child I prayed; and the Lord hath given me my petition which I asked of him: Therefore also I have lent him to the Lord; as long as he liveth he shall be lent to the Lord.

1 SAMUEL 1:27-28

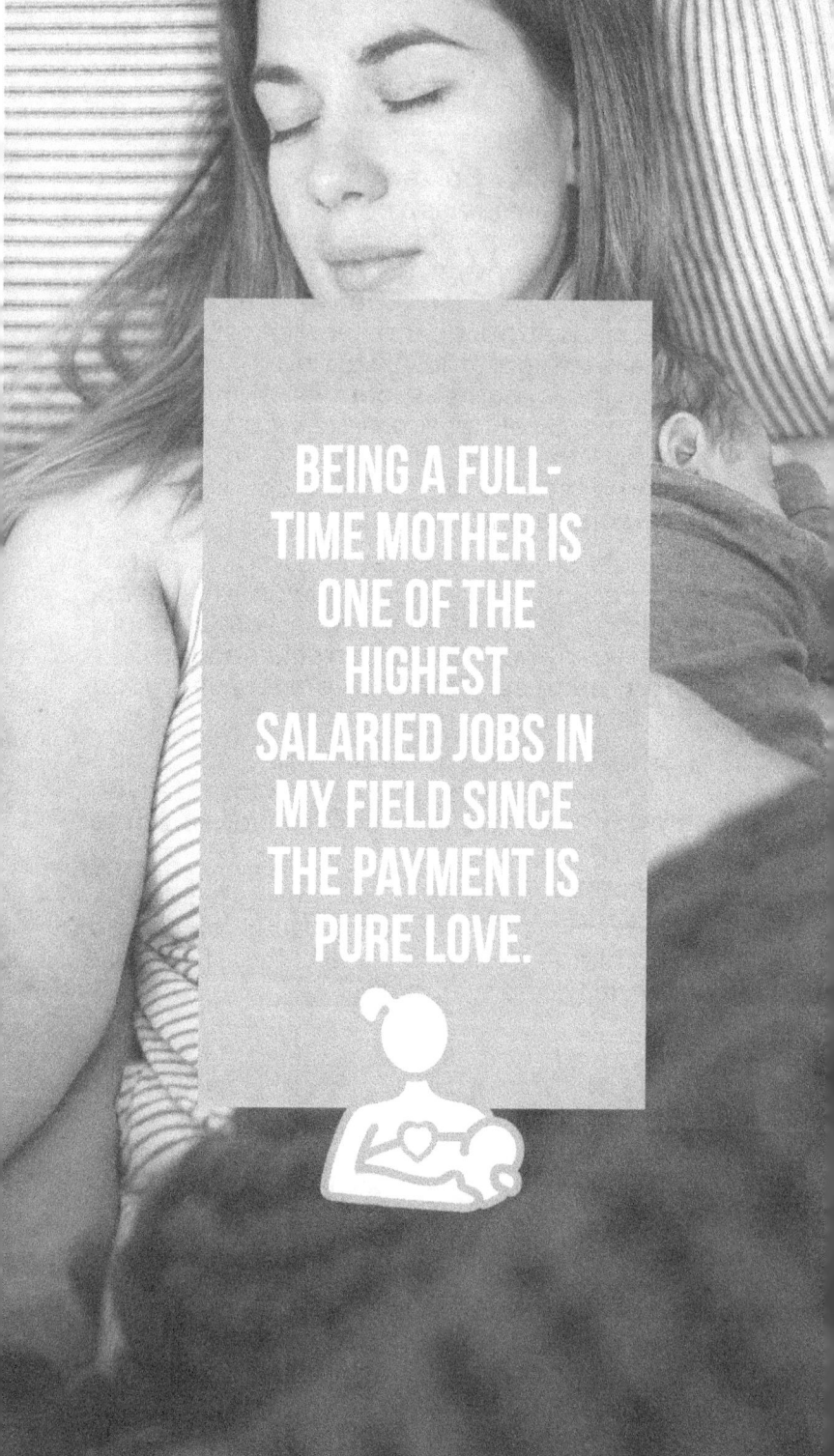

Perhaps the most famous "mother" in the world is Mother Teresa. As Sister Teresa in 1948, she was given permission to leave her order of nearly twenty years and travel to India. On her first day in Calcutta, Teresa picked up five abandoned children and brought them to her "school." Before the year ended, she had 41 students learning about hygiene in her classroom in a public park. Shortly thereafter, a new congregation was approved. Mother Teresa quickly named it "Missionaries of Charity." Within two years, their attention had turned to the care of the dying.

Once a poor beggar was picked up as he was dying in a pile of rubbish. He was reduced by suffering and hunger to a mere specter. Mother Teresa took him to the Home for the Dying and put him in bed. When she tried to wash him, she discovered his body was covered with worms. Pieces of skin came off as she washed him. For a brief moment, the man revived. In his semiconscious state, he asked, "Why do you do it?" Mother Teresa responded with the two words that are her hallmark: "For love."

Ask any mother why she does what she does and you are likely to receive the same answer. Love is both a mother's work . . . and a mother's reward.

For whatsoever a man soweth, that shall he also reap.

GALATIANS 6:7

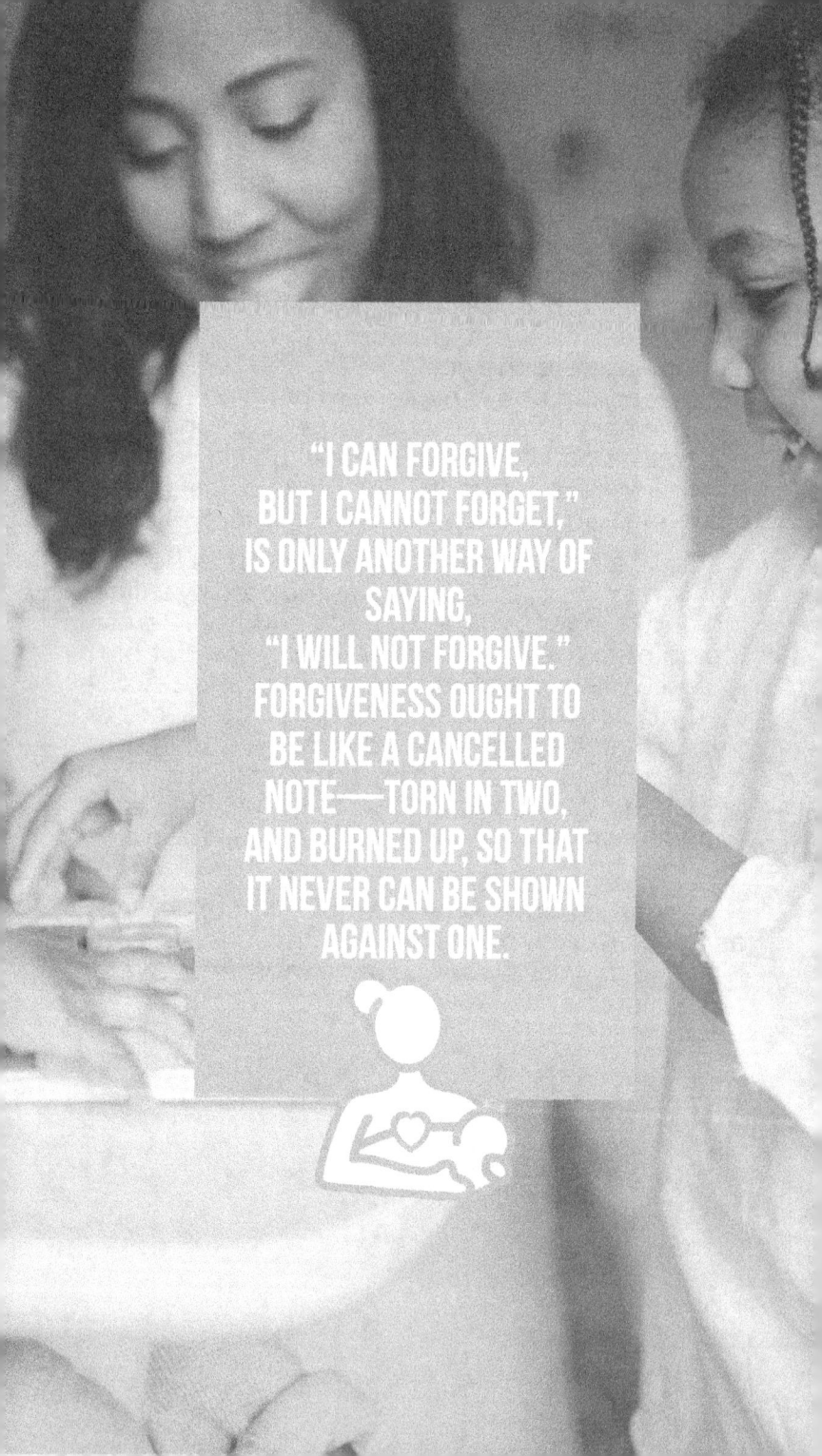

"I CAN FORGIVE,
BUT I CANNOT FORGET,"
IS ONLY ANOTHER WAY OF
SAYING,
"I WILL NOT FORGIVE."
FORGIVENESS OUGHT TO
BE LIKE A CANCELLED
NOTE—TORN IN TWO,
AND BURNED UP, SO THAT
IT NEVER CAN BE SHOWN
AGAINST ONE.

Years after her experience in a Nazi Germany concentration camp, Corrie ten Boom found herself standing face to face with one of the most cruel and heartless German guards she had ever met in the camps. This man had humiliated and degraded both her and her sister, jeering at them and visually "raping" them as they stood in the delousing shower.

Now he stood before her with an outstretched hand, asking, "Will you forgive me?"

Corrie said, "I stood there with coldness clutching at my heart, but I know that the will can function regardless of the temperature of the heart. I prayed, 'Jesus, help me!' Woodenly, mechanically I thrust my hand into the one stretched out to me and I experienced an incredible thing. The current started in my shoulder, raced down into my arm and sprang into our clutched hands. Then this warm reconciliation seemed to flood my whole being, bringing tears to my eyes. 'I forgive you, brother,' I cried with my whole heart. For a long moment we grasped each other's hands, the former guard, the former prisoner. I have never known the love of God so intensely as I did in that moment!"

When we forgive we set a prisoner free—ourselves!

And be ye kind one to another, tenderhearted, forgiving one another, even as God for Christ's sake hath forgiven you.
EPHESIANS 4:32

MANY PARENTS ARE FINDING OUT THAT A PAT ON THE BACK HELPS DEVELOP CHARACTER— IF GIVEN OFTEN ENOUGH, EARLY ENOUGH, AND LOW ENOUGH.

A number of years ago, a magnificent diamond was found in an African mine. It was presented to the king of England to be part of his crown. The king, in turn, sent it to Amsterdam to be cut. The stone was put into the hands of an expert lapidary. For weeks, he defects, its cleavage lines, its most minute details. Drawings and models were made of the stone. Then the day came when he cut a notch in this rock of priceless value, and struck a hard blow with one of his instruments. In less than a second, the superb jewel lay on his table in two pieces.

Was his blow a mistake? Far from it. In striking the rough, uncut stone with such precision, he brought forth from it two magnificent gems with perfect shape, radiance, and splendor. From a raw stone, he had created two priceless jewels. Rather than destroy the diamond, he had redeemed it to its full value.

The discipline we give our children must he done with like precision, thoughtfulness, and toward the same end—the bringing out of our child's best qualities so he or she might become a radiant "living stone" in God's eternal crown.

He that spareth his rod hateth his son: but he that loveth him chasteneth him betimes.

PROVERB 13:24

THE PERSONS HARDEST TO CONVINCE THEY'RE AT RETIREMENT AGE ARE CHILDREN AT BEDTIME.

The mother of three small children, each born only two years apart, often found herself exhausted by the end of a day. Along with the children's father, she had set strict rules that after a story time ... prayers ... one small drink of water ... and a final trip to the bathroom, each child must go to bed and stay there.

One night, after a particularly trying day, all three children were finally tucked into bed and the two parents headed to the kitchen for some cookies, milk, solitude, and a little time alone together. They had just started to relax when they suddenly found themselves surrounded by three little people, all standing in silence as they watched Mom and Dad each bite into a delicious home-baked cookie. Turning to Dad, Mom asked, "Well, do we relent, or do we stick with the rules?"

Before Dad could answer, their three-year-old daughter piped up, "Stick with the rules, Mom!"

Knowing that her daughter didn't really want to be sent back to bed, Mom asked, "And what exactly are those rules, dear?"

Her daughter replied without hesitation, "Share with one another."

Correct thy son, and he shall give thee rest; yea, he shall give delight unto thy soul.

PROVERBS 29:17

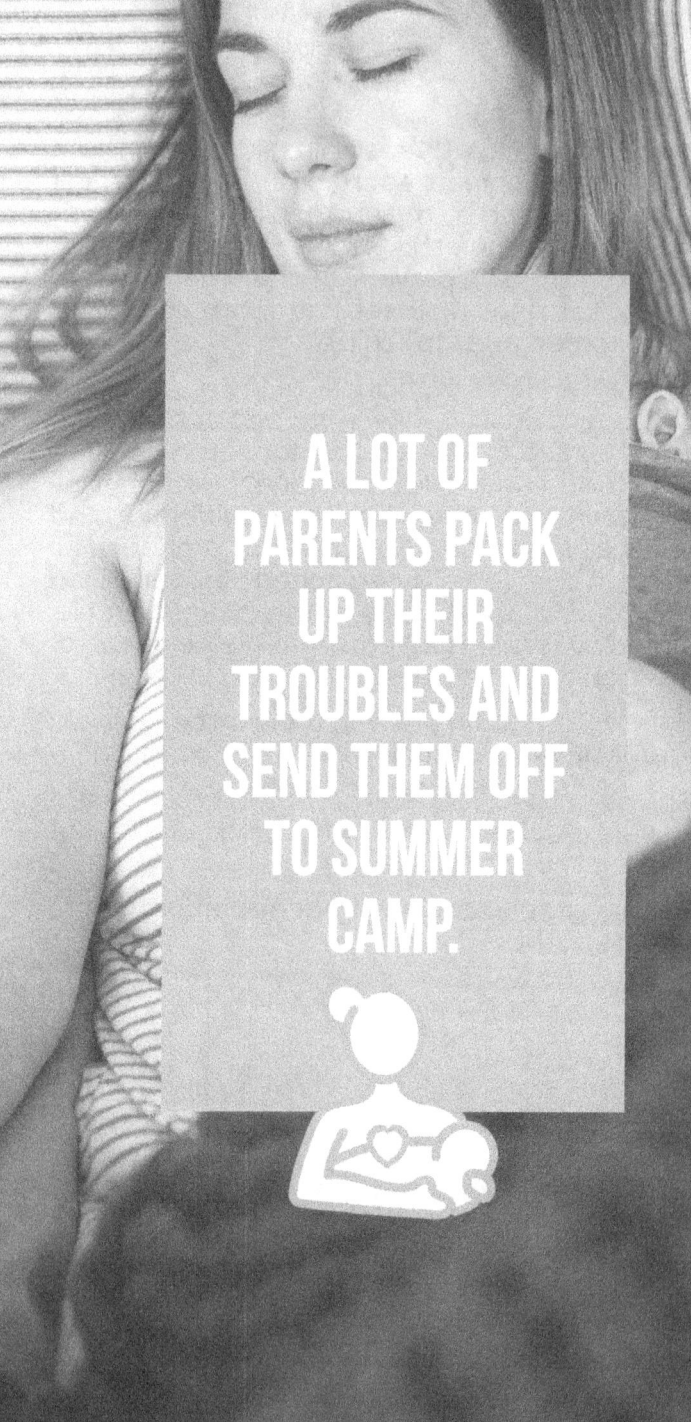

A LOT OF PARENTS PACK UP THEIR TROUBLES AND SEND THEM OFF TO SUMMER CAMP.

For all the "trouble" children can cause, they can also keep life "fun" with their unrehearsed quips and candid observations about life. Consider, for example, the little boy who was in a quandary about what to get his mother for Mother's Day.

The little girl next door asked, "You have any money?"

"Na-a-a," the boy said.

"What about making her something?" the girl asked.

"I'm not very good at arts and crafts," the boy admitted.

"I know!" the little girl said. "You could promise to keep your room clean and neat for a *whole week*. And if you really want to make it a special gift, you could remember to clean your goldfish bowl and put your dirty clothes in the laundry basket." The little boy just shrugged, unimpressed by her ideas. "Or," she continued doggedly, "You could go home the first time she calls you. Or . . . you could quit fighting with your brothers and sisters, especially at the dinner table."

The boy continued to shake his head. "No," he said. "I want to get my Mom something she will really use—and something she'll really *appreciate*!"

A merry heart doeth good like a medicine.

PROVERBS 17:22

CHILDREN ARE THE HANDS BY WHICH WE TAKE HOLD OF HEAVEN.

enry Ward Beecher, considered by many to be one of the most effective and powerful pulpit orators in the history of the United States, not only had a reputation for having an extremely sensitive heart, but also for having a great love of the sea. Many of his sermons were laced with loving anecdotes that had seafaring flavor.

Not only did Beecher make the statement on the facing page, but he had this to say about a mother's relationship with her child:

A babe is a mother's anchor. She cannot swing far from her moorings. And yet a true mother never lives so little in the present as when by the side of the cradle. Her thoughts follow the imagined future of her child. That babe is the boldest of pilots, and guides her fearless thoughts down through scenes of coming years. The old ark never made such voyages as the cradle daily makes.

What a wonderful image to think of a child as being on a voyage from Heaven, through life, to return to Heaven's port one day. What a challenge to think that our children have not come along to join us in our sail through life, but rather, we to join in their voyage!

Verily I say unto you, whosoever shall not receive the kingdom of God as a little child shall in no wise enter therein.

LUKE 18:17

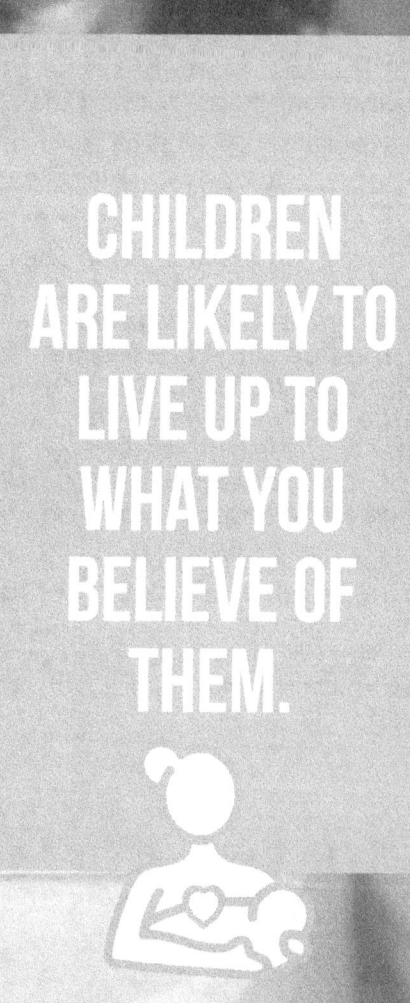

CHILDREN
ARE LIKELY TO
LIVE UP TO
WHAT YOU
BELIEVE OF
THEM.

A number of years ago, a young girl known as "Little Annie" was locked in the dungeon of a mental institution outside Boston —the only place, said the doctors, for the hopelessly insane. At times, Annie behaved like an animal, attacking those who came close to her "cage." At other times, she sat in a daze.

An elderly nurse held hope for all God's children and she began taking her lunch break in the dungeon, just outside Little Annie's cage. She hoped in some way to communicate love to her. One day she left her dessert—a brownie—next to Annie's cage. Annie made no response, but the next day, the nurse found the brownie had been eaten. Every Thursday thereafter, she brought a brownie to Annie.

As weeks passed, doctors noticed a change in Little Annie. After several months, they moved her upstairs. And eventually, the day came when this "hopeless case" was told she could return home. By that time, however, Annie was an adult and she chose to stay at the institution to help others. One of those she cared for, taught, and nurtured was Helen Keller. Little Annie's full and proper name was Anne Sullivan.

Your child becomes the embodiment of the love you pour into her. Pour generously!

For as he thinketh in his heart, so is he.

PROVERBS 23:7

During World War I, Eleanor Roosevelt made a valiant effort to conserve food, but things didn't turn out exactly as she had planned. In July 1917 the Food Administration picked their household as "a model for other large households." The *New York Times* sent a newswoman to interview Mrs. Roosevelt about her food-saving methods, and she later wrote: "Mrs. Roosevelt does the shopping, the cooks see that there is no food wasted, the laundress is sparing in her use of soap, each servant has a watchful eye … and all are encouraged to make helpful suggestions in the use of 'left-overs.'" The article ended with a quote from Mrs. Roosevelt: "Making ten servants help me do my saving has not only been possible but also highly profitable."

As might be expected, the story created a great deal of mirth in Washington. FDR joined in teasing his wife, saying, "Please have a photo taken showing the family, the ten cooperating servants, the scraps saved from the table, and the handbook." To which Mrs. Roosevelt moaned in reply, "I feel dreadfully about it because so much is not true and yet some of it I did say. I will never be caught again, that's sure, and Fd like to crawl away for shame."

When in doubt about what to say, say *nothing*.

In the multitude of words there wanteth not sin: but he that refrained his lips is wise.

PROVERBS 10:19

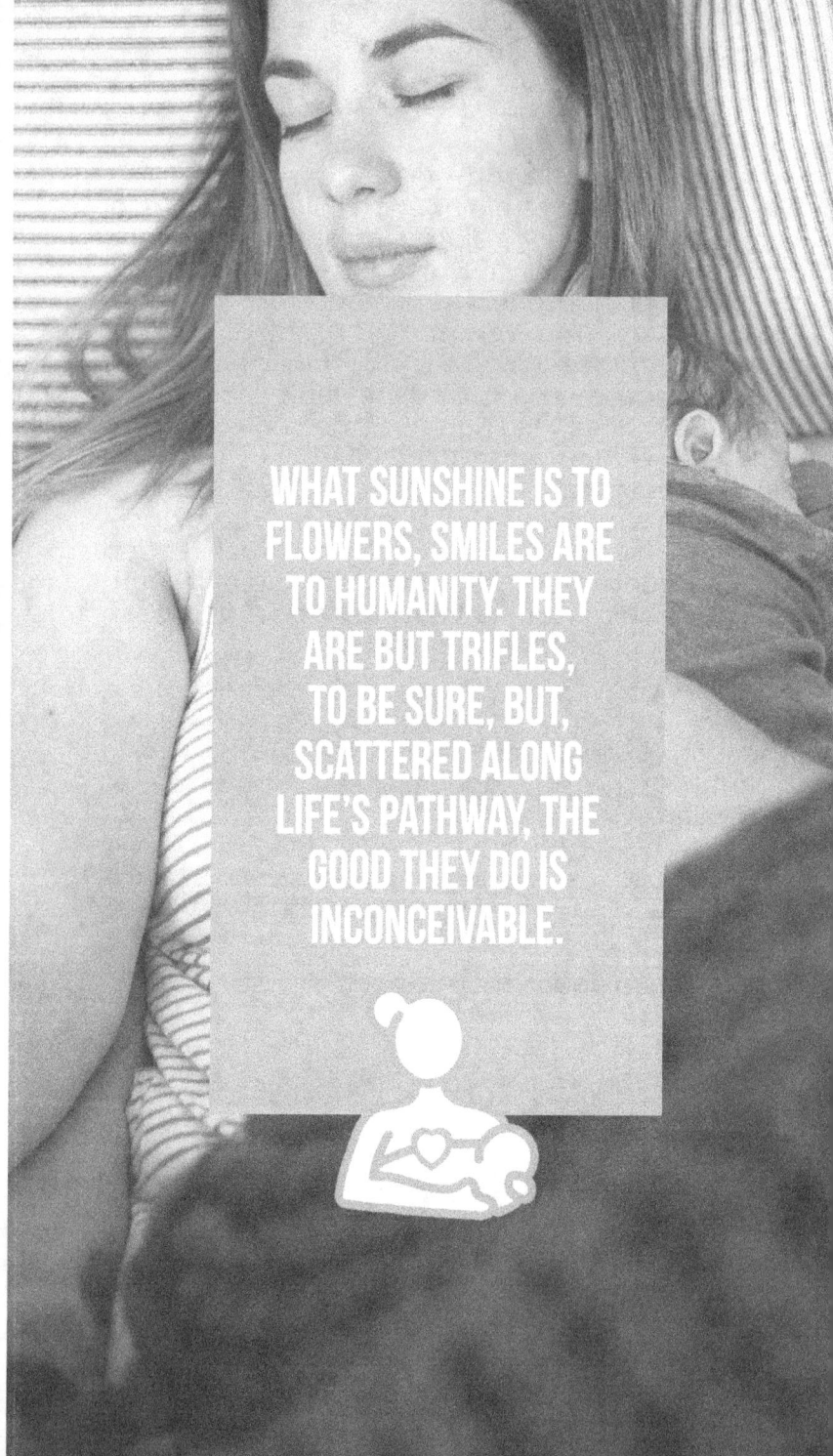

WHAT SUNSHINE IS TO
FLOWERS, SMILES ARE
TO HUMANITY. THEY
ARE BUT TRIFLES,
TO BE SURE, BUT,
SCATTERED ALONG
LIFE'S PATHWAY, THE
GOOD THEY DO IS
INCONCEIVABLE.

A pastor tells the story of how, during the twelve years of his pastorate at one particular church, he had a custom during the Sunday morning service of calling the children forward just before his sermon so that the children could go to a special "children's church" and hear a sermon geared especially for them. During their processional to their assembly hall, the children marched past the pulpit and the pastor made it a point to smile at each child. In return, he received their smiles. "It was one of the high points of the service," he recalled.

One day, however, the pastor apparently missed smiling at one child. A curly-headed four-year-old ran out of the procession and threw herself into the arms of her mother, sobbing as if her heart was broken.

After the service the pastor sought out the mother to find out what had happened. The mother explained that after her child had quieted, she asked what caused the tears. The child had said, "I smiled at God, but he didn't smile back at me!"

The pastor reflected, "To that child, I stood for God. I had failed with my smile, and the world went dark."

Smile at each person you meet today. You may never know how much you have brightened a life!

A happy heart makes the face cheerful.

PROVERBS 15:3 NIV

A LITTLE BOY'S MOTHER ONCE TOLD HIM THAT IT IS GOD WHO MAKES PEOPLE GOOD. HE LOOKED UP AND REPLIED, "YES, I KNOW IT IS GOD, BUT MOTHERS HELP A LOT."

Susie was orphaned after both of her parents died. With no other relatives to care for her, she was put into foster care. Eventually she came to live with the Weavers. Mrs. Weaver found Susie sullen, withdrawn, and uncommunicative. She asked to see her records. The first foster family wrote, "Susie is a quiet, shy girl." The second family wrote, "She obeys but she doesn't participate much in the family." Mrs. Weaver thought, *I doubt if Susie will be with us long.* Still, she decided to keep Susie through the Christmas holiday and then talk to her social worker about a transfer to another home.

At Christmas, the Weavers exchanged a number of lovely presents, including gifts for Susie. Then Susie handed Mrs. Weaver a brown paper sack with a rough drawing of a Christmas scene on it. She opened it to find a rhinestone necklace with a couple of stones missing and a little bottle of perfume, half empty. As she put on the necklace and dabbed perfume behind her ear, Susie said, "Mom's necklace looks good on you. You smell good like she did, too." Mrs. Weaver's heart melted. She vowed to renew her efforts to love Susie, and she succeeded! By the following Christmas, Susie had become her adopted daughter.

Reject not nor forsake the teaching of you mother.

PROVERBS 1:8 AMP

A college freshman once wrote the following to her parents:

Dear Mom and Dad,

Just thought I'd drop you a note to clue you in on my plans. I've fallen in love with a guy named Buck. He quit high school between his sophomore and junior year to travel with his motorcycle gang. He was married at 18 and had two sons. About a year ago he got a divorce.

We've been going steady for two months now and plan to get married in the fall. (He thinks he should be able to find a job by then.) Until then, I've decided to move into his apartment. I think I might be pregnant.

At any rate, I dropped out of school last week. I was just bored with the whole thing. Maybe I'll finish college sometime in the future.

[And then on the next page she continued . . .]

Mom and Dad, everything I've written so far in this letter is false. NONE OF IT IS TRUE! But, Mom and Dad, it IS true that I got a C in French and flunked my math test. And it IS true that I'm overdrawn and need more money for my tuition payments.

Your loving daughter.

There is a right time for everything: a time to laugh.

ECCLESIASTES 3:1,4 TLB

THE LORD CAN
DO GREAT
THINGS
THROUGH THOSE
WHO DON'T
CARE WHO GETS
THE CREDIT.

One night in 1837, she believed she heard the voice of God informing her that she had a mission. Nine years later, that mission began to take shape when a friend sent her information about the Institution of Protestant Deaconesses in Germany. She later entered that institution to learn how to care for the sick. In 1853 she became superintendent of a "woman's hospital" in London. But then the Crimean War broke out in 1854, and she volunteered at once to care for British soldiers, leaving for Constantinople almost immediately. Once in Turkey, she was given charge of the nursing at the military hospital. Even though doctors were hostile toward her and the hospital itself was deplorably filthy, she dug in her heels and began caring for her patients, at first using the provisions she had brought with her and then undertaking a correspondence campaign to resupply the hospital. She spent many hours each day in the wards, touching virtually every man who ever entered the hospital. The comfort she gave on night rounds earned her the nickname "The Lady with the Lamp."

Her selfless giving eventually made her name synonymous with compassionate nursing care. She was . . . Florence Nightingale.

A man's pride shall bring him low: but honour shall uphold the humble in spirit.

PROVERBS 29:23

CHILDREN ARE NATURAL MIMICS—THEY ACT LIKE THEIR PARENTS IN SPITE OF EVERY ATTEMPT TO TEACH THEM GOOD MANNERS.

If a child lives with criticism
He learns to condemn;
If a child lives with hostility
He learns to fight;
If a child lives with ridicule
He learns to be shy;
If a child lives with shame
He learns to feel guilty.
BUT
If a child lives with tolerance
He learns to be patient;
If a child lives with encouragement
He learns confidence;
If a child lives with praise
He learns to appreciate;
If a child lives with fairness
He learns justice;
If a child lives with security
He learns to have faith;
If a child lives with approval
He learns to like himself;
If a child lives with acceptance and friendship
He learns to find LOVE in the world!

DOROTHY LAWE HOLT

Beloved, follow not that which is evil, but
that which is good.

3 JOHN 11A

A MOTHER UNDERSTANDS WHAT A CHILD DOES NOT SAY.

A uthor and pastor's wife Colleen Townsend Evans has written, "Silence need not be awkward or embarrassing, for to be with one you love, without the need for words, is a beautiful and satisfying form of communication.

"I remember times when our children used to come running to me, all of them chattering at once about the events of their day—and it was wonderful to have them share their feelings with me. But there were also the times when they came to me wanting only to be held, to have me stroke their heads and caress them into sleep. And so it is, sometimes, with us and with God our Father."

Don't force your child to talk to you. Give him the respect and "space" to remain silent. Sometimes children need to work out their own ideas and opinions in quiet before voicing them. On the other hand, when he *does* talk, take time to listen intently, carefully, and kindly. In so doing, your child will know that he *can* talk to you whenever he wants or needs to, and you can rest assured that his silence is not rooted in suspicion or fear of you.

The language of silence is a language.

Serve him with a perfect heart and with a willing mind: for the Lord searcheth all hearts, and understandeth all the imaginations of the thoughts.

1 CHRONICLES 28:9

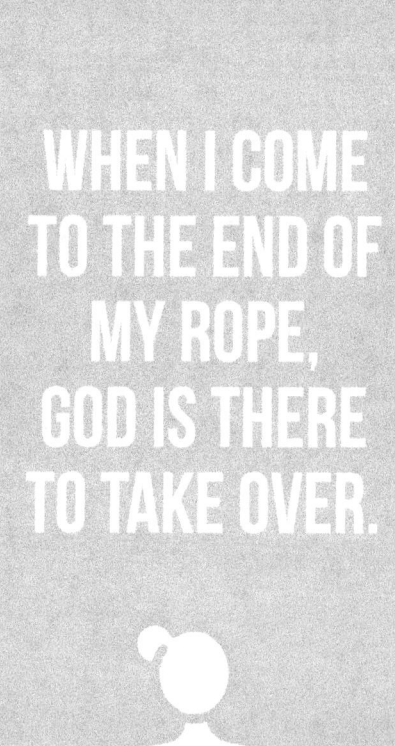

WHEN I COME
TO THE END OF
MY ROPE,
GOD IS THERE
TO TAKE OVER.

Leslie was born mentally retarded, without eyes, and with cerebral palsy. Vegetable-like, he was totally unresponsive to sound or touch. At the age of six months, he was expected to die shortly. A nurse, May Lemke, was asked if she could care for him at home until that time. She did . . . for more than thirty years.

When May accepted baby Leslie, she accepted him as just that, a baby—no different from others—to be taught and loved. Year after year she cared for him, but there was no movement or response. Even so, she never stopped talking to him, singing to him, or praying for him. Music filled their home . . . still, no response. She and her husband bought an old used piano and put it in his bedroom. She pushed his fingers against the keys. With quiet faith, she knew God would someday help Leslie to break out of his prison. She rejoiced when he began to walk at age 16.

Several years later, May and her husband were awakened one night by the sound of Tchaikovsky's Piano Concerto No. 1. Startled, they arose to find Leslie at the piano with a smiling glow on his face. Shortly thereafter he began to talk and to cry . . . and to sing. And at age 28, he began to talk in earnest. May's prayers were answered—in God's timing, God's way.

For he hath said, I will never leave thee, nor forsake thee.

HEBREWS 13:5

BABIES ARE SUCH A NICE WAY TO START PEOPLE.

Henry Kendall from Boston and Richard Taylor from Medicine Hat, Canada, achieved a breakthrough in man's understanding of matter, and furthered the theory of the structure of protons and neutrons.

Mikhail Gorbachev from Privolnoye, USSR, contributed to a breakthrough in man's understanding about how East and West might better relate through "glasnost," a policy of open political coexistence.

Octavio Paz from Mexico City, was a political commentator, diplomat, essayist, and poet who wrote passionately throughout his life about man's needs for "wider horizons."

Edward Donnall Thomas from Mart, Texas, proved that it was possible to transplant organs to save the lives of dying patients.

Harry M. Markowitz from Chicago, developed the theory that combinations of economic assets of differing risks could decrease the overall risk of investment.

What did these five men have in common? Two things. First, although they represented vastly diverse heritages, interests, and talents, all won Nobel prizes in 1990. And second, nobody could have predicted their success before they were born.

And she conceived . . . and said, I have gotten a man from the Lord.

GENESIS 4:1

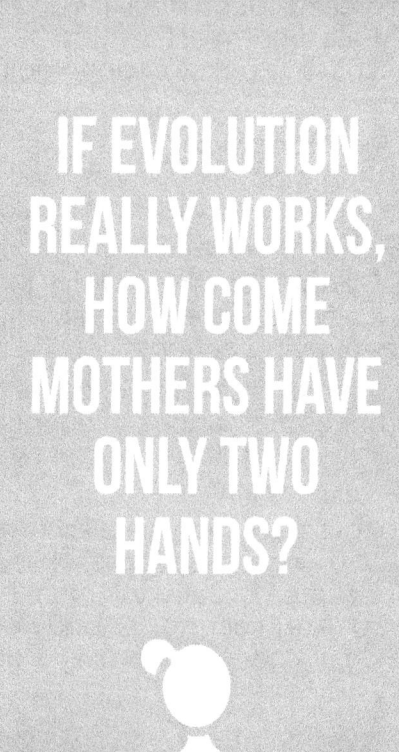

IF EVOLUTION REALLY WORKS, HOW COME MOTHERS HAVE ONLY TWO HANDS?

Harriet Rukenbrod Day's poem, "A Mother's Dilemma" says it well:

Baby's in the cookie jar
Sister's in the glue
Kitty's in the birdie's cage
And I am in a stew!
Time for dad to come to lunch
Someone's spilled the roses
Breakfast dishes still undone
The twins have drippy noses.
Junior has the stove apart
Dinner guests at eight
Neighbors' kids swoop in like flies
How can I concentrate?
Telephone keeps ringing wildly
Someone's in the hall
Fido's chewed the rug to bits
The preacher's come to call!
Would mothers like to chuck their load?
They couldn't stand the rap
Easy, mild existences
Would cause their nerves to snap!

A merry heart doeth good like a medicine.

PROVERBS 17:22

DEAR MOTHER—
YOU KNOW THAT
NOTHING CAN
EVER CHANGE
WHAT WE HAVE
ALWAYS BEEN AND
WILL ALWAYS BE
TO EACH OTHER.

The story is told of four scholars who were arguing over the beauty and accuracy of various Bible translations.

One scholar argued for the *King James Version*, citing its beautiful, eloquent old English.

The second scholar advocated for the *American Standard Bible*. He cited its literalism, the way it moved a reader from passage to passage with confident feelings of accuracy from the original texts.

The third scholar said he preferred the translation by Moffatt. He praised its quaint, penetrating use of words, the turn of a phrase that captured the attention of the reader.

After giving thought to each of the lengthy and impassioned arguments presented, the fourth scholar said, "Frankly, I have always preferred my mother's translation."

Knowing that his mother was not a Bible translator, nor a scholar, the other three chuckled and said, "No, seriously . . ." The man stood his ground. "I stand by my claim," he said. "My mother translated each page of the Bible into life. And it was the most convincing translation I have ever seen."

Her children stand and bless her.

PROVERBS 31:28 TLB

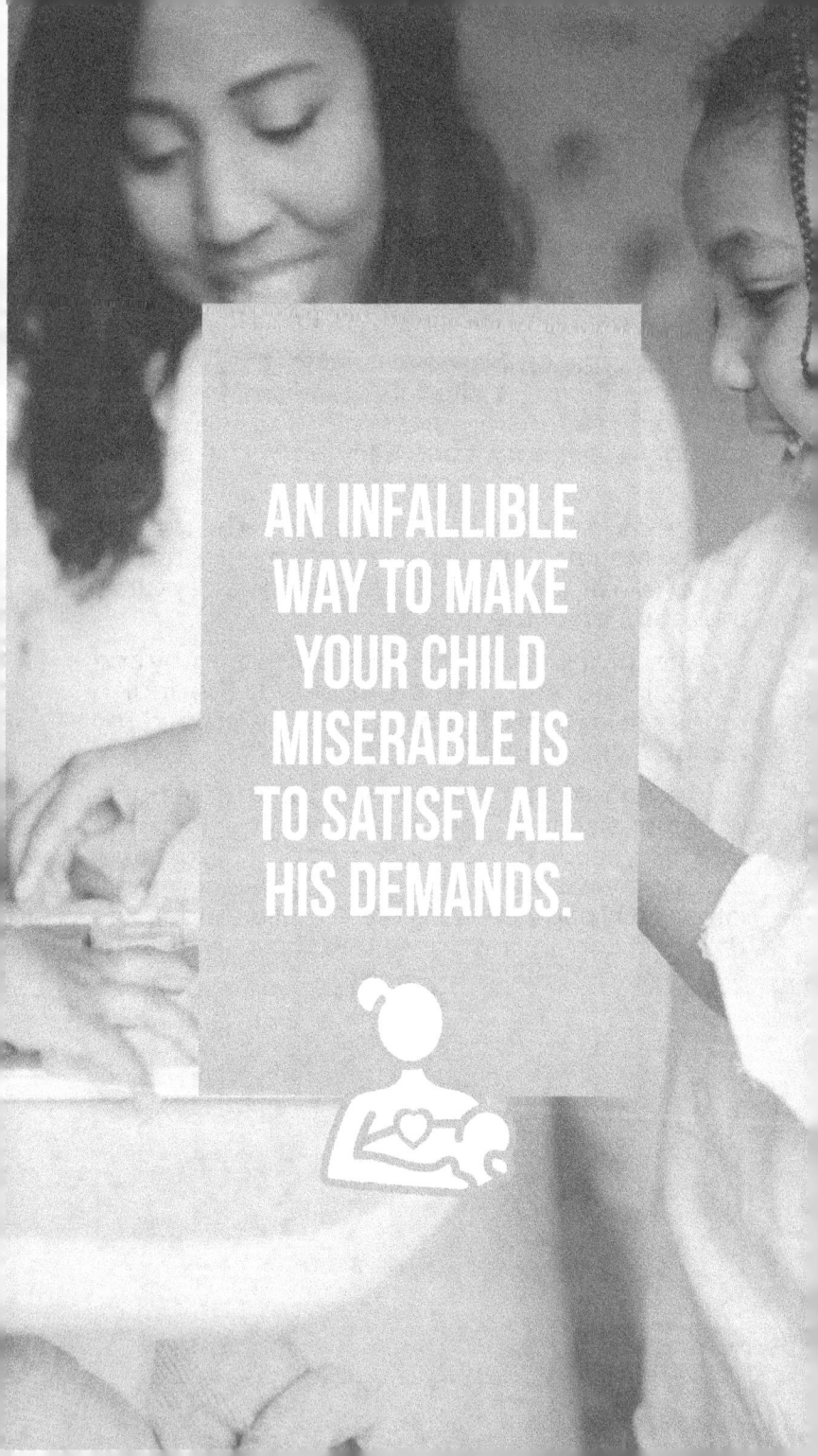

AN INFALLIBLE WAY TO MAKE YOUR CHILD MISERABLE IS TO SATISFY ALL HIS DEMANDS.

In *Little Women*, Mrs. March tells this story to her daughters, who unfortunately found they could "identify" with every word: "Once upon a time, there were four girls, who had enough to eat and drink and wear, a good many comforts and pleasures, kind friends and parents ... and yet they were not contented ... These girls ... made many excellent resolutions; but they ... were constantly saying, 'If we only had this,' or 'If we could only do that.' ... So they asked an old woman what spell they could use to make them happy, and she said, 'When you feel discontented, think over your blessings, and be grateful.'

"They decided to try her advice, and soon were surprised to see how well off they were. One discovered that money couldn't keep shame and sorrow out of rich people's houses; another that ... she was a great deal happier with her youth, health, and good spirits than a certain fretful, feeble old lady, who couldn't enjoy her comforts; a third that, disagreeable as it was to help get dinner, it was harder still to have to go begging for it; and the fourth, that even carnelian rings were not so valuable as good behavior. So they agreed to stop complaining, to enjoy the blessings already possessed."

Remember, not everything your child wants is best for him. The best way to bring happiness to your child is to teach him it comes from within.

The rod and reproof give wisdom: but a child left to himself bringeth his mother to shame.

PROVERBS 29:15

CHILDREN MISS NOTHING IN SIZING UP THEIR PARENTS. IF YOU ARE ONLY HALF CONVINCED OF YOUR BELIEFS, THEY WILL QUICKLY DISCERN THAT FACT.

Two boys were walking home from church one day. They began talking about the Sunday school lesson they had heard earlier in the morning.

"That would really be something," one of the boys said, "to be out in a wilderness for forty days and nights."

"Yeah," said the other boy, "and not eat. Jesus must have been real strong."

"It would have been kind of scary, too," said the first boy, "to have the devil show up and tempt you."

The second little boy didn't respond so the first boy asked, "Do you believe that stuff about the devil? Do you think there really is a devil?"

The second little boy looked at his friend and said, "Naaah, he's probably just like Santa Claus—it's really just your dad."

Not only do children copy the mannerisms of their parents, they are quick to zero in on their parents' traits, beliefs, and values. Would your child call you a Christian today? Does your child know what you believe, and why? Does your child know how important your faith is to you?

The most important person to whom you can witness about your faith is your own child.

Let us hold fast the profession of our faith without wavering.

HEBREWS 10:23

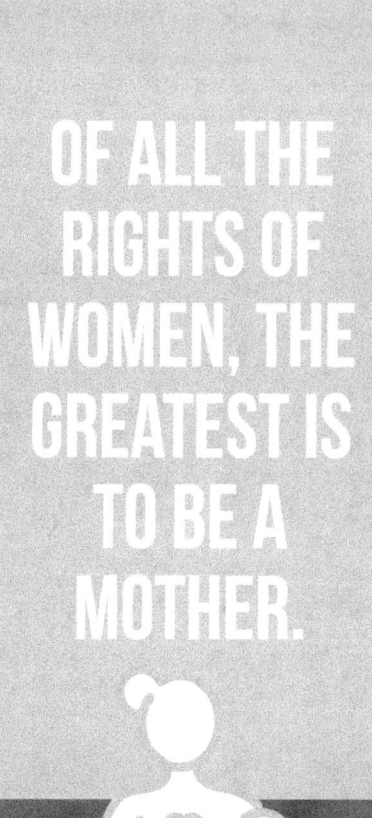

OF ALL THE RIGHTS OF WOMEN, THE GREATEST IS TO BE A MOTHER.

After the famous food distributor Henry J. Heinz died, his will was found to contain this confession:

"I desire to set forth at the very beginning of this will, as the most important item in it, a confession of my faith in Jesus Christ as my Savior. I also desire to bear witness to the fact that throughout my life, in which there were unusual joys and sorrows, I have been wonderfully sustained by my faith in God through Jesus Christ. This legacy was left me by my consecrated mother, a woman of strong faith, and to it I attribute any success I have attained."

Heinz is not the only famous American to credit his mother for his success, of course. Consider these words of another American hero, Thomas Edison: "I did not have my mother long, but she cast over me an influence which has lasted all my life. The good effects of her early training I can never lose. If it had not been for her appreciation and her faith in me at a critical time in my experience, I should never likely have become an inventor. I was always a careless boy, and with a mother of different mental caliber, I should have turned out badly. But her firmness, her sweetness, her goodness were potent powers to keep me in the right path. My mother was the making of me."

Although at times being a mother is the hardest job there is, it is also the *greatest* right.

Her children arise up, and call her blessed; her husband also, and he praiseth her.

PROVERBS 31:28

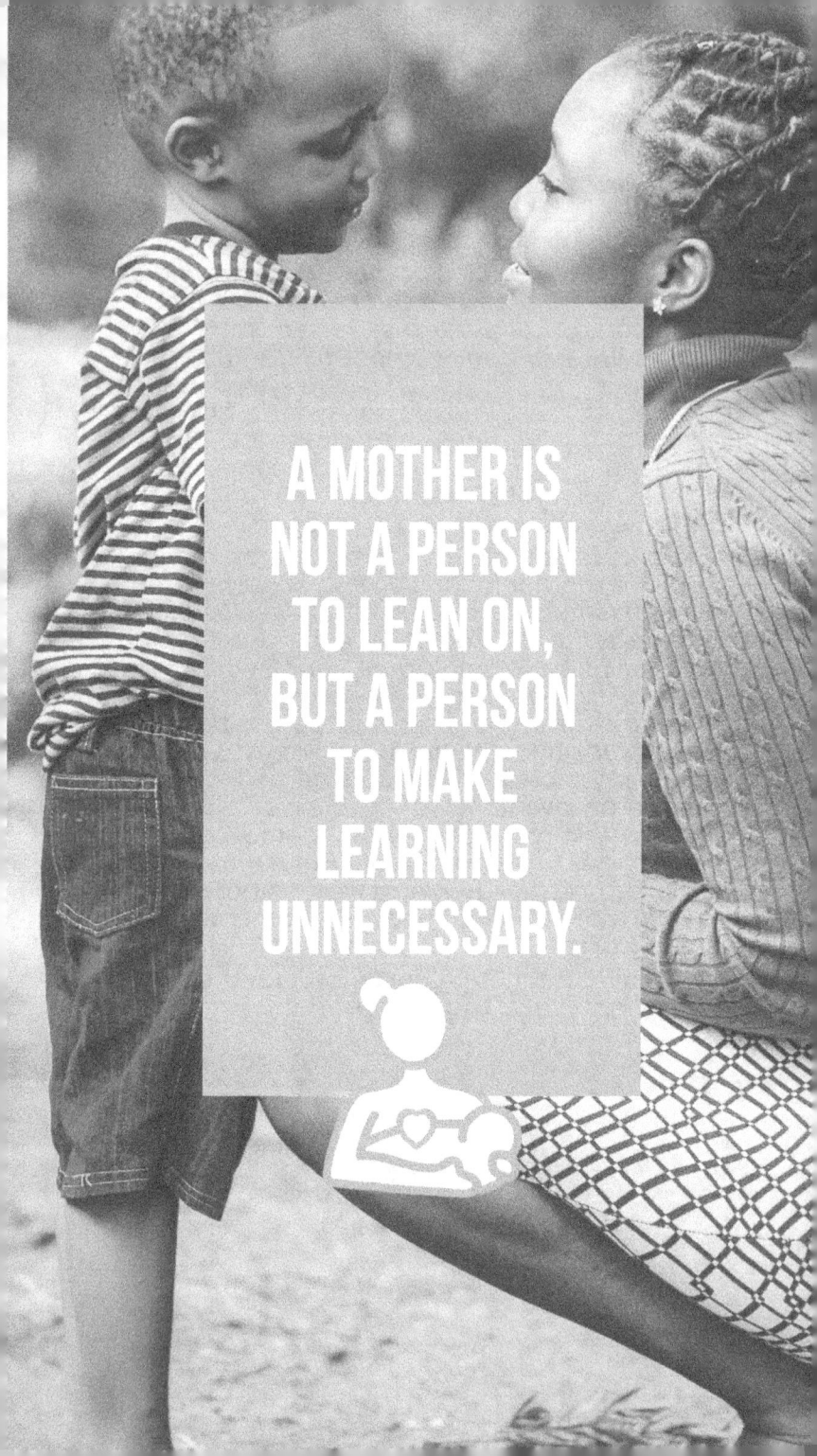

A MOTHER IS
NOT A PERSON
TO LEAN ON,
BUT A PERSON
TO MAKE
LEARNING
UNNECESSARY.

"Whenever I held my newborn baby in my arms," Rose once said, "I used to think that what I said and did to him could have an influence not only on him but on all whom he met, not only for a day or a month or a year, but for all eternity—a very, very challenging and exciting thought for a mother." Feeling this duty, Rose became a natural and determined teacher of her children, leading them by discovery, story, example, and inspiration to fulfill their own destinies.

Rose engaged her children in conversation about history and politics, and when guests visited their home, she expected her children to ask questions and offer opinions. Even though the family was wealthy, the boys were expected to fix their own bicycles and were required to earn their own pocket money. She gave each child a sense of independence and privacy, yet dressed them with similar clothes so they would feel a part of a whole family unit. Rose expected her children to be self-confident adults and independent thinkers, with compassion for those less fortunate.

And she succeeded. Among Rose Kennedy's children, son John became President of the United States, son Robert, Attorney General, and son Edward, a United States Senator.

Therefore shall a man leave his father and his mother, and shall cleave unto his wife: and they shall be one flesh.

GENESIS 2:24

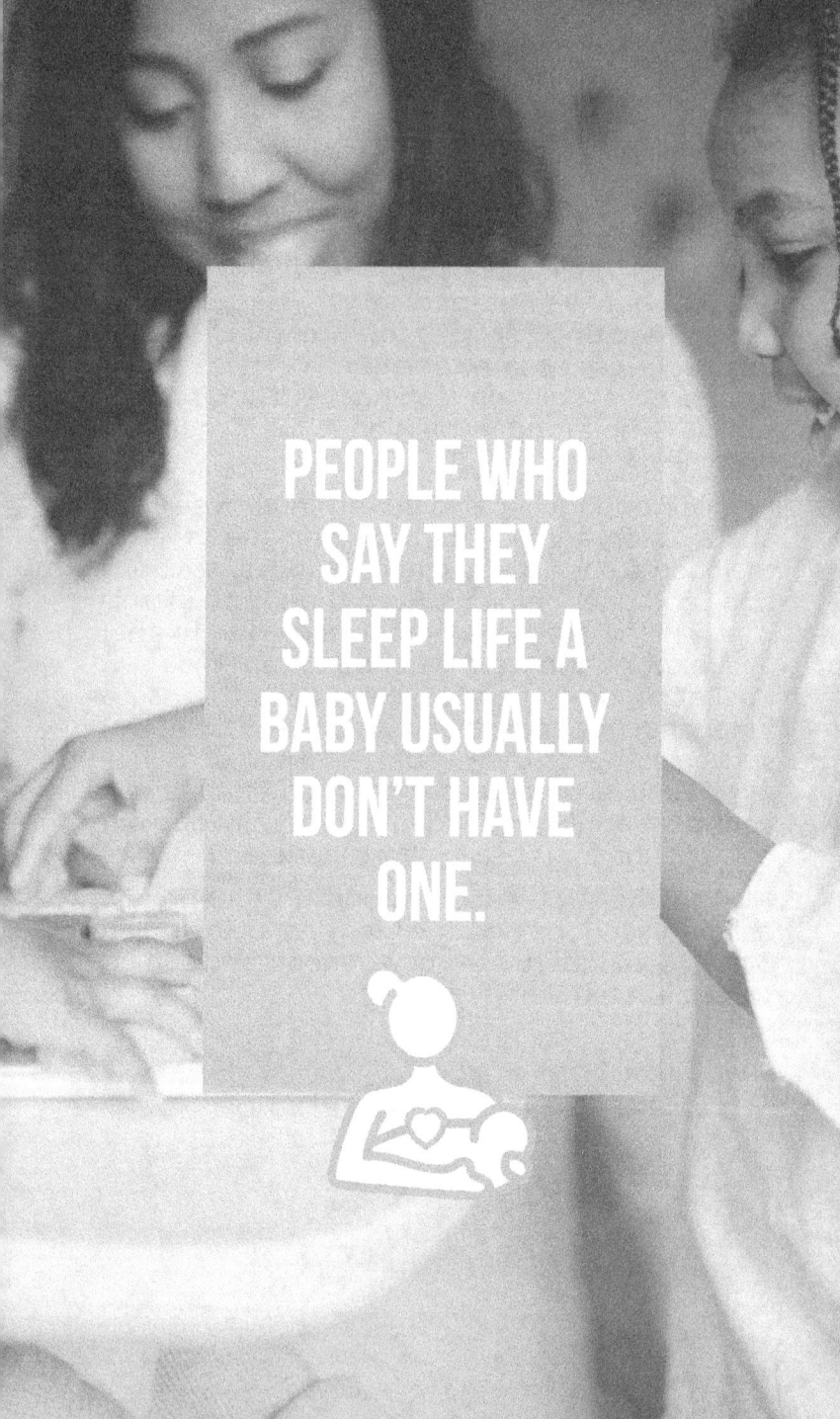

PEOPLE WHO SAY THEY SLEEP LIFE A BABY USUALLY DON'T HAVE ONE.

Kathy and Jim were longing for the day when their precious baby would eventually sleep all the way through the night. Originally they had agreed to take turns getting up when she cried. But Jim frequently gave in to the urge to prompt his wife into taking his turn by saying, "Honey, she's probably hungry." That, of course, was a problem only a nursing mother could address.

Their fatigue, however, was greatly mitigated by the considerable joy they had in watching little Anna grow and gain new skills, not the least of which was her attempt at learning to talk. Even though she knew that most babies have "Mama" as their first word, Kathy felt her beloved husband would be thrilled if Anna's first word was for him. So, day after day, she worked with her bright baby to teach her to say what she was sure would be a magical word to daddy's ears.

One night, all of Kathy's diligence paid off. At 2:15 AM, Anna awoke and cried "Da-da" at the top of her lungs. Kathy turned over and said softly to her husband beside her, "She's calling for *you*, dear, and I'm sure this is something only *you* can handle."

A merry heart doeth good like a medicine.

PROVERBS 17:22

A TORN JACKET IS SOON MENDED; BUT HARD WORDS BRUISE THE HEART OF A CHILD.

A poem first published in *The Bible Friend* speaks about the great influence that a mother has:

I took a piece of plastic clay
And idly fashioned it one day;
And as my fingers pressed it still,
It moved and yielded at my will.
I came again when days were past,
The form I gave it still it bore,
And as my fingers pressed it still,
I could change that form no more.
I took a piece of living clay,
And gently formed it day by day,
And molded with my power and art,
A young child's soft and yielding heart.
I came again when days were gone;
It was a man I looked upon,
He still that early impress bore,
And I could change it never more.

Every word . . . every action . . . leaves a mark upon your child, for good or for bad. Little things to an adult sometimes loom large for a child. What may seem to you an insignificant comment or deed may turn out to be the one thing your child remembers!

In accordance with the authority which the Lord gave me, for building up and not for tearing down.

2 CORINTHIANS 13:10 NASB

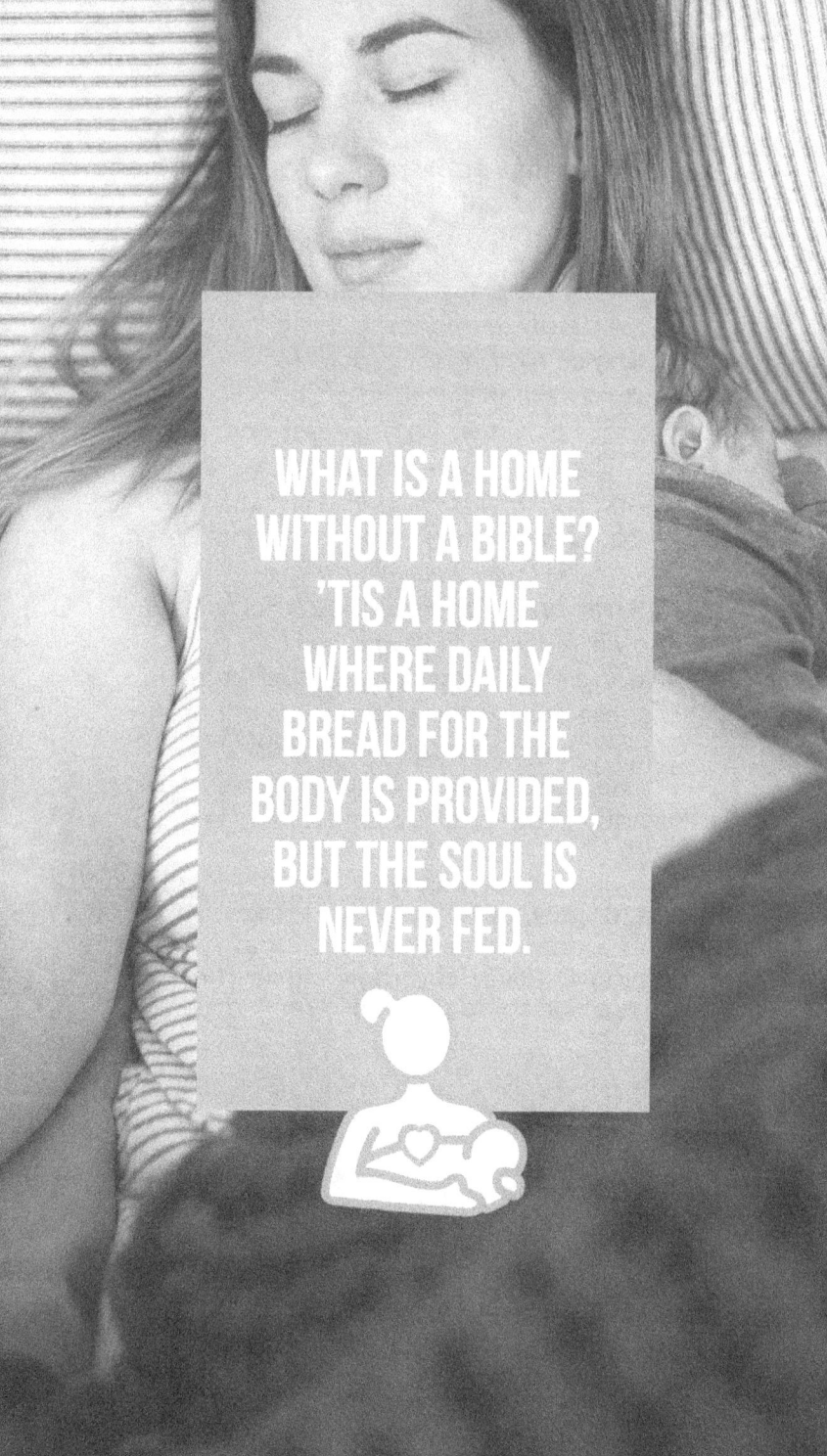

WHAT IS A HOME WITHOUT A BIBLE? 'TIS A HOME WHERE DAILY BREAD FOR THE BODY IS PROVIDED, BUT THE SOUL IS NEVER FED.

A young woman was packing a suitcase for a long trip. She said to a woman who was watching her, "I'm just about finished. I only have to put in a guidebook, a lamp, a mirror, my favorite love letters, a microscope, a telescope, a volume of fine poetry, a song book, a few biographies, a package of old letters, a sword, and a set of books I have been studying."

The onlooker gasped, "How do you intend to get all that in your suitcase? It's almost full now!"

The young woman replied, "Oh, all that won't take much room." She then walked over to a table, picked up her Bible, placed it in the corner of her suitcase, and closed the lid. Winking at her friend, she said, "And I even got in a loaf of living bread, too."

The Bible says of itself that it is "fresh" with every reading—it is never stale. The Bible is always applicable to life, no matter where one lives. And the truths of the Bible are unshakable—they will last forever and never go out of style. Voltaire once said that in a hundred years, the Bible would be a forgotten book, found only in museums. When the hundred years were up, however, Voltaire's home was occupied by the Geneva Bible Society! Feed your children a healthy portion of the Bible today. Consider it "heavenly food."

My son, attend to my words; incline thine ear unto my sayings. Let them not depart form thine eyes; keep them in the midst of thine heart. For they are life unto those that find them, and health to all their flesh.

PROVERB 4:20-22

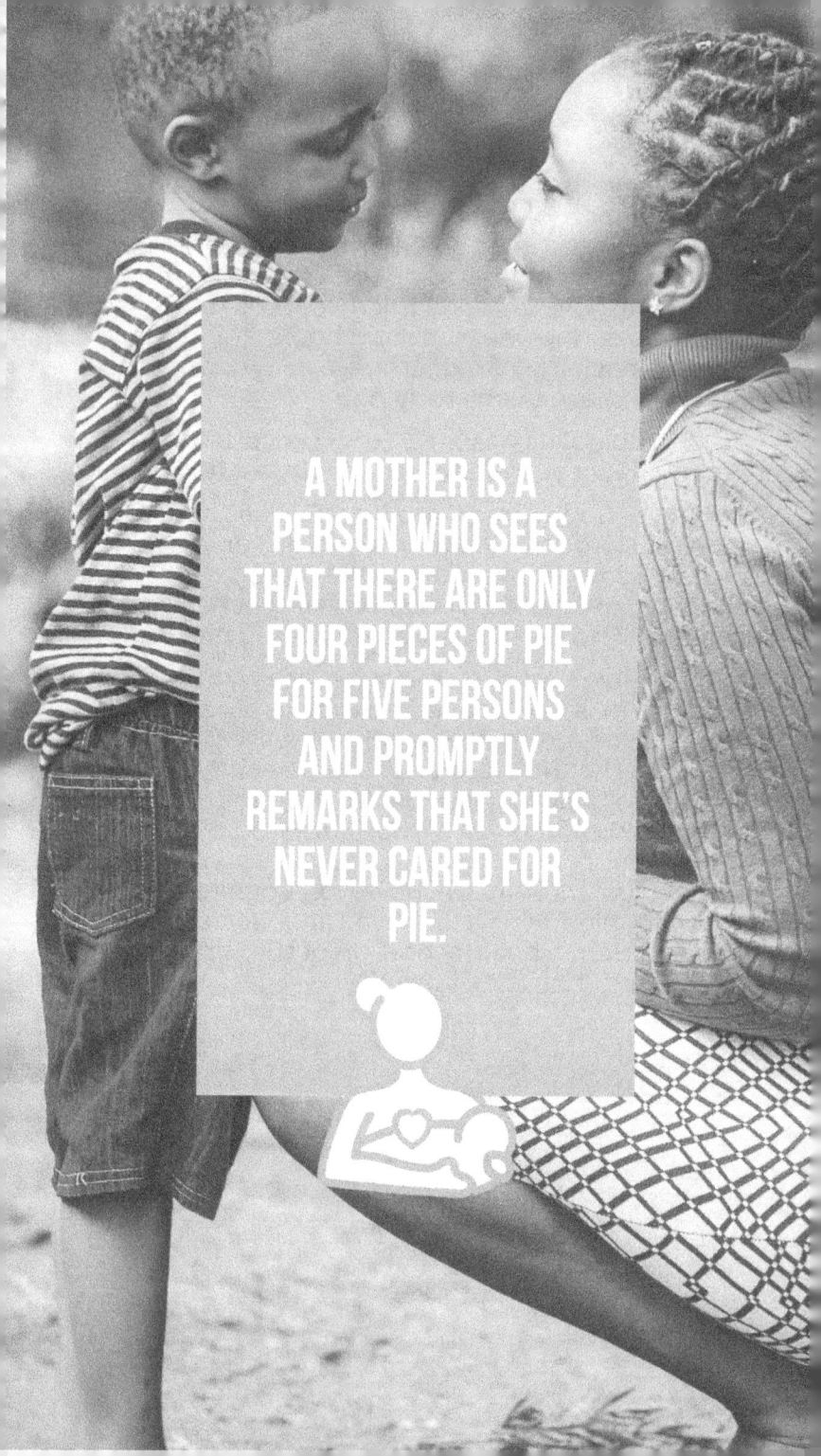

In 1932, Violet married a union organizer and within a few years, had four sons. When she was pregnant a fifth time, gangsters moved to take over the union and her husband left, feeling his family was safer without him. Violet and her sons moved into a tiny apartment and a few months later, a daughter was born. To feed her family, Violet worked days at the National Silver Company and nights at a drugstore. She would work, have bouillon for lunch, finish her first job, pick up a kidney for 25 cents and make soup, tell the children not to mind the taste, go to the second job, come home and wash out the children's socks and shirts, catch a couple of hours of sleep, and begin her next day. On days off, she waited tables, and holidays, she worked at a department store.

Over the years she worked in a cracker factory, hawked ice cream, labeled medicine bottles, cleaned offices, and pushed a coffee cart. In 1959 she became an orderly in a home for the aged and 17 years later she retired with a pension of $31-78 a month. For the first time since 1946 she had a week off! Thomas, her son, perhaps paid her the highest tribute possible, saying he had only "happy memories" of his childhood: "We didn't even know we were poor until years later."

It is more blessed to give than to receive.

ACTS 20:35

One evening just before Mary Martin, the great Broadway musical star, was to go on stage in *South Pacific*, a note was handed to her. It was from Oscar Hammerstein, who had written this to her from his deathbed:

Dear Mary, A bell's not a bell till you ring it. A song's not a song till you sing it. Love in your heart is not put there to stay. Love isn't love till you give it away.

After her performance that night a number of people rushed backstage, exclaiming, "Mary, what happened to you out there tonight? We have never heard anything like that performance! You sang with more power than you've ever sung!"

Blinking back tears, Mary then read them the note from Hammerstein and added, "Tonight, I gave my love away!"

Even the poorest person has something to give to others if he has love in his heart. Love's gifts take many forms—a smile, a hug, a note of thanks, "just being there" in tough times. Love is the one gift that always fits, is always appropriate, and is always in season and in fashion.

For God so loved the world, that he gave his only begotten Son, that whosoever believeth in him should not perish, but have everlasting life.

JOHN 3:16

MOTHER MEANS SELFLESS DEVOTION, LIMITLESS SACRIFICE, AND LOVE THAT PASSES UNDERSTANDING.

A number of years ago, a young mother was making her way on foot across the hills of South Wales, carrying her tiny baby in her arms. The wintry winds were stronger than she anticipated and her journey took much longer than planned. Eventually, she was overtaken by a blinding blizzard.

The woman never reached her destination. When the blizzard had subsided, those expecting her arrival went in search of her. After hours of searching, they finally found her body underneath a mound of snow.

As they shoveled the snow away from her frozen corpse, they were amazed to see that she had taken off her outer clothing. When they finally lifted her body away from the ground, they discovered the reason why. This brave and self-sacrificing young mother had wrapped her own cloak and scarf around her baby and then huddled over her child. When the searchers unwrapped the child, they found to their great surprise and joy that he was alive and well!

Years later, that child, David Lloyd George, became prime minister of Great Britain, and is regarded as one of England's greatest statesmen.

Greater love hath no man than this, that a man lay down his life for his friends.

JOHN 15:13

PARENTS OF TEENS AND PARENTS OF BABIES HAVE SOMETHING IN COMMON.
THEY SPEND A GREAT DEAL OF TIME TRYING TO GET THEIR KIDS TO TALK.

The name Albert Einstein is synonymous with that of "genius." Many don't know, however, that Einstein was a late talker. His parents grew quite worried about this. Then, at supper one night, he broke his silence with a full sentence, saying, "The soup is too hot." Overjoyed, his greatly relieved parents asked him why he hadn't spoken before. He said, "Because up to now everything was in order."

The difference in parents trying to get their babies and teens to talk is one of *language*. Babies are learning the parents' language. But parents end up trying to learn the language of their teens! This shift has several stages. First, a parent goes through the "Why?" stage. When parents don't have answers, the child enters his own "I know" stage. Next, he adds vocabulary words he doesn't learn from his parents. "Jam" and "cool" take on new meanings. A child then asks more questions using these words that parents can't answer, such as "Why are you jammin' fifty in a school zone?" and "Is it ever cool to break the law?" Finding that parents *still* don't have answers, teens take to the telephone to talk to someone who does—another teen. The solution to the communication gap may very well be: *make up some answers!*

There is a right time for everything: a time to laugh.

ECCLESIASTES 3:1,4 TLB

n *Dare to Discipline*, Dr. James Dobson tells about his own mother's approach: "I found her reasonable on most issues. If I was late coming home from school, I could just explain what had caused the delay . . . If I didn't get my work done, we could sit down and come to some kind of agreement for future action. But there was one matter on which she was absolutely rigid: She did not tolerate 'sassiness.'

"She knew that backtalk and 'lip' are the child's most potent weapons of defiance and they must be discouraged." Through the years, Dobson recalls having been spanked with a shoe, and often with a handy belt. He vividly recalls, however, one particular spanking. He made the costly mistake of sassing his mother when the only object nearby for a spanking was her girdle. He says, "Now those were the days when a girdle was a weapon. It weighed about sixteen pounds and was lined with lead and steel . . . with a multitude of straps and buckles. . . . She gave me an entire thrashing with one massive blow!"

While Jim may not have appreciated her principles about discipline at the time, he certainly did in later years. His book *The Strong-Willed Child* is dedicated to her!

Discipline your son, and he will give you peace; he will bring delight to your soul.

PROVERBS 29:17 NIV

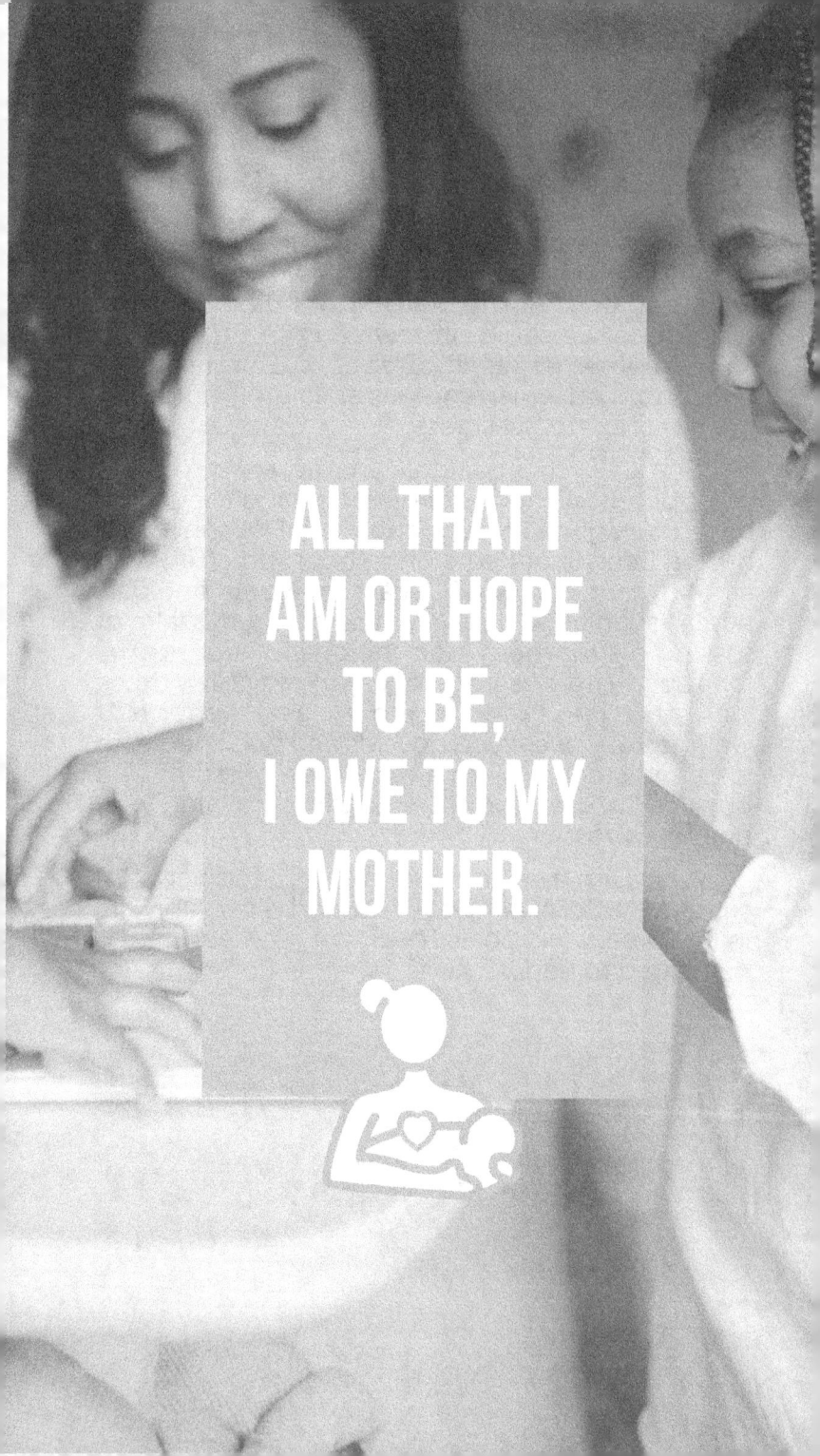

ALL THAT I
AM OR HOPE
TO BE,
I OWE TO MY
MOTHER.

ech Walesa, the first freely elected president of Poland in fifty years and the 1983 winner of the Nobel Prize for Peace, credits his mother for teaching him the values that led to his success. He writes about her in his book, *Lech Walesa: A Way of Hope*, "She is the only person from my childhood I still have a really clear recollection of. She took an interest in history and current affairs, and read a great deal. In the evenings, she would sometimes read to us. We took great pleasure in these moments. All the stories our mother told us had a moral in them: they taught one to be honest, to strive always to better oneself, to be just, and to call white white and black black. Mother was very religious. My faith can be said almost to have flowed into me with my mother's milk."

The children in the Walesa home were kept on a "tight rein," he recalls. Even the youngest had jobs to do—tending geese, taking the cows out to pasture, doing a variety of manual jobs.

Wisdom, faith, and discipline all have a mother's knee as their first foundation—and what a strong and wonderful foundation it can be if the mother is a woman who seeks those same qualities in her own life!

Get all the advice you can and be wise the rest of your life.

PROVERBS 19:20 TLB

NEVER DESPAIR OF A CHILD. THE ONE YOU WEEP THE MOST FOR AT THE MERCY SEAT MAY FULL YOUR HEART WITH THE SWEETEST JOYS.

A partially deaf boy came home from school one day carrying a note from officials at the school. The note suggested that the parents take the boy out of school, claiming that he was "too stupid to learn."

The boy's mother read the note and said, "My son Tom isn't 'too stupid to learn.' I'll teach him myself." And so she did.

When Tom died many years later, the people of the United States of America paid tribute to him by turning off the nation's lights for one full minute. You see, this Tom had invented the light bulb—and not only that, but motion pictures and the record player. In all, he had more than one thousand patents to his credit.

No child is beyond learning more than he knows today. No child is beyond finding a new way to express her creativity, and her love.

No child is beyond receiving affection and growing in self-esteem. No child is beyond experiencing the presence of Almighty God.

Never give up on any aspect of your child's growth and development. Your Heavenly Father hasn't, doesn't, and won't.

He that goeth forth and weepeth, bearing precious seed, shall doubtless come again with rejoicing.

PSALM 126:6

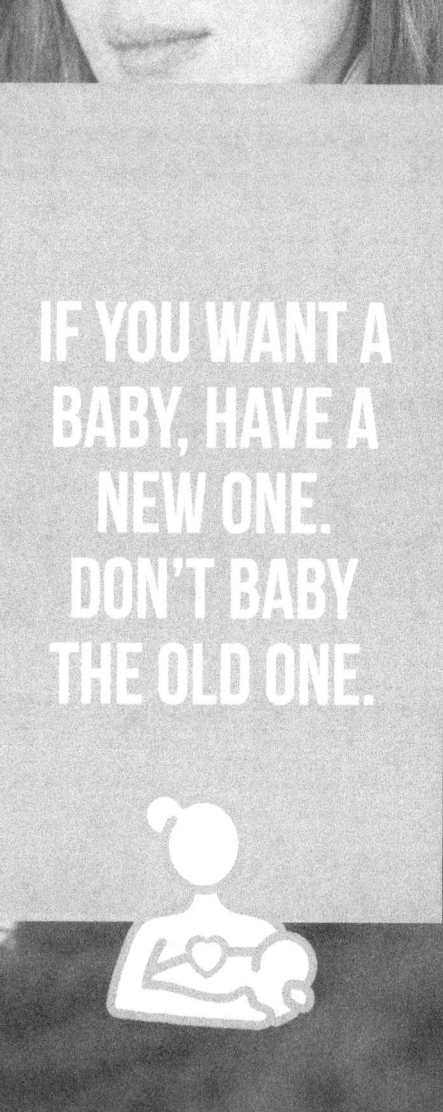

IF YOU WANT A BABY, HAVE A NEW ONE. DON'T BABY THE OLD ONE.

As her daughter Janet remembers her, Jane lavished on her children the kind of love that empowered, not enslaved. She taught all four of her children how to play baseball, bake a cake, and to play fair. As Janet recalls, "She beat the living daylights out of us sometimes, and she loved us with all her heart. She taught us her favorite poets. And there is no child care in the world that will ever be a substitute for what that lady was in our lives. . . . My mother always told me to do my best, to think my best, and to do right and consider myself a person."

Another daughter, Maggy, recalls, "What gave us our self-confidence was the absolute certainty that every adult in our world loved us absolutely. They weren't always perfect, and we weren't always perfect. But we could count on that love."

Jane received love in return. Her daughter Janet declined to be considered for a job in President Clinton's administration until after her mother's death so she might remain by her ailing mother's side. When Janet Reno finally did accept a position, it was as Attorney General of the United States, the first woman to head the Justice Department.

Chasten thy son while there is hope, and let not thy soul spare for his crying.

PROVERBS 19:18

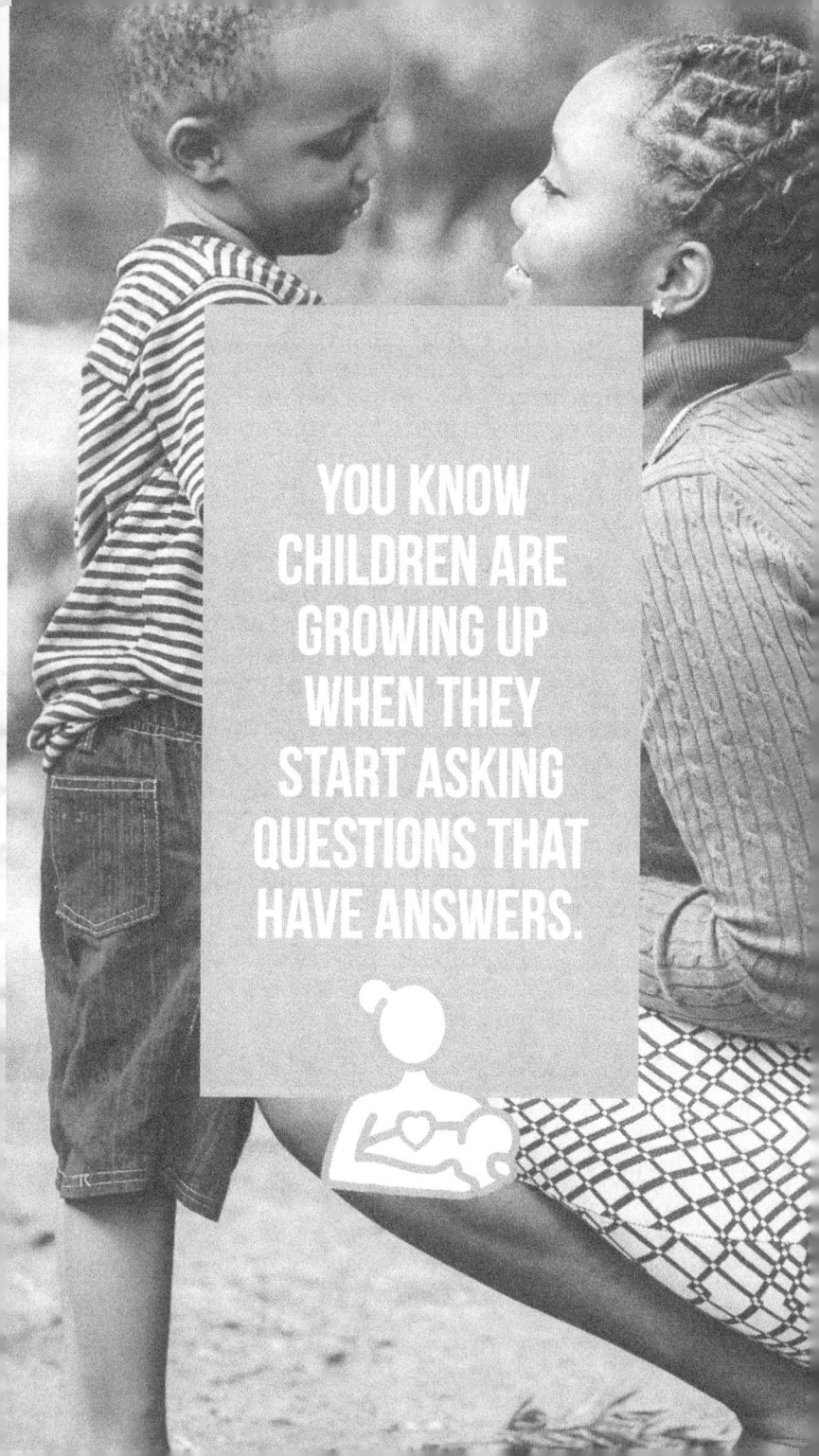

YOU KNOW CHILDREN ARE GROWING UP WHEN THEY START ASKING QUESTIONS THAT HAVE ANSWERS.

A little girl once asked her grandmother, "How old are you?" The grandmother replied, "Now dear, you shouldn't ask people that question. Most grown-ups don't like to tell their age."

The next day the little girl had another question. She asked, "Grandma, how much do you weigh?" The grandmother said, "Oh, honey, you shouldn't ask grown-ups how much they weigh. It isn't polite."

The third day the little girl came to her grandmother with a big smile and announced, "Grandma, I know how old you are. You're sixty-two. And I also know that you weigh 140 pounds."

"My goodness," the grandmother said, "how do you know all that?"

The little girl replied, "You left your driver's license on the table and I read it." And then the little girl added, "And I also saw on your driver's license that you flunked sex."

Three of the greatest things a parent can ever do are:

1) answer a child's questions to the full extent the child is capable of understanding an answer, 2) give a child information he needs to have and spare him knowledge he doesn't need, and 3) take time to converse with your child. Each is a genuine act of love!

When I was a child, I spake as a child, I understood as a child, I thought as a child: but when I became a man, I put away childish things.

1 CORINTHIANS 13:11

THE BEST WAY TO KEEP CHILDREN AT HOME IS TO MAKE HOME A PLEASANT ATMOSPHERE— AND TO LET THE AIR OUT OF THE TIRES.

In his bestseller, *Fatherhood*, Bill Cosby tells of a decision that he and his wife made about their children using the family car:

"We would not allow any of the children to have a driver's license as long as he or she was living with us." He asks, "Does this sound unreasonable to you?" Cosby goes on to write:

> One memorable day, one of these children did drive to town just to see if she could do it while unencumbered by a license. It was a Saturday morning and my wife and I had just finished breakfast. I walked over to the sink to rinse out a glass and there I suddenly saw our car going past the kitchen window. Turning to my wife, I said, "Dear, did you just drive by here?"

> "No," she replied.

> "Well, am I in this kitchen?"

> "As far as I can tell."

> "Then why did I just go by in the car?"

A merry heart doeth good like a medicine.

PROVERBS 17:22

WE SHOULD
SEIZE EVERY
OPPORTUNITY
TO GIVE
ENCOURAGEMENT.

C hildren's stories often provide profound insights into life. The tales of Winnie the Pooh are a good source for friendly and warm words, as evidenced by the following story told on a Pooh Bear recording:

One day Pooh Bear is about to go for a walk in the Hundred Acre wood.

It's about 11:30 in the morning. It is a fine time to go calling—just before lunch. So Pooh sets out across the stream, stepping on the stones, and when he gets right in the middle of the stream he sits down on a warm stone and thinks about just where would be the best place of all to make a call.

He says to himself, "I think I'll go see Tigger." No, he dismisses that. Then he says, "Owl!" Then, "No, Owl uses big words, hard-to-understand words."

At last he brightens up! "I know! I think I'll go see Rabbit. I like Rabbit. Rabbit uses encouraging words like, 'How's about lunch?' and 'Help yourself, Pooh!' Yes, I think I'll go see Rabbit."

Give some oxygen—in the form of encourage-ment—to your child daily.

Encouragement is oxygen to the soul. A man hath joy by the answer of his mouth: and a word spoken in due season, how good is it!

PROVERBS 15:23

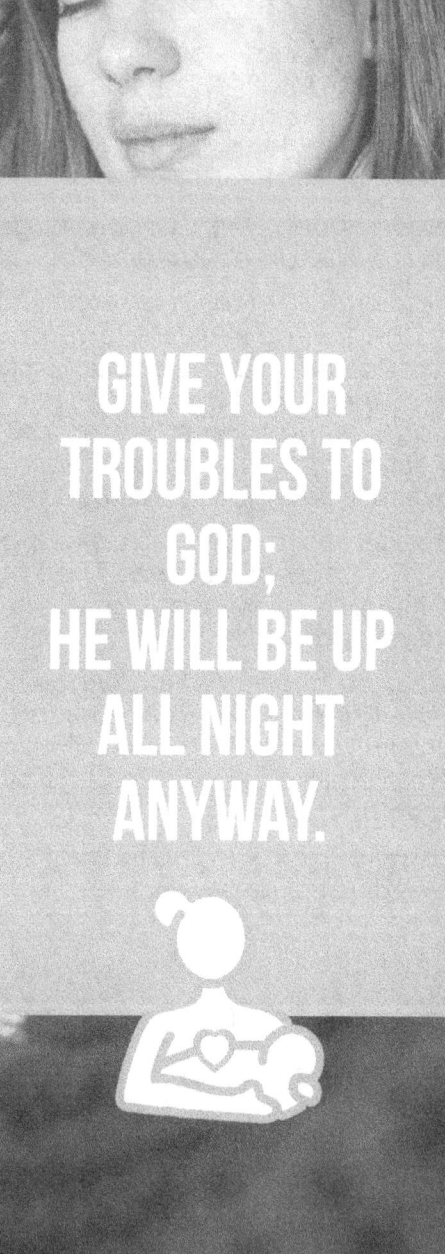

GIVE YOUR
TROUBLES TO
GOD;
HE WILL BE UP
ALL NIGHT
ANYWAY.

When Penny saw her daughter's scarlet cheeks, she became alarmed instantly. Candi had undergone a liver transplant as an infant and when Penny rushed Candi to the hospital, her fears were confirmed: the fever signaled a serious infection. Six-year-old Candi would need another liver transplant!

The same day, Candi's best friend Jason also became ill. He, too, had undergone a liver transplant. Penny and Jason's mom, Nancy, spotted each other in a hospital corridor, in the heat of crisis, each unaware of the other's latest problem. Then, the children's surgeon presented Penny with the toughest choice of her life. A liver had been found, and it was suitable for either child. The medical team had assigned the liver to Candi, but now the team felt Jason's need was more urgent. Was Penny willing to give up the liver intended for Candi so Jason might have it? She said yes.

Jason's transplant went smoothly, hut after two weeks, no liver had been found for Candi, whose condition was becoming desperate. At what seemed the last moment, a liver was found. Three weeks after the operation, Candi went home. Penny recalls, "I gave Candi's liver to Jason knowing that somehow God would provide for Candi. I thank Him every day!"

He will not allow your foot to slip; He who keeps you will not slumber.

PSALM 121:3 NASB

When Dwight D. Eisenhower was Supreme Commander of the Allied invasion of Europe during World War II, he was faced with the responsibility of making one of the most far-reaching decisions ever posed to a single man: the decision to change the date of D-Day at the last moment. The consequences of a *wrong* decision were so overwhelming, in his opinion, that he felt crushed by the weight of the decision before him. Still, he was the Supreme Commander and the only man who could make the decision that would impact millions of lives. He later wrote:

I knew I did not have the required wisdom. But turned to God. I asked God to give me the wisdom. I yielded myself to Him. I surrendered myself. And He gave me clear guidance. He gave me insight to see what was right, and He endowed me with courage to make my decision. And finally He gave me peace of mind in the knowledge that, having been guided by God to the decision, I could leave the results to Him.

Few decisions you face in life will ever approach the magnitude of the decision General Eisenhower faced. But whatever size problem we face, God wants us to trust Him enough to leave our problem with Him.

Devote yourselves to prayer, keeping alert in it with an attitude of thanksgiving.

COLOSSIANS 4:2 NASB

THE BEST
THINGS YOU CAN
GIVE CHILDREN,
NEXT TO GOOD
HABITS,
ARE GOOD
MEMORIES.

The bed was about 45 years old when Elaine's mother offered it to her. Elaine decided to refinish it for her daughter to use. Then, as she prepared to strip the wood, she noticed that the headboard was full of scratches. She deciphered one scratch as the date her parents were married. Above another date was a name she didn't recognize. A call to her mother revealed the details of a miscarriage before Elaine was born. Elaine suddenly realized the headboard had been something of a diary for her parents! She wrote down all the scratches she could decipher and over lunch with her mother, she heard stories about the times when her mother lost her purse at a department store . . . a rattlesnake was shot just as it was poised to strike her brother . . . a man saved her brother's life in Vietnam . . . her sister nearly died after falling from a swing . . . a stranger broke up a potential mugging.

Elaine couldn't strip and sand away so many memories—so she moved the headboard into her own bedroom. She and her husband began to carve their own dates and names. "Someday," she says, "we'll tell our daughter the stories from her grandparents' lives and the stories from her parents' lives. And someday the bed will pass on to her."

The memory of the just is blessed.

PROVERBS 10:7

WHEN HOME IS RULED ACCORDING TO GOD'S WORD, ANGELS MIGHT BE ASKED TO STAY WITH US, AND THEY WOULD NOT FIND THEMSELVES OUT OF THEIR ELEMENT.

Corrie ten Boom's character was shaped to a great extent by the people who visited in her home. Her mother, a gentle and compassionate woman, was able to bring harmony even to cramped quarters filled with divergent personalities. She loved guests and had a gift for "stretching a guilder until it cried." Those who came to their home found music, fun, food, and interesting conversations. Corrie kept a "blessing box" to collect coins for missionary projects and she always gave guests an opportunity to be a blessing, even as they were blessed by the ten Boom hospitality. The soup may have been watered down, but the oval table always had room for unexpected guests who arrived just before meal time. The atmosphere was one of *gezellig*, of warm exuding friendship, and it wove its way into the very fabric of Corrie's personality.

In later years as Corrie ten Boom traveled the world and was dependent upon the invitations of other Christians, she seldom stayed in hotels. Instead, she graciously accepted food and lodging from others. She once said, "I think that I am enjoying the reward for the wide open doors and hearts of our home." To those she visited, however, she was now the angel unaware, bringing with her welcome *gezellig*.

I will meditate in thy precepts, and have respect unto thy ways. I will delight myself in thy statutes: I will not forget thy word.

PSALM 119:15-16

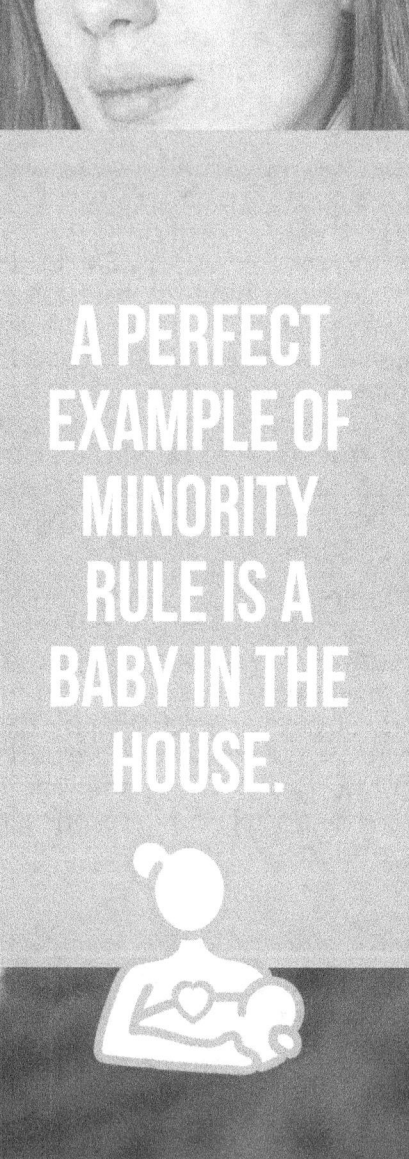

A PERFECT EXAMPLE OF MINORITY RULE IS A BABY IN THE HOUSE.

Jean Kerr shares these secrets about feeding an infant in *How I Got To Be Perfect*: "Some adults who find themselves uneasy in the silence have discovered that it is helpful to intone, rhythmically, the names of the entire family: 'Here's a bite for Grandma, here's a bite for Daddy.' . . . If the family should be small and the dish of Pablum large, the list can be padded by adding the names of all the deliverymen. A friend of mine has worked out a variant of this for her little boy. With the first bite of food she says, 'Open up the garage doors, here comes the Chevy, here comes the Cadillac,' and so forth. That child took the game so seriously that eventually he would eat only foreign cars.

"Any method is better than the method I used on our first baby. In those days I believed in enthusiasm and the hard sell . . . 'Oooh, yummy, yummy,' I would say, sounding like some manic commercial. 'Oooh, what have we got *here*? Tasty, tasty Pablum. Oooh, I wish I could have some of this delicious Pablum.' Then, to indicate that all was on the level, I would actually eat a spoonful or two. Even when I didn't gag, my expression would give the whole show away. In due time that baby found out who was in charge. He was."

There is a right time for everything: A time to laugh . . .

ECCLESIASTES 3:1,4

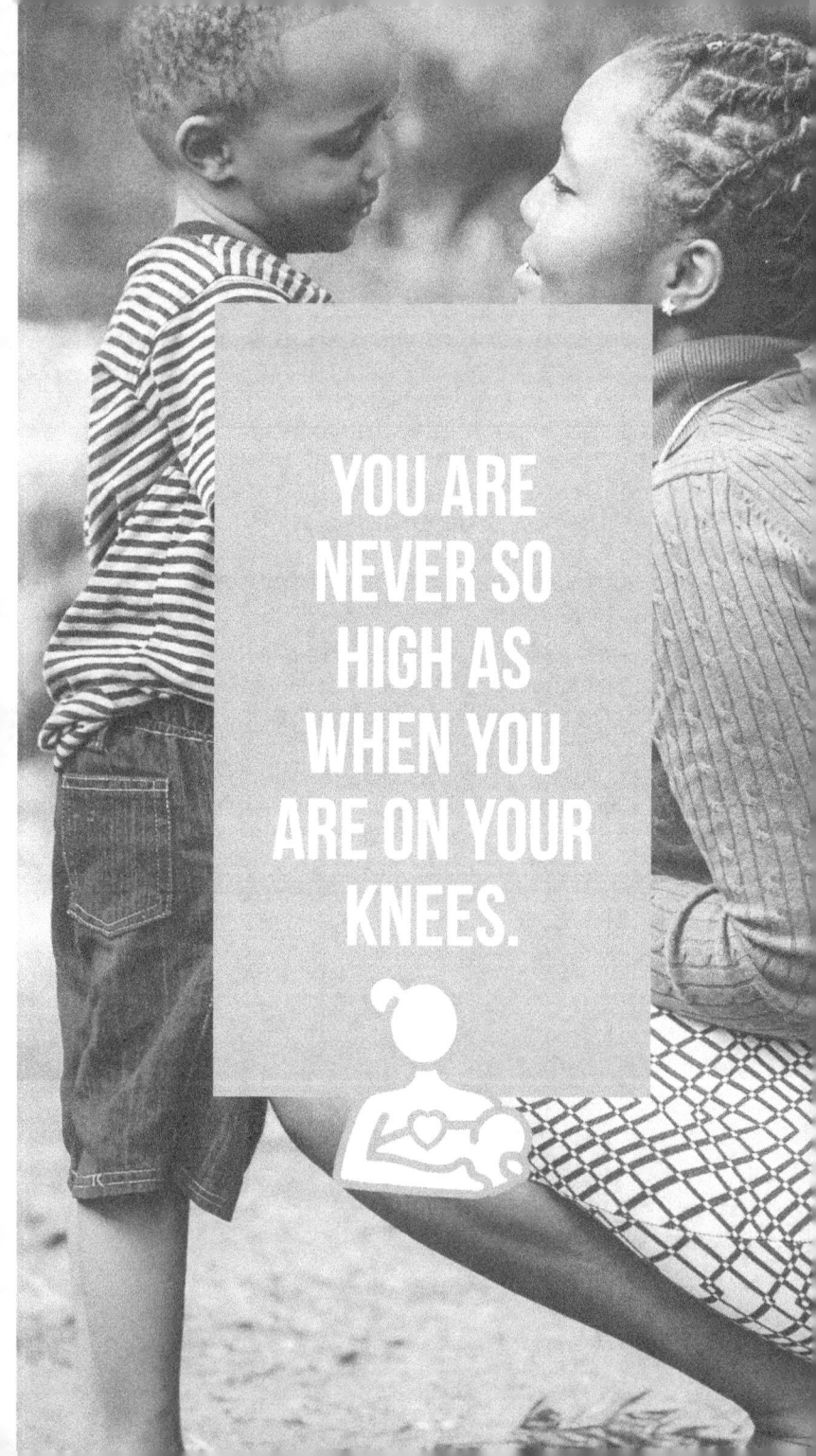

The great preacher Billy Sunday told the story of a minister who was making calls one day. He came to one home and when a child answered the door, he asked for her mother. She replied, "You cannot see Mother for she prays from nine to ten." The minister waited forty minutes. When the woman finally came out of her "prayer closet," her face was filled with such light and glory that the minister said he knew immediately why her home was so peaceful, a haven of strength and light, and why her elder daughter was a missionary and her two sons were in the ministry. Billy Sunday added his comment, "All hell cannot tear a boy or girl away from a praying mother."

Remember to pray these things for your child:
- physical, emotional, and spiritual health
- an abiding sense of safety and security
- courage to face the problems of each day
- a calm spirit to hear the voice of the Lord
- a willingness to obey
- a clear mind, both to learn and to recall
- a generous spirit toward family and friends
- wise teachers, mentors, and counselors
- unshakable self-worth and personal dignity
- eternal salvation and a home in heaven one day

Humble yourselves in the sight of the Lord, and he shall lift you up.

JAMES 4:10

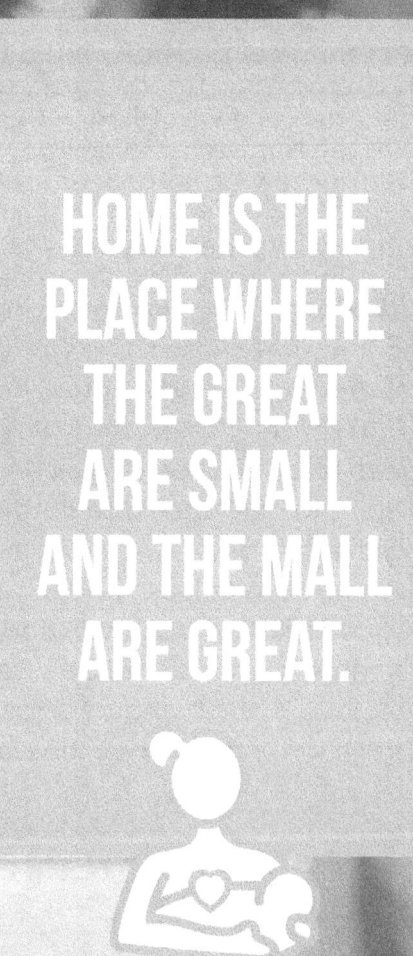

HOME IS THE
PLACE WHERE
THE GREAT
ARE SMALL
AND THE MALL
ARE GREAT.

Two well-bred, blue-blooded dogs were walking primly along the street with their noses held high. They encountered a big scruffy dog who obviously was of the Heinz-57-Varieties pedigree. At first they tried daintily to sidestep the friendly alley dog, but they were unable to do so. He was eager to make friends and trotted alongside them. One of the lady dogs said, "We really must go," to which the alley dog replied, "Well, all right, but first tell me your names so I'll know what to call your dames if I see you again."

The purebred replied haughtily, "My name is Miji, spelled M-I-J-I."

The other said daintily, "My name is Miki, spelled M-I-K-I."

"Pleased to meet you," said the low-class dog, and then he added, "My name is Fido— spelled P-H-Y-D-E-A-U-X."

Home should be a place where there's no room for pride. Respect and self-dignity, yes, but haughty arrogance born of position? No! Respect your little ones and serve them. Honor your elders and give your best to them. Don't play favorites in relationships, or allow a child to think he is favored. Ultimately, home should be a place marked by "equal-opportunity love."

But many that are first shall be last; and the last shall be first.

MATTHEW 19:30

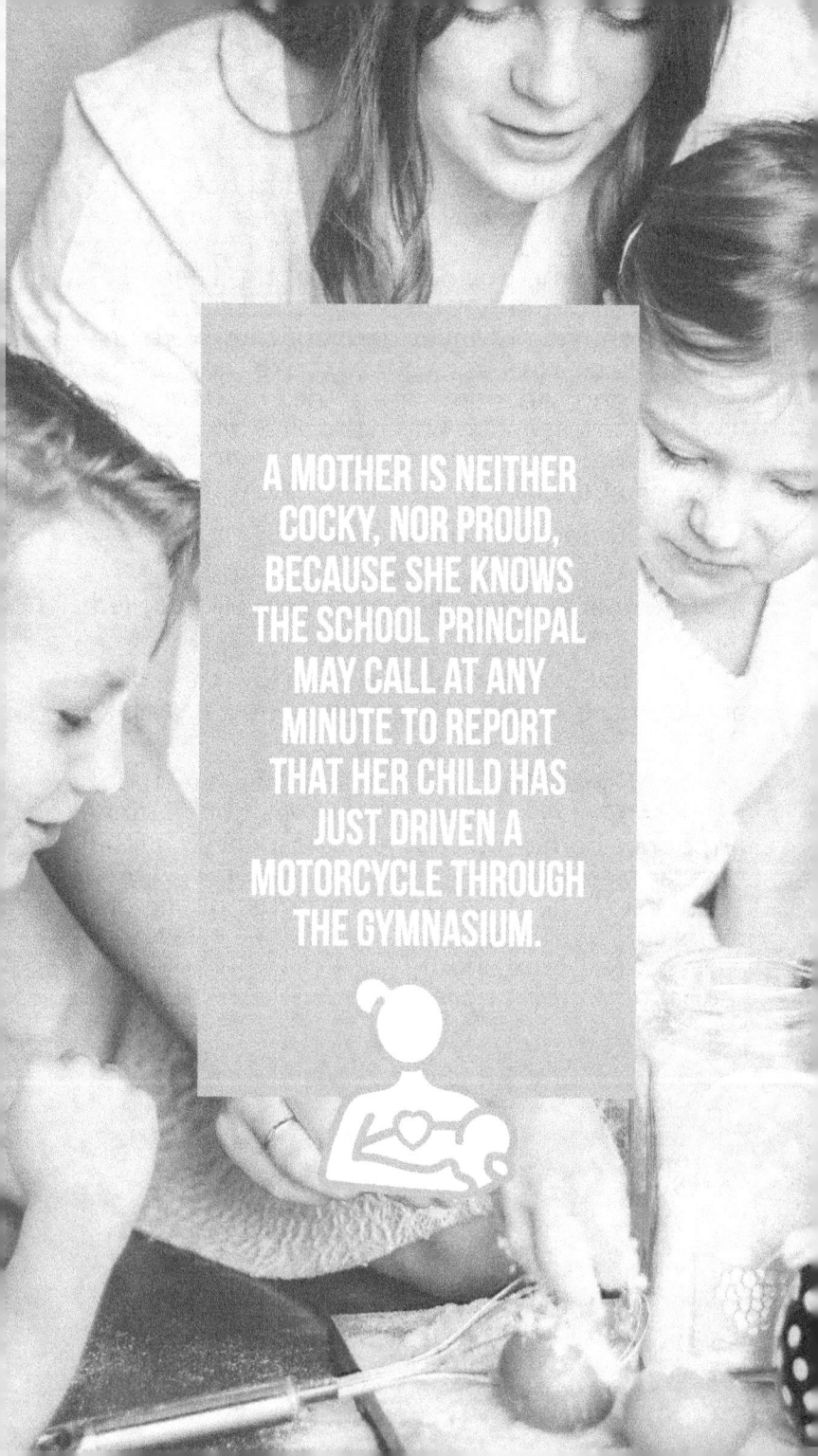

A MOTHER IS NEITHER COCKY, NOR PROUD, BECAUSE SHE KNOWS THE SCHOOL PRINCIPAL MAY CALL AT ANY MINUTE TO REPORT THAT HER CHILD HAS JUST DRIVEN A MOTORCYCLE THROUGH THE GYMNASIUM.

After picking up their three-year-old daughter after her first day of nursery school, Rosanna Smith's husband left this message for her on the voice mail system at her office:

Hi, honey. The good news is that Amanda got through her first day at school. The bad news is the principal wants to meet with us.

A second message, recorded awhile later, updated the story:

The good news is that the parents of the boy she bit aren't suing. The bad news is that he had to go to the doctor because of it, and we'll be paying the bill.

Yet a third message, recorded minutes later, added:

The good news is that once we see her teacher, the school will accept Amanda back. The bad news is that Amanda has decided to drop out.

The message ended, "Have a good day!"

A mother once noted that her favorite passage in the Bible was this: "And this too shall pass." It's a good thought to keep in mind when life takes unexpected twists and turns!

Boast not thyself of tomorrow; for thou knowest not what a day may bring forth.

PROVERBS 27:1

A CHILD IS FED WITH MILK AND PRAISE.

Consider these "Commandments for Parents," written from a child's point of view!

1. My hands are small; please don't expect perfection whenever I make a bed, draw a picture, or throw a ball. My legs are short; slow down so that I can keep up with you.

2. My eyes have not seen the world as yours have; let me explore it safely; don't restrict me unnecessarily.

3. Housework will always be there; I'm little only for a short time. Take time to explain things to me about this wonderful world, and do so willingly.

4. My feelings are tender; don't nag me all day long (you would not want to be nagged for your inquisitiveness). Treat me as you would like to be treated.

5. I am a special gift from God; treasure me as God intended you to do— holding me accountable for my actions, giving me guidelines to live by, and disciplining me in a loving manner.

6. I need your encouragement (but not your empty praise) to grow. Go easy on the criticism; remember, you can criticize the things I do without criticizing me.

Let no corrupt communication proceed out of your mouth, but that which is good to the use of edifying, that it may minister grace unto the hearers.

EPHESIANS 4:29

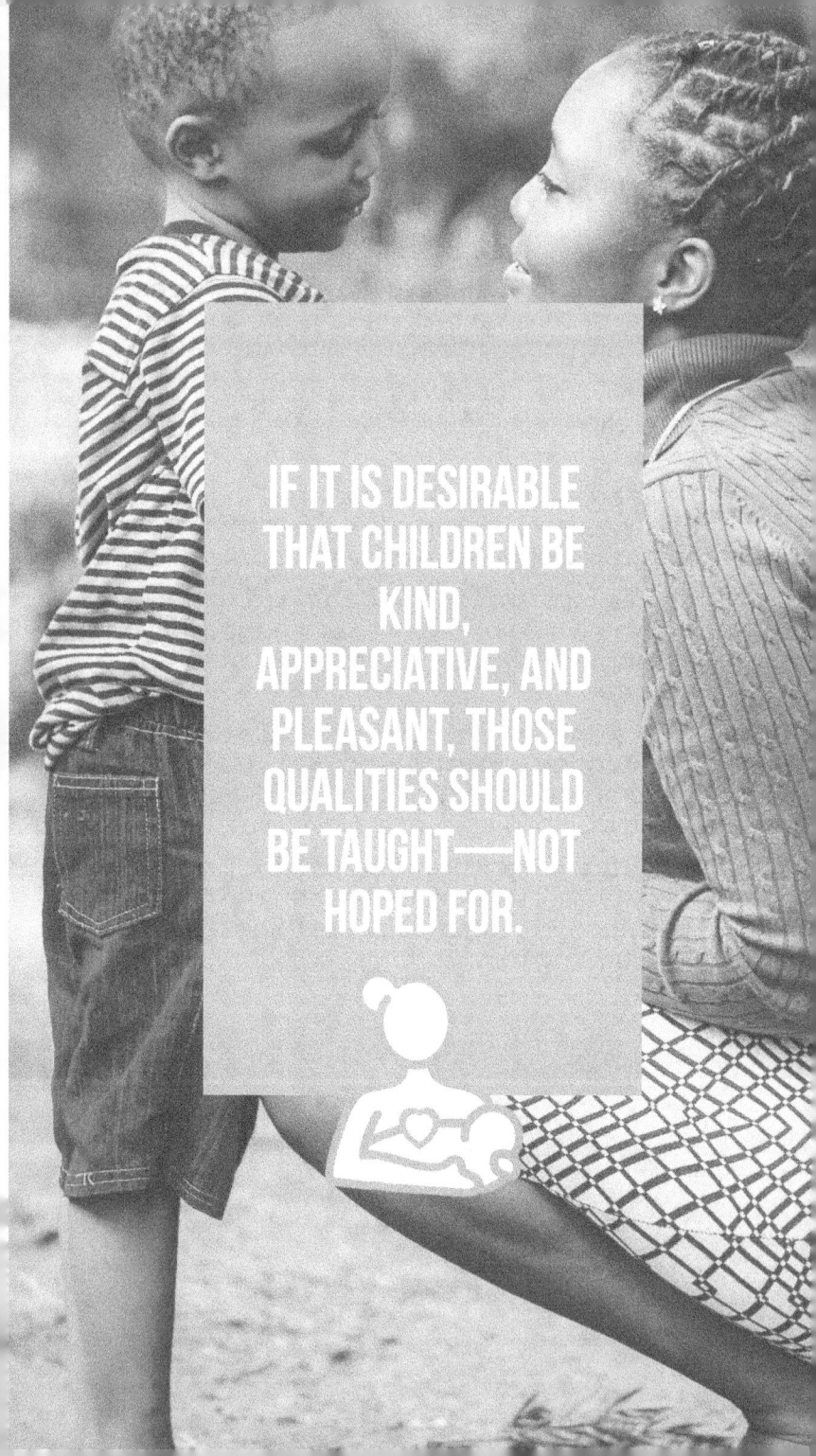

IF IT IS DESIRABLE
THAT CHILDREN BE
KIND,
APPRECIATIVE, AND
PLEASANT, THOSE
QUALITIES SHOULD
BE TAUGHT—NOT
HOPED FOR.

M ary Dow Brine's *Somebody's Mother*— here abbreviated—is a classic worthy to be memorized:

She stood at the crossing and waited long,
Alone, uncared for, amid the throng.
Past the woman so old and gray
Hastened the children on their way.
No one offered a helping hand to her—
So meek, so timid, afraid to stir
Lest the carriage wheels or the horses' feet
Should crowd her down in the slippery street.
He paused beside her and whispered low,
"I'll help you cross, if you wish to go."
Her aged hand on his strong young arm
She placed, and so, without hurt or harm,
He guided the trembling feet along,
Proud that his own were firm and strong.
Then back again to his friends he went,
His young heart happy and well content.
"She's somebody's mother, boys, you know.
For all she's aged and poor and slow.
And I hope some fellow will lend a hand
To help my mother, you understand,
If ever she's poor and old and gray,
When her own dear boy is far away."

This boy's parents taught him to be not only kind, appreciative and pleasant to his *own* family and friends but to even see a stranger as someone special.

For the commandment is a lamp; and the law is light; and reproofs of instruction are the way of life.

PROVERBS 6:23

NEVER LEND YOUR CAR TO ANYONE TO WHOM YOU HAVE GIVEN BIRTH.

Author Teresa Bloomingdale writes about driving with her teenager:

"The worst 'first' has to be the first time your child drives your car with you sitting beside him. (I do wish they would not call that the 'death seat.') I have tried to avoid this traumatic 'first' by refusing to get into a car with any of my children until they have taken Driver's Education and been duly licensed. But it doesn't help, because if there is anything more nerve-racking than riding with a nervous teenager who is learning to drive, it is riding with a self-confident kid who thinks he knows everything.

"I wish I could say that the more a mother rides with her teenager, the easier it gets to climb into that car, but such is not the case. Every time I get into a car beside one of my driving children, I am convinced that before we travel six blocks we shall both be killed. Thus, whenever possible, I think up an excuse to stay home . . . I am fully aware that his chances of having an accident will not be decreased by my absence, but since I am sure that he will have an accident with or without me, I would prefer that it be without me. After all, I have nine other children to think of. (And oh, dear God, nine other children who will all be driving someday!)"

A merry heart doeth good like a medicine.

PROVERBS 17:22

Some years ago a boy in a small town in Florida heard that the Russians were our enemies. He began to wonder about the Russian children, finding it hard to believe they were his enemies, too. He wrote a short note: "Dear Comrade in Russia, I am seven years old and I believe that we can live in peace. I want to be your friend, not your enemy. Will you become my friend and write to me?"

He closed the letter "Love and Peace" and signed his name. He then folded the note, put it neatly into an empty bottle, and threw it into an inland lake near his home. Several days later, the bottle and note were retrieved on a nearby beach. A story about the note appeared in a local newspaper and a wire service picked up the story and sent it nationwide. A group of people from New Hampshire who were taking children to the Soviet Union as ambassadors of peace read the article, contacted the boy and his family, and invited them to go with them. In the end, the little boy, accompanied by his father, traveled to Moscow and became a peacemaker to the Soviet Union!

One boy decided he could make a difference and he acted on that. When we act with purity of heart, nothing becomes impossible to us—child or adult!

Behold, children are a gift of the Lord.

PSALM 127:3A NASB

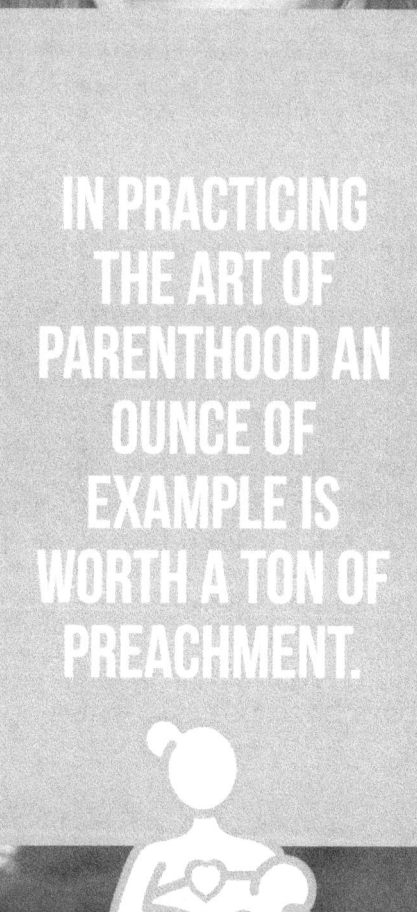

IN PRACTICING THE ART OF PARENTHOOD AN OUNCE OF EXAMPLE IS WORTH A TON OF PREACHMENT.

Jane Goodall spent more than thirty years in Africa and became the world's top authority on chimpanzees. She writes about the support that helped her get started:

"When I decided that the place for me was Africa, everybody said to my mother, 'Why don't you tell Jane to concentrate on something attainable?' But I have a truly remarkable mother.

"When I was two years old, I took a crowd of earthworms to bed to watch how they wriggled in the bedclothes. How many mothers would have said 'ugh' and thrown them out the window? But mine said, 'Jane, if you leave the worms here they'll be dead in the morning. They need the earth.' So I quickly gathered them up and ran with them into the garden. My mother always looked at things from my point of view."

"Seeing things from your child's point of view" is one of the most valuable ways to interact with your child! Periodically get down on the floor and play with your child. As you do, show by example how to play, how to share, how to interact, how to cooperate or compete in a friendly manner, and how to put away toys or organize a play space. What you do, your child will do!

Let your light so shine before men, that they may see your good works, and glorify your Father which is in heaven.

MATTHEW 5:16

CHILDREN
SPELL "LOVE"

...

T-I-M-E.

A father called his young son while out of town on business and asked, "What would you like for me to bring you?"

The two-year-old whispered, "Come out clock." The father wasn't sure he had understood him, so he asked his son to repeat his request. Again the boy said, "Come out clock."

The man thought this fairly odd, but the next day on his way to the airport, he bought a large toy clock for his son. His son happily opened the present, played with it a few minutes, and then returned to doing what he had done virtually nonstop since his father had walked in the door: tug at his pants leg. The man looked at his wife as if to say, *What's going on? I don't get it.*

At that moment their cuckoo clock began to strike the hour and on cue, figurines of a woodcutter and his wife popped out, chasing a little boy and girl, with all four then retreating into their cottage. The little boy looked up at the clock, then beamed at his father. The mother suddenly understood. "Each time the clock has struck the hour," she explained, "I've been telling our son, 'It's about time for Daddy to come home.' I think he must have been waiting for you to come out of the clock and chase him around the house!" The father promptly did, to glees of laughter!

Children soon learn how *precious* time is—that's why when a parent gives it to them they feel so loved!

Don't be fools; be wise: make the most of every opportunity you have for doing good.

EPHESIANS 5:16 TLB

THE MOTHER'S LOVE IS LIKE GOD'S LOVE; HE LOVES US NOT BECAUSE WE ARE LOVABLE, BUT BECAUSE IT IS HIS NATURE TO LOVE, AND BECAUSE WE ARE HIS CHILDREN.

Sarah's second child was born with a club-foot, just as her first child had been. At that time, such a child was called a "child of the devil." But that wasn't true in Sarah's thinking. When she saw that her son had a quick mind, she worked night and day for many years as a maid in other people's homes to pay for his education. She taught her son Thad to keep on fighting, no matter how great the odds against him, and she loved him with all her heart.

When young Thad was cruelly taunted as a "cripple" by his classmates, Sarah comforted and encouraged him, and with each passing year, he became more confident. Thaddeus eventually went to law school. His interest turned to those he saw as less fortunate than himself, especially black slaves.

He often paid the doctor bills of crippled boys, and he once spent $300 of his savings, intended for law books, to buy the freedom of a black man about to be sold away from his family. Over the years, Thaddeus Stevens became loved by American blacks as a hero second only to Abraham Lincoln, and he was considered the greatest defender of former slaves.

A mother's love truly can redeem a child's weakness, and turn it into a strength!

Herein is love, not that we loved God, but that he loved us, and sent his Son to be the propitiation for our sins. Beloved, if God so loved us, we ought also to love one another.

1 JOHN 4:10-11

THERE IS ONLY ONE PRETTY CHILD IN THE WORLD, AND EVERY MOTHER HAS IT.

During World War I, one of the most popular songs was that about a rookie named Jim. The song recounts a mother telling a friend how she stood on the sidewalk and watched her son's regiment march by. Oh, how proud she was of him! But, as Jim came marching by, she noticed something amiss. All the other young men were putting down their right foot when Jim was putting down his left. When all the others were going right-left, Jim was marching left-right. She concludes, as many a proud mother might:

"Were you there?

And tell me did you notice?

They were all out of step but Jim!"

Mothers should never live in denial about their children's mistakes or faults. Facing weaknesses, and helping a child to face them, is one of the best ways to help a child grow strong. At the same time, the Scriptures tell us that "love covers a multitude of sins." In truly loving a person, we are not to deny their flaws, but to say instead, "I choose to love this person in spite of their mistakes and flaws, and to focus instead, on all the things that make this person beautiful, wonderful, and lovable!"

He hath made every thing beautiful in his time.

ECCLESIASTES 3:11

THE BEST TIME TO
GIVE CHILDREN
YOUR ADVICE IS
WHEN THEY ARE
YOUNG ENOUGH TO
BELIEVE YOU KNOW
WHAT YOU ARE
TALKING ABOUT.

Through the years, one of the most popular comic strips about family life was that of "Momma," by Mel Lazarus. Momma was always trying to straighten out her three grown children. Of major concern to her was the proper courtship and marriage of her daughter, Mary Lou.

In one strip, Mary Lou is shown on the front porch saying good night to her boyfriend. He is whispering sweet nothings in her ear. Momma is trying to eavesdrop from the window, but can't quite hear what's going on.

Once Mary Lou is inside the house, Momma asks, "Mary Lou, what did he whisper to you?"

Mary Lou answers, "Ah, just 'love stuff,' Momma."

Momma then says, "Decent 'love stuff' can be spoken freely, out loud . . . Decent 'love stuff' can be shouted from rooftops." In the final frame of the comic strip Momma's voice crescendos to a climax: "decent 'love stuff' can be embroidered on samplers!"

There is a right time for everything: a time to laugh.

ECCLESIASTES 3:1,4 TLB

THE FAMILY TREE
IS WORTH
BRAGGING ABOUT
IF IT HAS
CONSISTENCY
PRODUCED GOOD
TIMBER, AND NOT
JUST NUTS.

The children of a prominent family thought hard and long about what they could give to their father as a present. They finally decided to commission a professional biographer to write a book detailing the family history. In meeting with the biographer, the children gave him numerous documents and anecdotes to weave into the account, as well as scores of photographs. Then one of the children said, "We have one more matter we need to discuss with you—the family's black sheep." In hushed whispers, they told about an uncle who had been convicted of first degree murder and executed in the electric chair.

"No problem," the biographer assured the children, "I can handle this situation so there will be no embarrassment."

"We don't want to lie," said one of the children.

The biographer agreed, "I'll merely say that Uncle Samuel occupied a chair of applied electronics at an important government institution. He was attached to his position by the strongest of ties and his death came as a real shock."

A good reputation is something that can never be purchased or traded. It can only be acquired by choices rooted in integrity and morality.

A good name is rather to be chosen than great riches.

PROVERBS 22:1

A HAPPY CHILDHOOD IS ONE OF THE BEST GIFTS THAT PARENTS HAVE IT IN THEIR POWER TO BESTOW.

His mother, Eliza, was an intelligent woman with strong common sense and strait-laced conduct. A disciplinarian, she was devoutly religious, and a believer in hard work and thrift. Her strong will and deep piety gave her a remarkable serenity, which she transmitted to her son, John. A diligent and serious student. John was trained by his mother in matters of piety, neatness, and industry. Attendance at church and Sunday school was weekly.

His father was full of the joy of life and loved song, talk, and sociability. He taught John to develop his innate gift for business. William was as anxious as Eliza that all their children grow up self-reliant, honest, keen-witted, and dependable. John recalled later that both of his parents were examples of courtesy and patience. He said, "I cannot remember to have heard the voices of either Father or Mother raised in anger or complaint in speaking to any of us."

William and Eliza also instilled in their son a rich heritage of giving to church and charities, the gifts being made from their childhood earnings. In all, William and Eliza gave their son, John D. Rockefeller, a happy childhood—a gift he valued throughout his life far more than the millions of dollars he made.

Withhold not good from them to whom it is due, when it is in the power of thine hand to do it.

PROVERBS 3:27

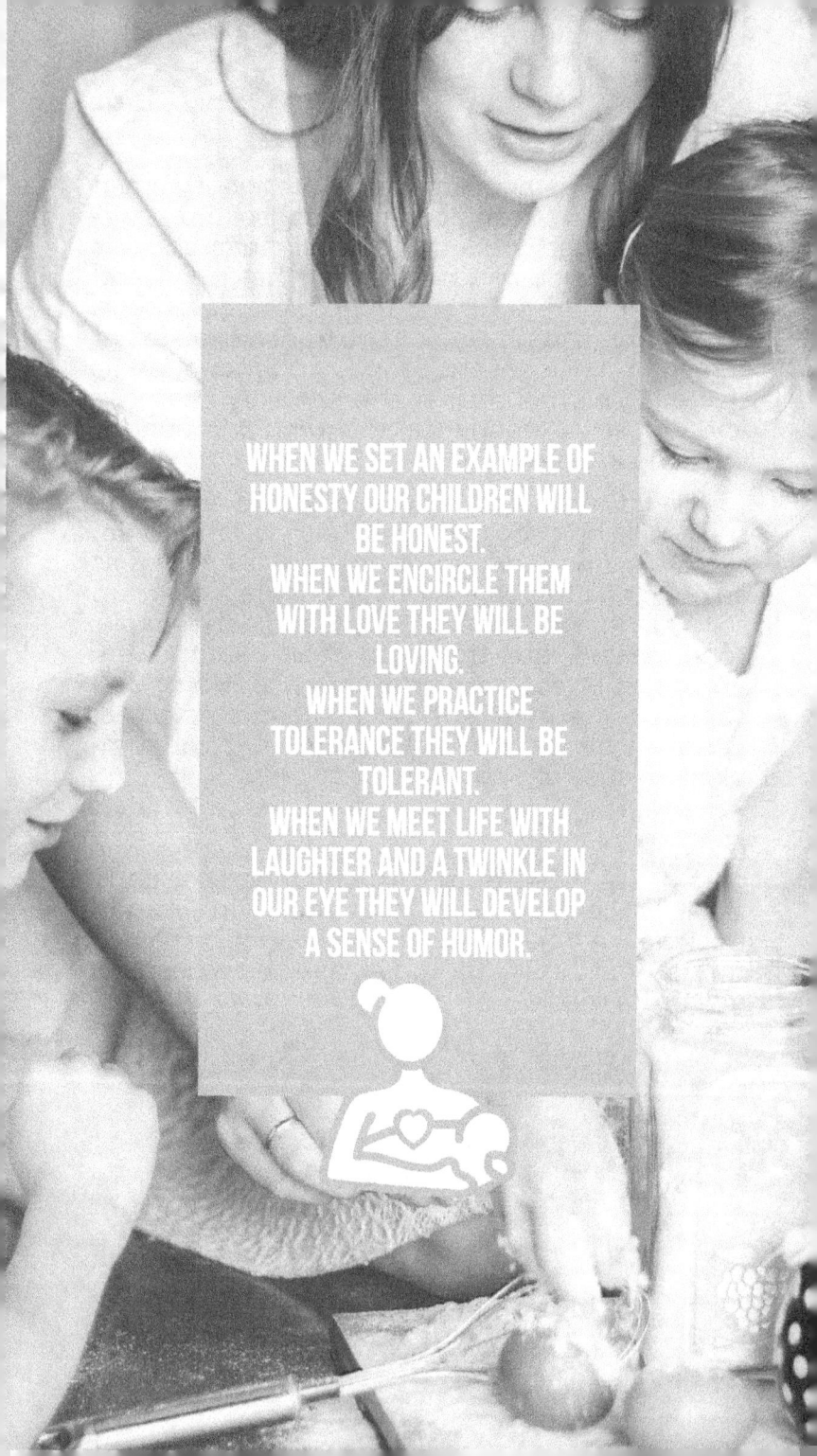

WHEN WE SET AN EXAMPLE OF HONESTY OUR CHILDREN WILL BE HONEST.
WHEN WE ENCIRCLE THEM WITH LOVE THEY WILL BE LOVING.
WHEN WE PRACTICE TOLERANCE THEY WILL BE TOLERANT.
WHEN WE MEET LIFE WITH LAUGHTER AND A TWINKLE IN OUR EYE THEY WILL DEVELOP A SENSE OF HUMOR.

Behavioral pediatrician John Obedzinski saw two types of families in his practice. On one hand were well-educated parents who raised their children "progressively," allowing their children total freedom of choice and expression. Their children were often sullen, arrogant, and totally self-absorbed. On the other hand were parents who were harsh disciplinarians and who made all their children's decisions. These children were often rebellious. Obedzinski set out to study resilient, happy families that seemed to weather life's ups and downs with loyalty and love. In doing so, he found these seven traits to be common:

· the children knew their place—a family is not a democracy and children do not have total freedom,

· the family values tradition and keeps treasured rituals, especially at holiday time,

· family members admit their mistakes openly,

· family members acknowledge their differences and try to accommodate them,

· children are taught to compete against each other in ways that are fair and friendly,

· children have chores and responsibilities, and

· family members tease one another and laugh at their own foibles, but the humor is never malicious.

Be thou an example of the believers, in word, in conversation, in charity, in spirit, in faith, in purity.

1 TIMOTHY 4:12

WOMEN SHOULD NOT HAVE CHILDREN AFTER 35—35 CHILDREN IS ENOUGH.

A mother already had five children under the age of ten, when she gave birth to twins. The minister who came to see her in the hospital said, "I see the Lord has smiled on you again."

"Smiled?" the woman shrieked. "He laughed right out loud!"

Another woman once said to her visiting minister, "I thank God for my sons."

The minister replied, "I'm sure they're all good, productive citizens."

She replied, "Oh, yes. The firstborn is a doctor, the second became a lawyer, the third is a chemist, the fourth an artist, and the fifth a writer." The minister was obviously impressed and then she added, "But thank God my husband and I had a dry goods store. Not a big one, mind you, but it's still enough for us to be able to support them all."

And finally there was the mother who remarked, "When I was young, my parents told me what to do. Now my children all tell me what to do. When is it that I get to do what I want to do?"

Happy is the man that hath his quiver full of them.

PSALM 127:5

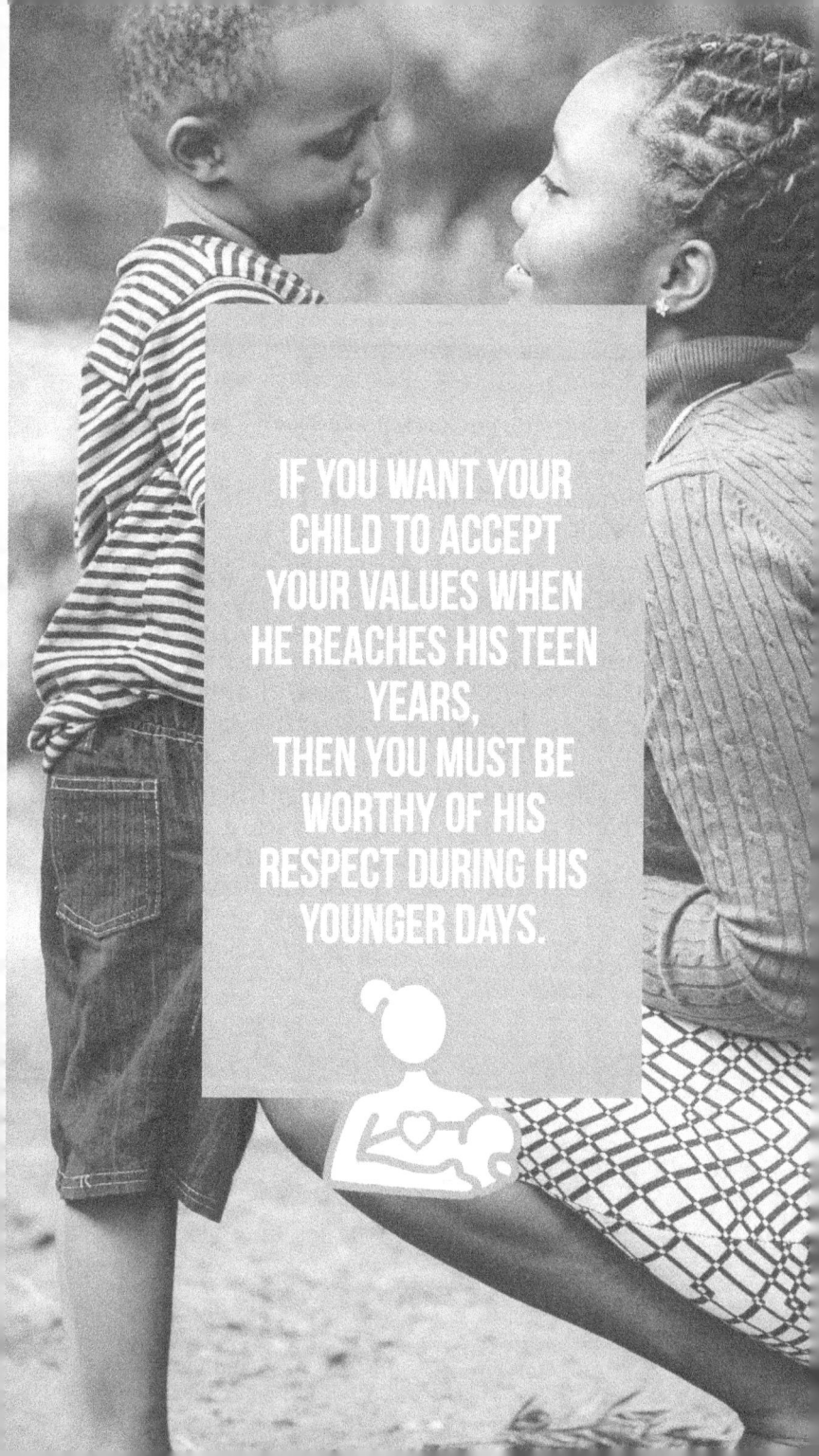

IF YOU WANT YOUR CHILD TO ACCEPT YOUR VALUES WHEN HE REACHES HIS TEEN YEARS,
THEN YOU MUST BE WORTHY OF HIS RESPECT DURING HIS YOUNGER DAYS.

Benjamin Franklin came to a personal conclusion that the lighting of streets would not only add gentility to his city, hut also make his city safer. In seeking to interest the people of his native Philadelphia in street lighting, however, he didn't try to persuade them by *talking* about street lighting. Instead, he hung a beautiful lantern on a long bracket before his own door. Then he kept the glass brightly polished, and carefully and diligently lit the wick every evening just as dusk approached.

People wandering down the dark street saw Franklin's light a long way off. They found its glow not only friendly and beautiful, but a point of helpful guidance. Before long, other neighbors began placing lights on long brackets before their own homes. Soon, the entire city was dotted with such lights and the entire city awoke to the value of street lighting. The matter was taken up with interest and enthusiasm as a citywide, city-sponsored endeavor.

Just as Franklin lit a lantern for his city, so too, our actions as parents are like beacons to our children. What they see, they copy. And when what they see is good, what they copy is also *good*!

In order to offer ourselves as a model for you, that you might follow our example.

2 THESSALONIANS 3:9 NASB

A MOTHER FINDS OUT WHAT IS MEANT BY SPITTING IMAGE WHEN SHE TRIES TO FED CEREAL TO HER BABY.

In *The Christian Mother*, Jacky Hertz writes: *"However sweet and lovable, babies are still very inconsiderate and often dirty creatures. Will I ever forget one day as we were living in Sitka, Alaska? All I had to do while Bill worked eight hours a day on a new naval base nearby was to keep up the tiny two-room house and care for our first baby, then eleven months old. Surely, some would say, I could have cleaned the entire 20-by-20-foot house in two hours a day and had leisure to spare. But life doesn't give us what we'd like.*

"One day the baby had been quiet too long. I went to the bedroom to see if all that silence was really sleep. . . . The view that met my eyes made me want to turn and run crying, or beat my head against the wall. . . . But I only began to laugh, and then to dissolve in hysterical giggles. Being fairly new to motherhood, I'd carelessly pinned his diaper with only two pins, one on either side. Now I saw he had soiled the diaper and, being wide awake, had begun to play. . . . He'd smeared the sheet . . . the mattress . . . the bars of the crib . . . the bottoms of his feet . . . between his toes . . . his hands . . . his clothes . . . his face . . . his hair. Yet from the middle of all this unholy mess his eyes were so innocent!"

There is a right time for everything: a time to laugh.

ECCLESIASTES 3:1,4 TLB

LOVING A CHILD IS A CIRCULAR BUSINESS . . . THE MORE YOU GIVE, THE MORE YOU GET, THE MORE YOU GET, THE MORE YOU GIVE.

A reporter once interviewed the famous contralto Marion Anderson and asked her to name the greatest moment in her life. The reporter knew she had many big moments to choose from. He expected her to name the private concert she gave at the White House for the Roosevelts and the King and Queen of England. He thought she might name the night she received the $10,000 Bok Award as the person who had done the most for her hometown, Philadelphia. Instead, Marion Anderson shocked him by responding quickly, "The greatest moment in my life was the day I went home and told my mother she wouldn't have to take in washing anymore."

The circular pattern of love between a parent and child is more than a matter of "what goes around, comes around." Rather, it stems from the principle that what a child sees, a child copies. Children are not born to be selfless and generous. Their more common cries are rooted in "Me first! Mine! I want." A child must learn to share, to sacrifice for others, to give spontaneously and from the heart. And a child learns that lesson quickly and most easily by copying someone else . . . usually his or her mother!

Give, and it will be given to you . . . For by your standard of measure it will be measured to you in return.

LUKE 6:38 NASB

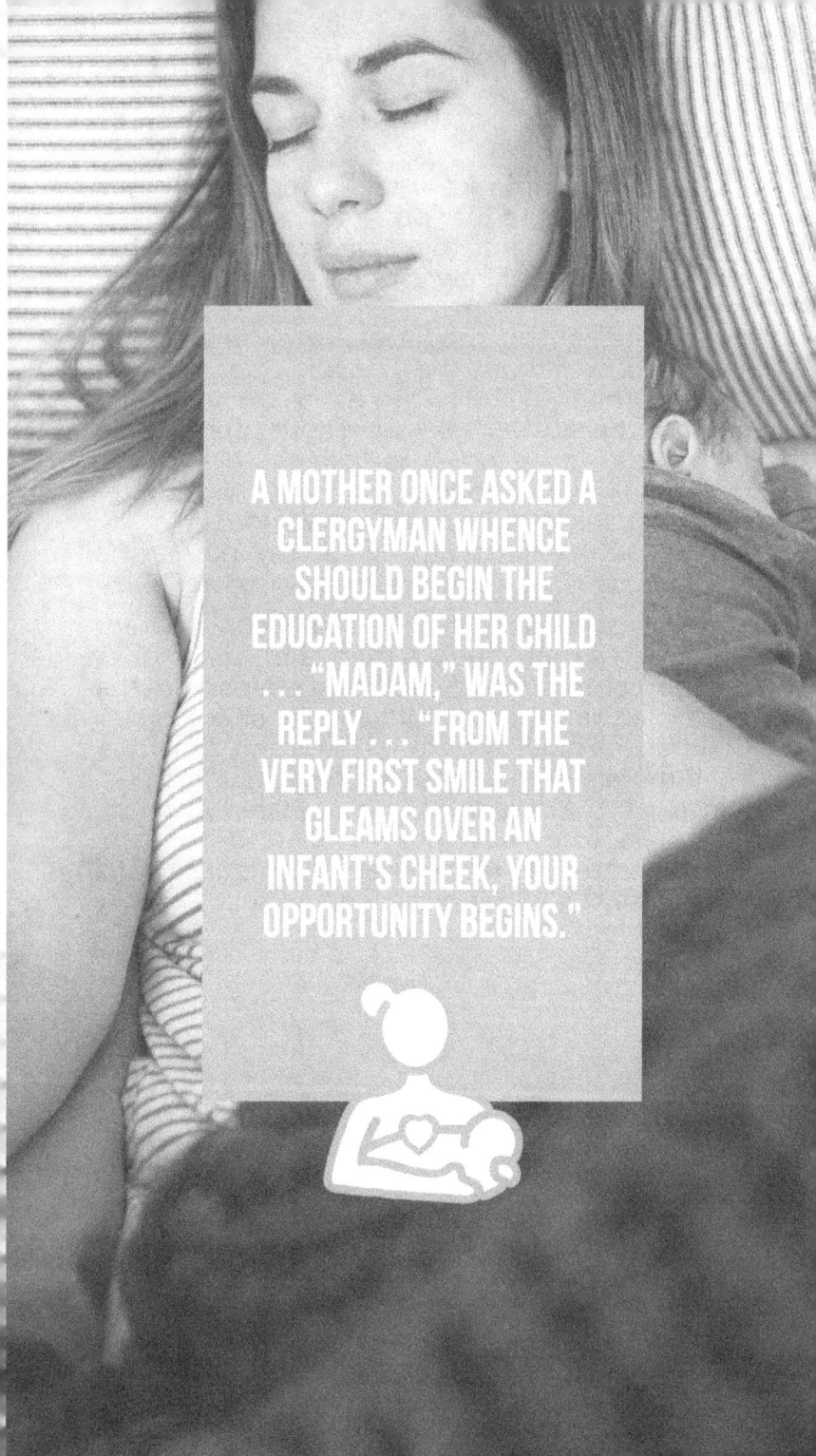

A MOTHER ONCE ASKED A CLERGYMAN WHENCE SHOULD BEGIN THE EDUCATION OF HER CHILD . . . "MADAM," WAS THE REPLY . . . "FROM THE VERY FIRST SMILE THAT GLEAMS OVER AN INFANT'S CHEEK, YOUR OPPORTUNITY BEGINS."

D r. Albert Siegel was quoted by the *Stanford Observer* as saying: "When it comes to rearing children, every society is only 20 years away from barbarism. Twenty years is all we have to accomplish the task of civilizing the infants who are born into our midst each year. These savages know nothing of our language, our culture, our religion, our values, our customs of interpersonal relations communism, fascism, democracy, civil liberties, the rights of the minority, respect, decency, honesty, customs, conventions, and manners. *The barbarian must be tamed if civilization is to survive.*"

A report from the Minnesota Crime Commission echoes this sentiment: "Every baby . . . wants what he wants when he wants it: his bottle, his mother's attention, his playmate's toy, his uncle's watch. Deny these and he seethes with rage and aggressiveness which would be murderous were he not so helpless. This means that all children, not just certain children, are born delinquent. If permitted to continue in the self-centered world of infancy . . . every child would grow up a criminal."

The parent who does not punish wrongdoing by an infant, permits it to be done by their teenager.

Train up a child in the way he should go, even when he is old he will not depart from it.

PROVERBS 22:6 NASB

SIMPLY HAVING CHILDREN DOES NOT MAKE MOTHERS.

Rachel had a close relationship with her mother, Maria, and after graduating from college, Rachel invited her mother to live with her. When her sister died, Rachel and Maria took in her two young daughters. Later. Rachel also took in her young nephew Roger and raised him as her own son. Maria kept house and typed Rachel's first two books, *Under the Sea-Wind* and *The Sea Around Us*.

When her mother died in 1958, Rachel wrote: "Her love of life and of all living things was her outstanding quality ... And while gentle and compassionate, she could fight fiercely against anything she believed wrong, as in our present Crusade! Knowing how she felt about that will help me to return to it soon, and to carry' it through to completion." Return, she did, writing *Silent Spring*, a book about the dangers of chemical pesticides— taking time out only to explore the woods with, read to, and play with Roger. The Environmental Protection Agency was formed in 1970, largely as a result of public outcry in the wake of her book.

Although she never married or bore children of her own, Rachel Carson is called by many, "mother of the age of ecology"—a genuine mother *at heart*.

Teach the young women to be sober . . . . to love their children.

TITUS 2:4

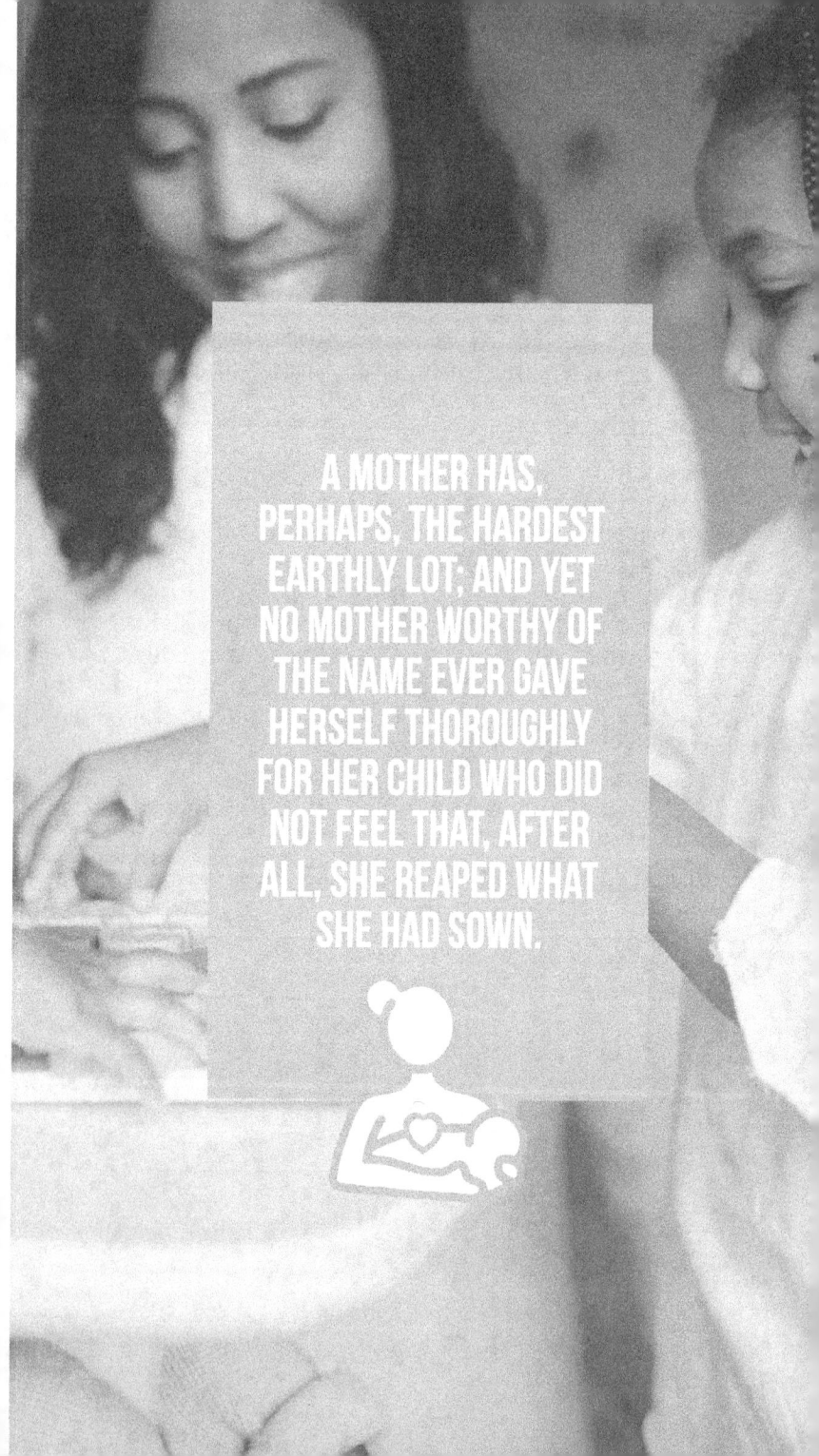

A MOTHER HAS, PERHAPS, THE HARDEST EARTHLY LOT; AND YET NO MOTHER WORTHY OF THE NAME EVER GAVE HERSELF THOROUGHLY FOR HER CHILD WHO DID NOT FEEL THAT, AFTER ALL, SHE REAPED WHAT SHE HAD SOWN.

As a boy in Naples, he worked long hours in a factory, all the while yearning to be a singer. When he was ten years old, he took his first voice lesson. The teacher promptly concluded, "You can't sing. You haven't any voice at all. Your voice sounds like the wind in the shutters."

The boy's mother, however, heard greatness in her son's voice. She believed in his talent, and even though they were poor, she put her arms around him and said encouragingly, "My boy, I am going to make every sacrifice to pay for your voice lessons."

This mother's confidence in her son and her constant encouragement of him through the years paid off! Her boy became one of the most widely acclaimed singers around the world. His name? Enrico Caruso.

What is your child's special talent? His desire?

What are your child's unique gifts—mentally, physically, spiritually?

What more can you do to nurture them, even as you nurture your child?

Unearth and foster your child's gifts and you tally have brought rare riches to the world.

And let us not be weary in well doing: for in due season we all reap, if we faint not.

GALATIANS 6:9

THE HIGHEST PINNACLE OF THE SPIRITUAL LIFE IS NOT JOY IN UNBROKEN SUNSHINE BUT ABSOLUTE AND UNDOUBTING TRUST IN THE LOVE OF GOD.

As Louisa Stead, her husband, and their young daughter were enjoying an ocean-side picnic one day. they noticed a young boy struggling in the surf. As the drowning boy cried out for help, Mr. Stead rushed to save him. Unfortunately, he was pulled under the waves by the terrified boy and both drowned as Louisa and her daughter watched helplessly from the shore.

In the sorrowful days that followed, the grief-stricken widow began to put pen to paper and the result was a hymn known to millions:

'Tis so sweet to trust in Jesus, just to take Him at His word, just to rest upon His promise, just to know, "Thus saith the Lord."

O how sweet to trust in Jesus, just to trust His cleansing blood, just in simple faith to plunge me 'neath the healing, cleansing flood!

Yes, tis sweet to trust in Jesus, just from sin and self to cease, just from Jesus simply taking life and rest and joy and peace.

I'm so glad I learned to trust Thee, Precious Jesus, Savior, Friend; and I know that Thou art with me, wilt be with me to the end.

Trusting Jesus, Louisa went as a missionary to Africa, where she served the Lord for 25 years!

For whatsoever is born of God overcometh the world: and this is the victory that overcometh the world, even our faith.

1 JOHN 5:4

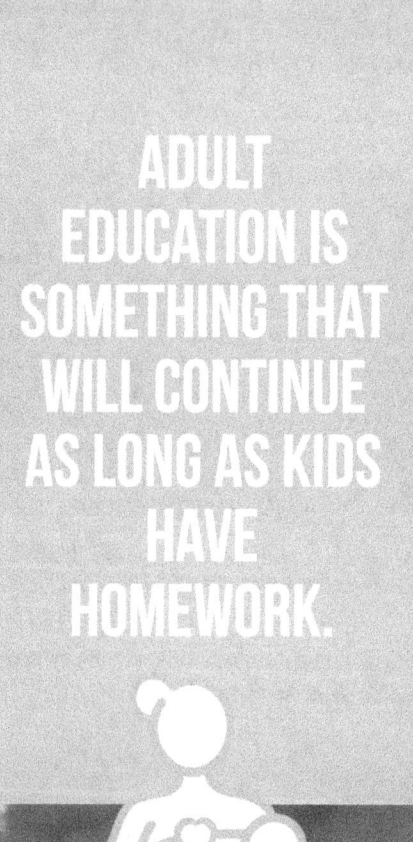

ADULT
EDUCATION IS
SOMETHING THAT
WILL CONTINUE
AS LONG AS KIDS
HAVE
HOMEWORK.

B ill Cosby has written in *Fatherhood* this humorous account about parents and homework:

When your child is struggling in school, you have such a strong desire to help that you often find it easier just to do the work yourself than to use a middleman. A few weeks ago my daughter came to me and said, "Dad, I'm in a bind. I've got to do this paper right away."

"All right," I said, "what's your plan of work?"

"You type it for me."

Once again, I typed her paper; but when I had finished and looked at the work, I said, "I'm afraid there's just one problem."

"What's that?" she said.

"This is awful. As your secretary, I can't let you turn this in."

"Needless to say, I rewrote it for her and I picked up a B minus. I would have had a B plus if I hadn't misspelled all those words.

"And so, I've now done high school at least twice, probably closer to three times; and I've gone through college a couple of times, too."

There is a right time for everything: a time to laugh.

ECCLESIASTES 3:1,4 TLB

IF A CHILD LIVES WITH APPROVAL, HE LEARNS TO LIVE WITH HIMSELF.

Samuel Blackwell was an intelligent and warm-hearted man, an enthusiastic supporter of religious tolerance, women's rights, and the abolition of slavery. When his children were barred from public schools because of his religious convictions, he hired private tutors for them. As a result, they received an even better education than they would have had—the girls pursuing the same course of study as the boys. His wife Hannah encouraged a love of music and reading in her children. Their home was a magnet for intellectuals of the period, and from their earliest years, the children were exposed to people who valued clear thinking, social awareness, and new ideas. Above all, the Blackwell children were accepted as equals by their parents and given major doses of loving approval.

Five Blackwell girls had careers: Elizabeth and Emily as doctors, Anna a newspaper correspondent, Marian a teacher, Ellen an author and artist. One son, Samuel, married America's first woman minister, Antoinette Brown. Son Henry married Lucy Stone, the women's rights leader. All this in an age when women were not allowed to serve on juries, cast ballots, testify in courts, and were barred from most higher education and from many professions!

When a parent shows their approval of a child and their talents they never learn to limit their abilities.

Wherefore, accept one another, just as Christ also accepted us to the glory of God.

ROMANS 15:7 NASB

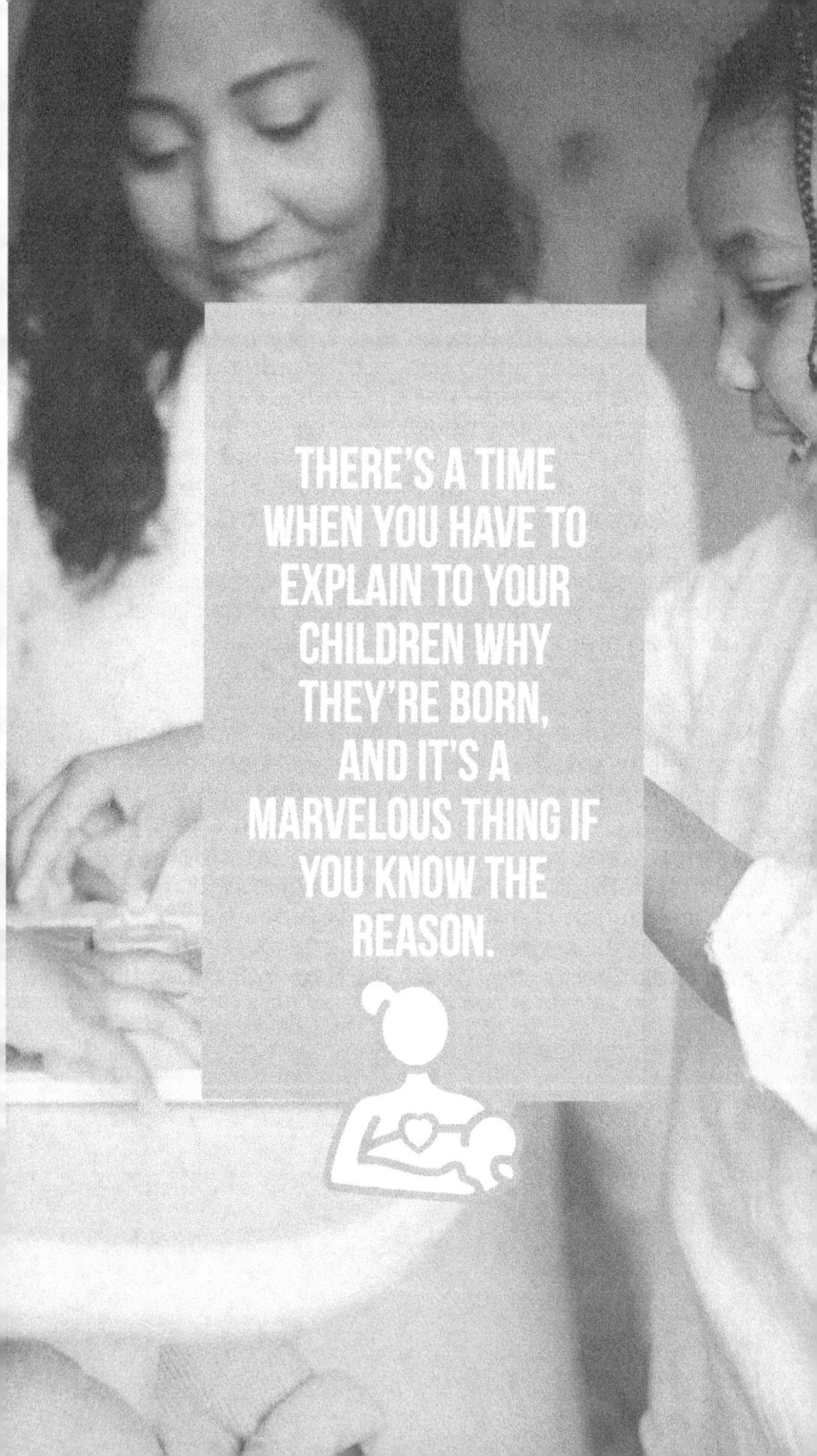

THERE'S A TIME WHEN YOU HAVE TO EXPLAIN TO YOUR CHILDREN WHY THEY'RE BORN, AND IT'S A MARVELOUS THING IF YOU KNOW THE REASON.

D r. Walter L. Wilson tells the story of a woman who attended one of his meetings. She waited after the service so she could have a few private moments with him since she felt as if her life had no meaning and no purpose—that she was invisible to God. As part of his counseling. Dr. Wilson asked the woman if she could quote any of the Scriptures. She replied that she had once learned John 3:16 in Sunday school.

Dr. Wilson then asked the woman to recite the verse. She said, "For God so loved the world, that he gave his only forgotten Son, that whosoever believeth in him should not perish, but have everlasting life."

Immediately Dr. Wilson noticed that she had used the word *forgotten* instead of *begotten* in quoting the verse. He asked, "Do you know why God forgot His Son?"

She said, "No, I don't."

He replied, "It was because He wanted to remember *you*."

Apart from your personal and family reasons for bearing your child, the Lord has a divine reason for your child's birth. He has a place for your child to fill and a role for your child to fulfill. Every child is planned and wanted from God's perspective!

Before I (God) formed thee in the belly, I knew thee; and before thou camest forth out of the womb I sanctified thee, and I ordained thee.

JEREMIAH 1:5

NEVER, NEVER BE TOO PROUD TO SAY, "I'M SORRY," TO YOUR CHILD WHEN YOU'VE MADE A MISTAKE.

In 1957 Ford bragged about producing "the car of the decade": the Edsel. One analyst likened its sales graph to a very dangerous ski slope. There is only one recorded case of an Edsel being stolen. These and many other such "failures" are listed in a book entitled *The Incomplete Book of Failures*. Appropriately, the book itself had two missing pages when it was printed! The book reports mistakes and errors in a variety of categories, including a memo from a record company that turned down the Beatles in 1962: "We don't like their sound. Groups of guitars are on their way out."

On a more personal note, Maxie Baughan, a former all-pro linebacker, once came off the field and disgustedly threw his helmet to the ground. What he didn't know was that cameras had caught his display of bad temper. A few days later, he was watching his 5-year-old son play and suddenly the boy took off his helmet and gave it a heave. Baughan scolded him for poor sportsmanship, but then the boy told his dad about watching him do the same thing . . . on TV.

Baughan promptly apologized!

Not apologizing for a mistake . . . is to make two mistakes, and the second can be far more damaging!

Confess your faults ones to another, and pray one for another.

JAMES 5:16

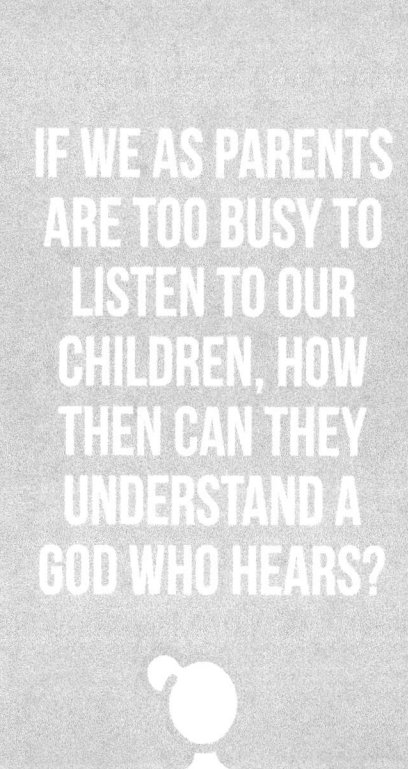

IF WE AS PARENTS ARE TOO BUSY TO LISTEN TO OUR CHILDREN, HOW THEN CAN THEY UNDERSTAND A GOD WHO HEARS?

A young boy came down to a pier on the mighty Mississippi River where an old man was fishing. He began to ask the man a myriad of questions, and with patience, the old man answered him. Their conversation was interrupted, however, by the shrill whistle of the *River Queen* as she came paddling down river. Both the old man and boy stopped to stare in wonder as the gleaming ship splashed spray into the sunshine.

Above the noise of the paddle wheel, the boy began to call across the water, "Let me ride! Let me ride!" The old man tried to calm him, explaining that the *River Queen* didn't just stop anywhere and give rides to little boys. The boy cried all the louder, "Let me ride!" The old man stared in amazement as the great ship pulled toward shore and lowered a gangplank to the pier. In a flash the boy scampered onto the deck. As the gangplank was pulled aboard and the ship began to pull back into the mainstream, the boy called back to his new-found friend, "I knew this ship would stop for me, Mister. The captain is my father!"

The young boy was confident in his relationship with his father. As your child becomes confident that you will listen to him he will be able to understand that his Heavenly Father will listen as well.

Let the wise listen.

PROVERBS 1:5 NIV

THE CURE OF
CRIME IS NOT IN
THE ELECTRIC
CHAIR,
BUT IN THE
HIGH CHAIR.

The importance of the first few years of a child's life cannot be overestimated. It is during those years that the foundation is laid for a child's language ability, ethics, morality, and value systems. In his book, *All Men Are Brothers*, Mahatma Gandhi said this about the instilling of values in very early childhood: "I am convinced that for the proper upbringing of children the parents ought to have a general knowledge of the care and nursing of babies . . . We labour under a sort of superstition that the child has nothing to learn during the first five years of its life. On the contrary, the fact is that the child never learns in later life what it does in its first five years. The education of the child begins with conception."

The famous psychoanalyst Sigmund Freud agreed. A Viennese woman once asked him, "How early should I begin the education of my child?"

Freud replied with a question of his own. "When will your child be born?"

"Born?" the woman asked. "Why, he is already five years old!"

"My goodness, woman," Freud cried, "don't stand there talking to me—hurry home! You have already wasted the five best years!"

Train up a child in the way he should go: and when he is old, he will not depart from it.

PROVERBS 22:6

PARENTHOOD: THAT STATE OF BEING BETTER CHAPERONED THAN YOU WERE BEFORE MARRIAGE.

A couple returned home after a week's vacation to the mountains feeling more exhausted than ever. All week they ran up and down mountain trails, valiantly struggling to keep their four children in line and safe from danger. Their tent had afforded them no privacy, and they were exhausted from playing referee around the campfire. The children, however, had had a great time. They bubbled over with enthusiasm as they told their grandparents about all the new sights, sounds, and experiences they had encountered—from roasting marshmallows to sleeping under the stars. The grandparents took one look at the parents, however, and said, "You need a vacation." The parents agreed and with the grandparents volunteering to babysit, they headed for a few days of rest at the beach.

After they had been there three days, they were sunning themselves one afternoon when the wife said dreamily, "Three whole days without the kids. That must be a record. I can't remember three whole days without the kids since the first one was born."

"Right," sighed her husband, and then added, "Believe it or not, I kind of miss them. Throw some sand in my face, will you?"

There is a right time for everything: a time to laugh.

ECCLESIASTES 3:1,4 TLB

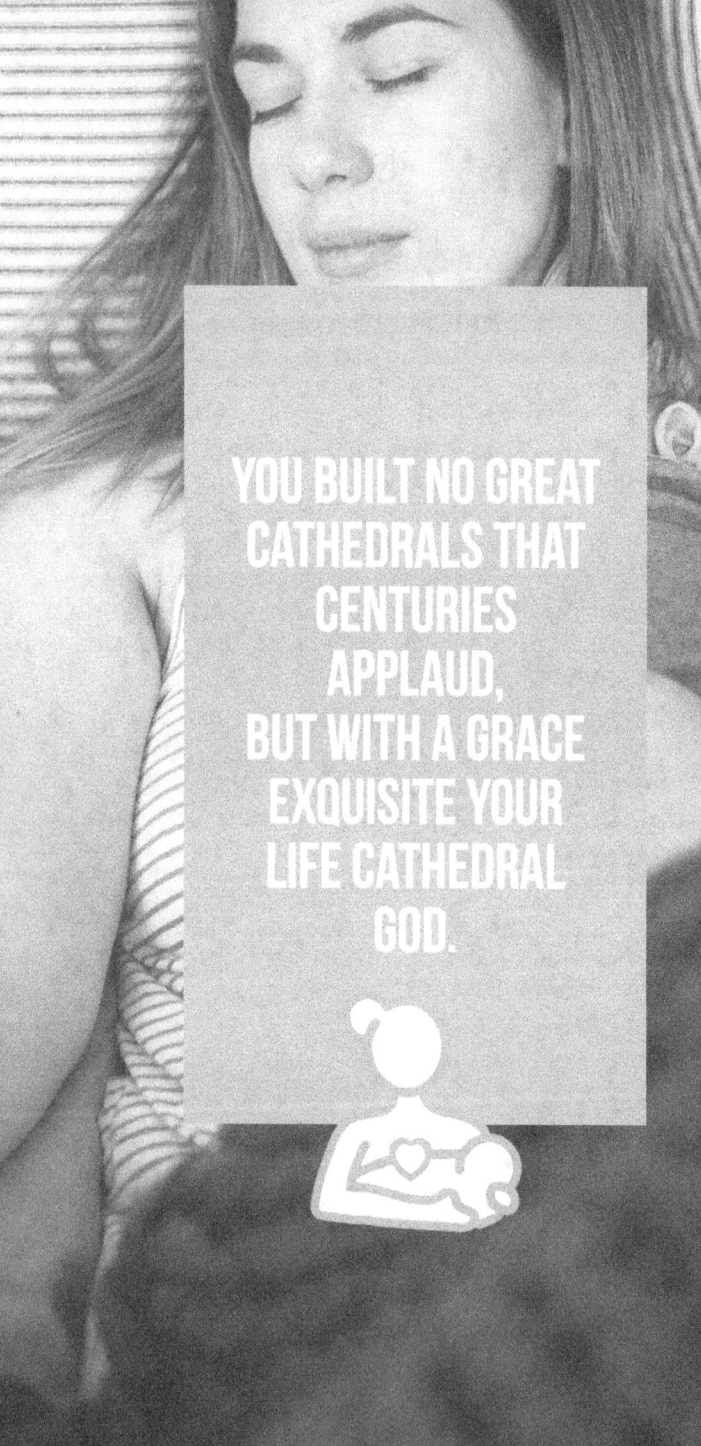

YOU BUILT NO GREAT
CATHEDRALS THAT
CENTURIES
APPLAUD,
BUT WITH A GRACE
EXQUISITE YOUR
LIFE CATHEDRAL
GOD.

When John Todd was only six, both his parents died. A loving aunt sent her horse and a slave, Caesar, to get John. On the way home, John asked Caesar if his aunt would be there . . . if he would like living with her . . . if she would love him . . . if she would have things ready for him. Each time Caesar replied, "Oh, yes. You fall into good hands." When they arrived, his aunt was waiting with open arms and heart. She became his second mother and he loved her dearly. Years later, as his aunt was nearing death, John wrote:

"My Dear Aunt, Years ago I left a house of death not knowing where I was to go, whether anyone cared, whether it was the end of me. The ride was long but . . . there we were in the yard and you embraced me and took me by the hand into my own room that you had made up. After all these years I still can't believe it—how you did all that for me! I was expected; I felt safe in that room—so welcomed. It was my room. Now it's your turn to go, and as one who has tried it out, I'm writing to let you know that Someone is waiting up. Your room is all ready, the light is on, the door is open, and as you ride into the yard—don't worry, Auntie. You're expected! I know. I once saw God standing in your doorway—long ago!"

For ye are the temple of the living God; as God hath said, I will dwell in them, and walk in them.

2 CORINTHIANS 6:16

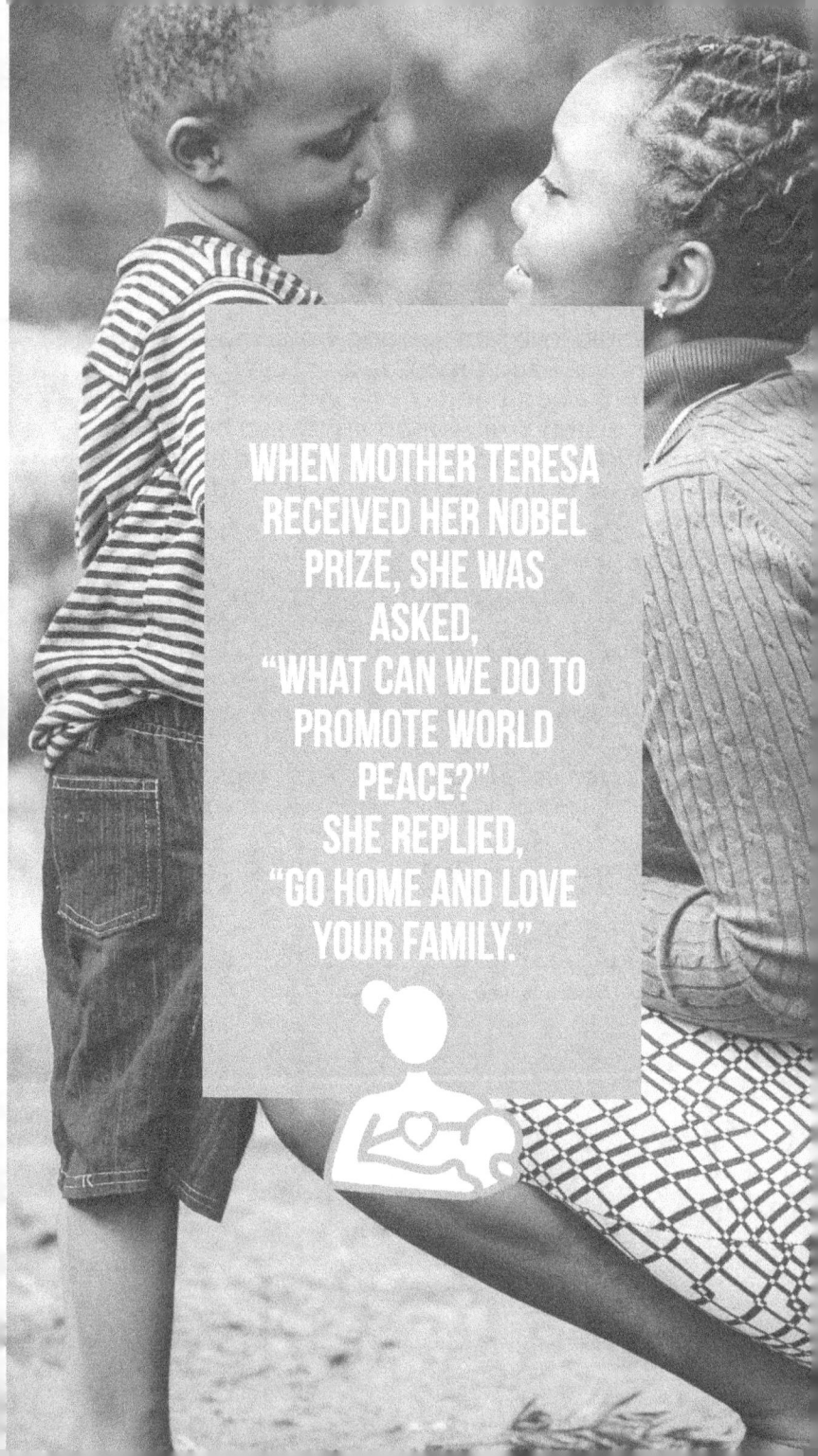

H er letters to her son Johannes give a strong impression of her clear common sense and her great kindheartedness. In these long letters carefully preserved, she tells her son all the interesting news from Hamburg, and never speaks ill of anybody. When son Fritz lost an excellent job, she wrote to Johannes: "Fritz must put his trust in God. who guides all human destinies. He will lead him out of this darkness." She remembered Johannes daily in her prayers, as well as Elise and Fritz, and tried to keep a tight bond among her children, reminding Johannes to remember their birthdays. There is no sign in her letters of any disharmony in her marriage, which lasted thirty-four years, and generally speaking, peace and cheerfulness seemed to prevail in her household.

In sharp contrast was the world outside their home: a poverty-stricken slum with narrow, crooked streets and grime-encrusted, "blackened" frame houses. Disease was rampant and if fire broke out, the effects in the neighborhood were devastating.

What was the impact of this mother's goodness and nurture on her son? There's no telling. Through the centuries, the compelling, beautiful music of Johannes Brahms has touched countless millions.

Let love and faithfulness never leave you; bind them around your neck, write them on the tablet of your heart.

PROVERB 3:3 NIV

During a long, winding drive through the Italian Alps, two-year-old Alexandra Chalupa slept safely buckled in her back-seat car seat. When she awoke, she pleaded to be allowed to sit up front, snuggled between her parents. Tanya Chalupa said no to her toddler's further protests. Moments later, their car skidded in the rain, lurched across traffic lanes, barely missed a deep gorge, and came to rest against a solid wall of rock. Her parents were bruised and shaken, but Alexandra remained firmly fastened and unhurt. Tanya shuddered to think what would have happened if she had been holding her daughter in her lap.

After the family returned to California, Tanya began a one-woman campaign to enact legislation requiring automobile safety seats for children under four years old or weighing less than 40 pounds. The memory of the accident and a conviction that such a law would save lives gave her the courage for a four-year campaign, even though she had no political know-how or financial backing. In 1983, the Child Restraint Law went into effect in California, and by year's end, child-passenger injuries had declined by more than 400 from the previous year!

And they that know thy name will put their trust in thee: for thou, Lord, hast not forsaken them that seek thee.

PSALM 9:10

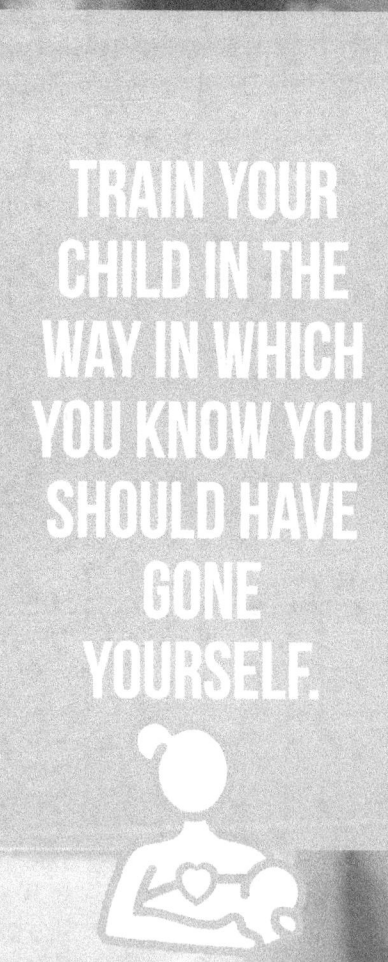

TRAIN YOUR CHILD IN THE WAY IN WHICH YOU KNOW YOU SHOULD HAVE GONE YOURSELF.

Near the top of one of the highest peaks in the Rocky Mountain range—more than 10,000 feet above sea level—are two natural springs. They are so close together and level in height, that it would not take a great deal of effort to divert one streamlet toward the other. Yet ... if you follow the course of one of these streams, you will find that it travels easterly, and after traversing plateaus and valleys, receiving water from countless tributaries, it becomes part of the great Mississippi River and empties into the Gulf of Mexico.

If you follow the water from the other fountain, you will find that it descended gradually in a westerly direction, again combining with other tributaries until it becomes part of the Columbia River, which empties into the Pacific Ocean.

The terminal points of the two streams are more than five thousand miles apart, separated by one of the highest ranges of mountains in the world. And yet in their onset, the two streams were close neighbors. Very little effort would be required to make the easterly stream run west, or the westerly stream run east.

If you want to impact the course of a life ... start at birth!

I will instruct thee and teach thee in the way which thou shalt go: I will guide thee with mine eye.

PSALM 32:8

The first memory that John H. Johnson has of his mother is of gripping her hand as they ran from the rampaging waters of a broken Mississippi River levee. The family lost everything, but "Miss Ger" was not one to quit. A field worker and later a domestic, she had known little but backbreaking work in her life. She had a dream, however, that her son would one day live in a city and become "somebody." She saved her money until she could move her family to Chicago. There, John graduated from high school with honors. When John had an idea for a magazine, it was his mother who came to his aid. allowing her new furniture to be used as collateral for a start-up loan. After *Negro Digest* became a success, John was able to do what he had dreamed about for years: he "retired" his mother, putting her on his personal payroll.

For 59 years, John saw or talked to his mother almost every day. Even when he found himself in other nations, he called his mother daily—once, from atop a telephone pole in Haiti. He continued to draw upon her spiritual and physical toughness until she died. John went on to publish *Ebony* and *Jet* magazines, and his company owns three radio stations. He says, "Not a day passes that I don't feed off the bread of her spirit."

Despise not thy mother when she is old.

PROVERBS 23:22

I REMEMBER MY MOTHER'S PRAYERS AND THEY HAVE ALWAYS FOLLOWED ME. THEY HAVE CLUNG TO ME ALL MY LIFE.

Abraham Lincoln is not the only president who has paid tribute to his mother's faith. President Reagan was also reverential about his mother, calling her "one of the kindliest persons I've ever known."

After an assassination attempt on President Reagan's life in March, 1981, he spoke of his mother in a letter: "I found myself remembering that my mother's strongest belief was that all things happen for a reason. She would say we may not understand the why of such things, but if we accept them and go forward, we find, down the road a ways, there was a reason and that everything happens for the best. Her greatest gift to me was an abiding and unshakable faith in God."

There are many things that a child doesn't remember. He rarely remembers every scraped knee, every reprimand, every home- cooked meal. What a child tends to remember are character traits of a parent, and the way they manifested themselves in a pattern of consistency. Make prayer a daily habit— and let your child overhear you praying for him on a daily basis. He may not remember each and every prayer . . . but he will remember yon as a praying person! And that example will never depart from him.

I prayed for this child, and the Lord has granted me what I asked of him.

1 SAMUEL 1:27 NIV

A businessman once made a "Worry Chart" on which he kept a record of all his worries. After a year, he tabulated the results. He found that 40 percent of the things he had worried about were now things that were very unlikely to happen . . . 30 percent were worries about past decisions he had made and which he could not now unmake . . . 12 percent dealt with other people's criticism of him . . . and 10 percent were worries about his future health, only about half of which he could do anything about in the present. In all, he concluded that only about 8 percent of his worries over the previous year had been legitimate.

What is it that you are worried about today? Most days? Keeping a worry chart might be a good way of discovering what it is that truly concerns you most.

Of equal interest in weighing one's worries would be a "Prayer Chart." What is it that you pray about the most? When asked to tabulate their prayers, many people seem to find that they actually spend very little time praying about the things that concern them the most!

Convert your worry time into prayer time. It's not only a more productive activity, but a healthier and more enjoyable one.

Be careful for nothing; but in every thing by prayer and supplication with thanksgiving let your requests be made known unto God.

PHILIPPIANS 4:6

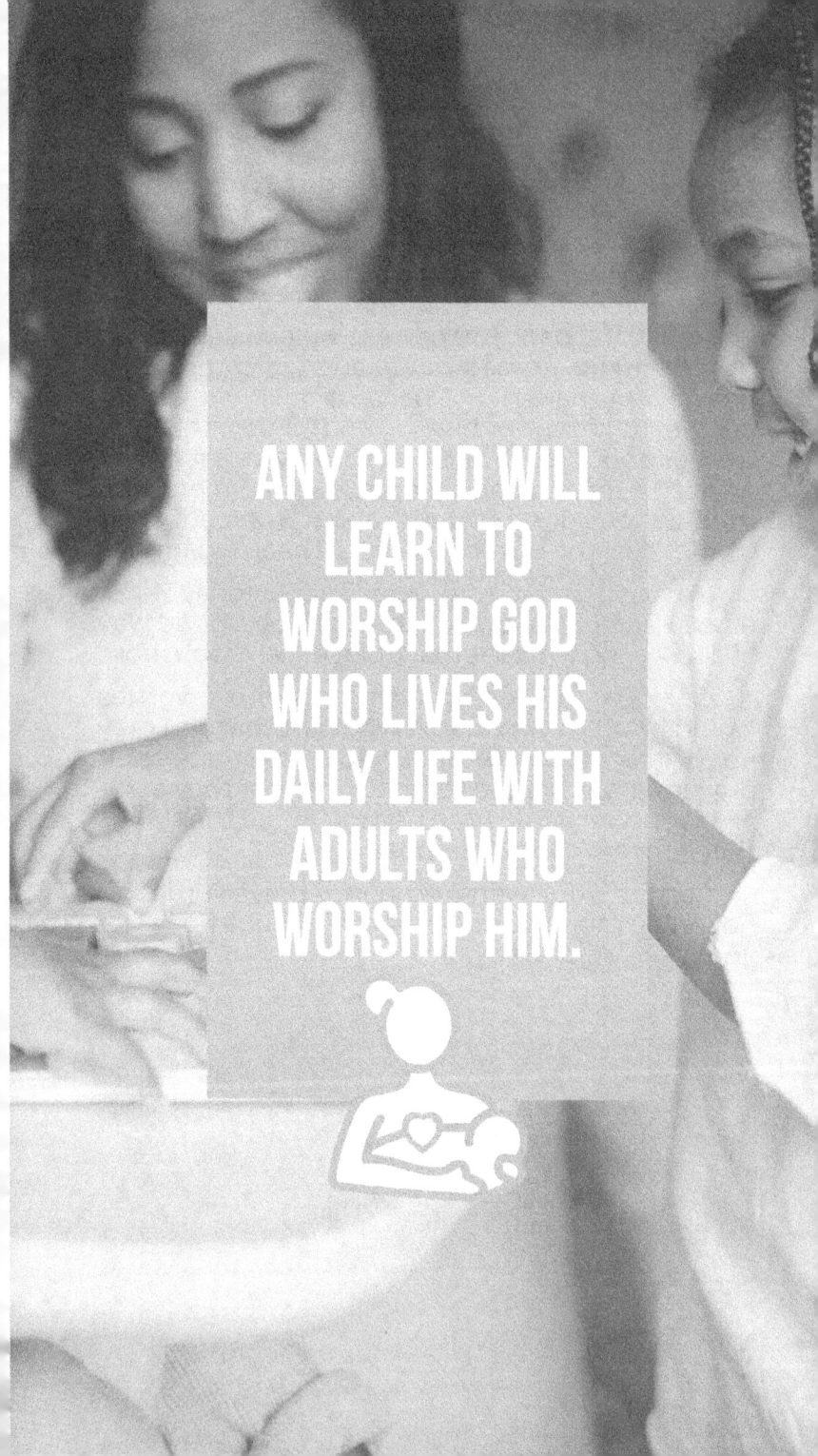

ANY CHILD WILL LEARN TO WORSHIP GOD WHO LIVES HIS DAILY LIFE WITH ADULTS WHO WORSHIP HIM.

Little Danny, only six months old, was bitten on the hand by a rat as he lay in his crib. His screams awakened everyone in the house. His parents rushed him to the hospital and the doctors did all they could do with the limited medical techniques available at the time, but the poor baby was just about given up for dead. His mother fell to her knees and screamed aloud, "Please, God, spare him and I will vow to you that I will beg pennies from door to door for a whole year to give to the poor. Spare my baby. Please, God, spare my baby." His father, too, dropped to his knees, prayed, and vowed that he would never gamble again.

Miraculously, Danny lived, perhaps even with rabies from the rat. And for an entire year, his mother took the streetcar to the end of the line, and walked all the way back downtown, begging pennies from door to door. Sometimes, doors were slammed in her face, but she persevered for a full year, pleading in her Middle Eastern accent, "Please give pennies to the poor. I promise God." His father never again gambled.

The memory is the chief reason Danny Thomas cites for keeping his vow to St. Jude and for his generous fundraising on behalf of the St. Jude Children's Research Hospital in Memphis, Tennessee.

He who walks with the wise grows wise.

PROVERBS 13:20 NIV

THE QUICKEST WAY FOR A PARENT TO GET A CHILD'S ATTENTION IS TO SIT DOWN AND LOOK COMFORTABLE.

Teresa Bloomingdale offers these humorous suggestions for improving family communication:

1. If you have tiny children who won't give you their attention, simply place a long-distance telephone call to somebody important, preferably their grandmother.

2. Your toddlers will immediately climb up on your lap and become all ears.

3. If you have older children who avoid you like the plague, buy yourself some expensive bath salts, run a hot tub, and settle in ... Teenagers who haven't talked to you since their tenth birthday will bang on the door, demanding your immediate attention.

4. Lure your husband into the bedroom and lock the door. The entire family will immediately converge in the hallway, insisting they must talk to you.

5. Get a job in an office which discourages personal phone calls. Your kids will then call you every hour on the hour.

6. Send them away to college, or let them move into an apartment. They can then be counted on . . . for long chats, during which they will expound at length on what wonderful parents you were, and what happened, because you certainly are spoiling their younger siblings rotten.

A merry heart doeth good like a medicine.

PROVERBS 17:22

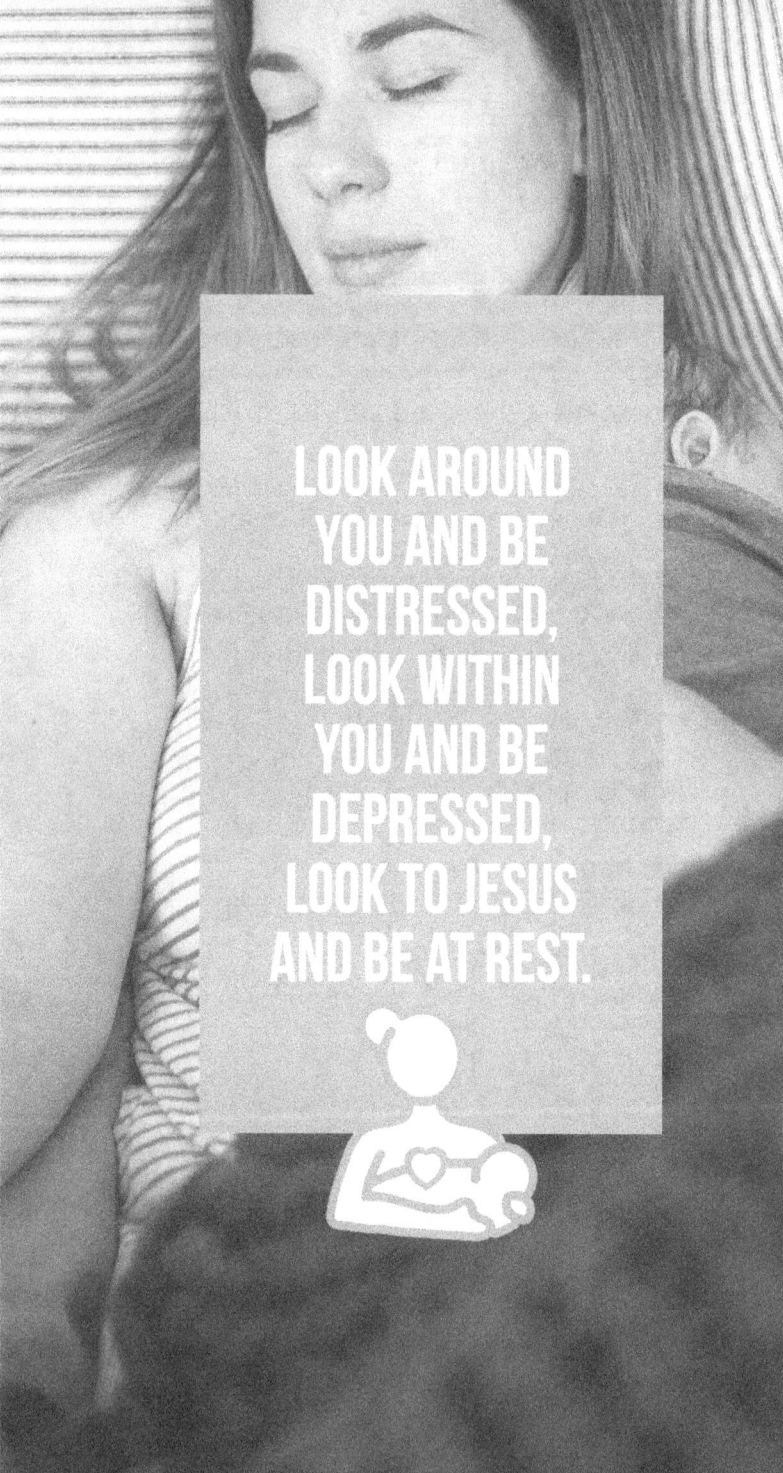

LOOK AROUND YOU AND BE DISTRESSED, LOOK WITHIN YOU AND BE DEPRESSED, LOOK TO JESUS AND BE AT REST.

J.C. Penney was well advanced in years before he committed his life fully to Jesus Christ. A good honest man, he was primarily interested in his early years in becoming a success and making money. As a clerk working for six dollars a week at Joslin's Dry Goods Store in Denver, he had an ambition to one day be worth one hundred thousand dollars. When he reached that goal he felt temporary satisfaction, but soon set his sights on being worth a million dollars.

Both Mr. and Mrs. Penney worked hard to expand their business, but one day Mrs. Penney caught cold and developed pneumonia, which subsequently caused her death. "When she died," J. C. recalled, "my world crashed about me. To build a business, to make a success in the eyes of men, to accumulate money— what was the purpose of life? . . . I felt mocked by life, even by God Himself." Before long, Penney was ruined financially and in deep distress. It was at that point that he turned to God and experienced a true spiritual conversion. He said, "When I was brought to humility and the knowledge of dependence on God, sincerely and earnestly seeking God's aid, it was forthcoming, and a light illumined my being. I cannot otherwise describe it than to say that it changed me as a man."

Jesus gives meaning and purpose to life. He brings calm to the storm. He brings rest to the soul.

Looking unto Jesus the author and finisher of our faith.

HEBREWS 12:2

A MOTHER'S LOVE IS PATIENT AND FORGIVING WHEN ALL OTHERS ARE FORSAKING, AND IT NEVER FAILS OR FALTERS, EVEN THOUGH THE HEART IS BREAKING.

An angel strolled out of heaven one beautiful day and winged its way to earth. On a quest for beauty, he wandered through both fields and cities beholding the glories of nature and the finest works of art. As sunset approached, he thought, *What memento can I take back to show my heavenly friends the beauty of earth?*

He noticed a patch of beautiful and fragrant wildflowers in the field where he was standing, and he decided to pluck them to make a bouquet. Then, passing a home, he saw through the open door a baby smiling from its crib. He took the smile with him, too. At another home, he saw through an open window a mother pouring out her love to her precious child as she stooped to kiss him "Goodnight." The angel decided to take the mother's love, too.

As the angel flew homeward through the pearly gates, he noticed to his astonishment that the flowers in his hand had withered. The baby's smile had changed into a frown. Only the mother's love remained as he had found it. He said to those who greeted him, "Here is the only thing I found today on earth that could retain its beauty and goodness all the way to heaven—the sweetness of a mother's love!"

Love is patient, love is kind, it does not envy, it does not boast, it is not proud. Love never fails.

1 CORINTHIANS 13:4,8A NIV

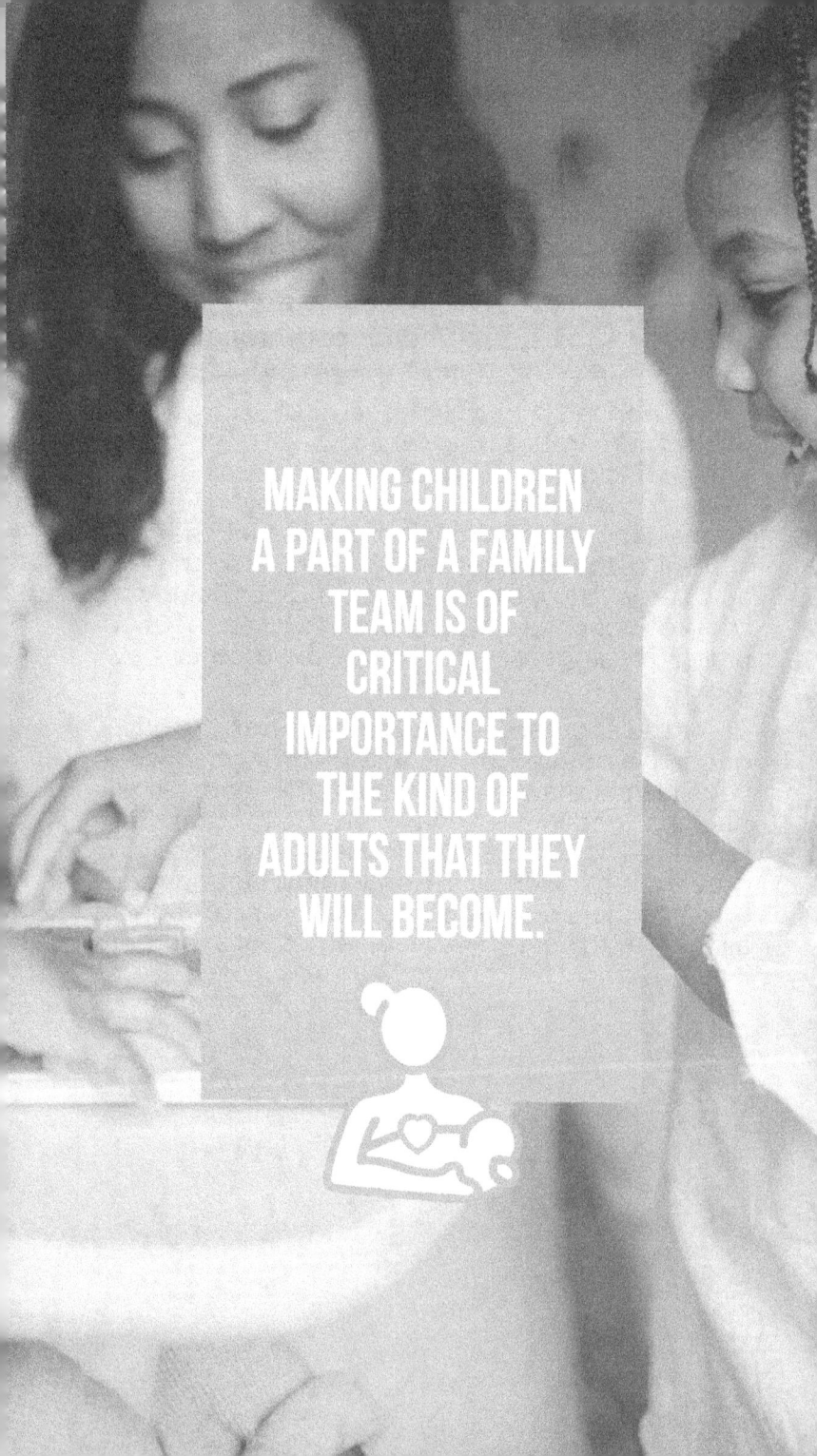

MAKING CHILDREN
A PART OF A FAMILY
TEAM IS OF
CRITICAL
IMPORTANCE TO
THE KIND OF
ADULTS THAT THEY
WILL BECOME.

t was a long hard road that took the Chandler children out of the cotton fields and out of poverty in Mississippi. All nine children have memories of a sharecropper's cabin and nothing to wear and nothing to eat. But today, all nine are college graduates! Their parents borrowed two dollars to buy a bus ticket for son Cleveland. He worked his way through school and became chairman of the economics department at Howard University. Luther went to the University of Omaha and became the Public Service Employment Manager for Kansas City. He helped brother James get to Omaha, and then to Yale for graduate work. James, in turn, helped Herman, who is now a technical manager in Dallas. Donald works in Minneapolis. The children also helped themselves—picking cotton, pulling corn, stripping millet, digging potatoes. Fortson went to Morehouse and is a Baptist minister in Colorado. Princess has a MA from Indiana and is a schoolteacher. Gloria is also a teacher. Bessie has a MA and is the dietitian at a veterans' hospital.

Together, the children bought a house for their parents in 1984. Nine players make a baseball team, but nine Chandler children have made an *unbeatable* team for the game of life!

Behold, how good and how pleasant it is for brethren to dwell together in unity!

PSALM 133:1

THERE IS NO GREATER LOVE THAN THE LOVE THAT HOLDS ON WHERE THERE SEEMS NOTHING LEFT TO HOLD ON TO.

Wavie intended only to skip a day of school, but friendly strangers offered her a ride, and with each mile she traveled, the more difficult it became for her to turn around. Her parents, thinking she had been abducted, almost immediately began to search for her. Several times they thought they were close to finding her, only to have their hopes dashed. Still, they never quit praying for their daughter. They prayed that God would send their love to Wavie and that He would protect her. And, they never quit believing that each ring of the phone, each delivery of the mail might bring word that their daughter was safe and well.

One day Wavie *did* return. She told of writing hundreds of letter to her parents, ones never mailed. Still, one of her tear-stained messages did come home with her. She had written, in part: "I love and miss you more than I could ever explain. I'm ashamed of what I've done. I pray every night that God will send you my love and take care of you so that one day I'll see all of you again."

Throughout the time she was away, Wavie's prayer for her parents had been nearly identical to that of her parents for her!

Love never fails—never fades out of becomes obsolete or comes to an end.

1 CORINTHIANS 13:8A AMP

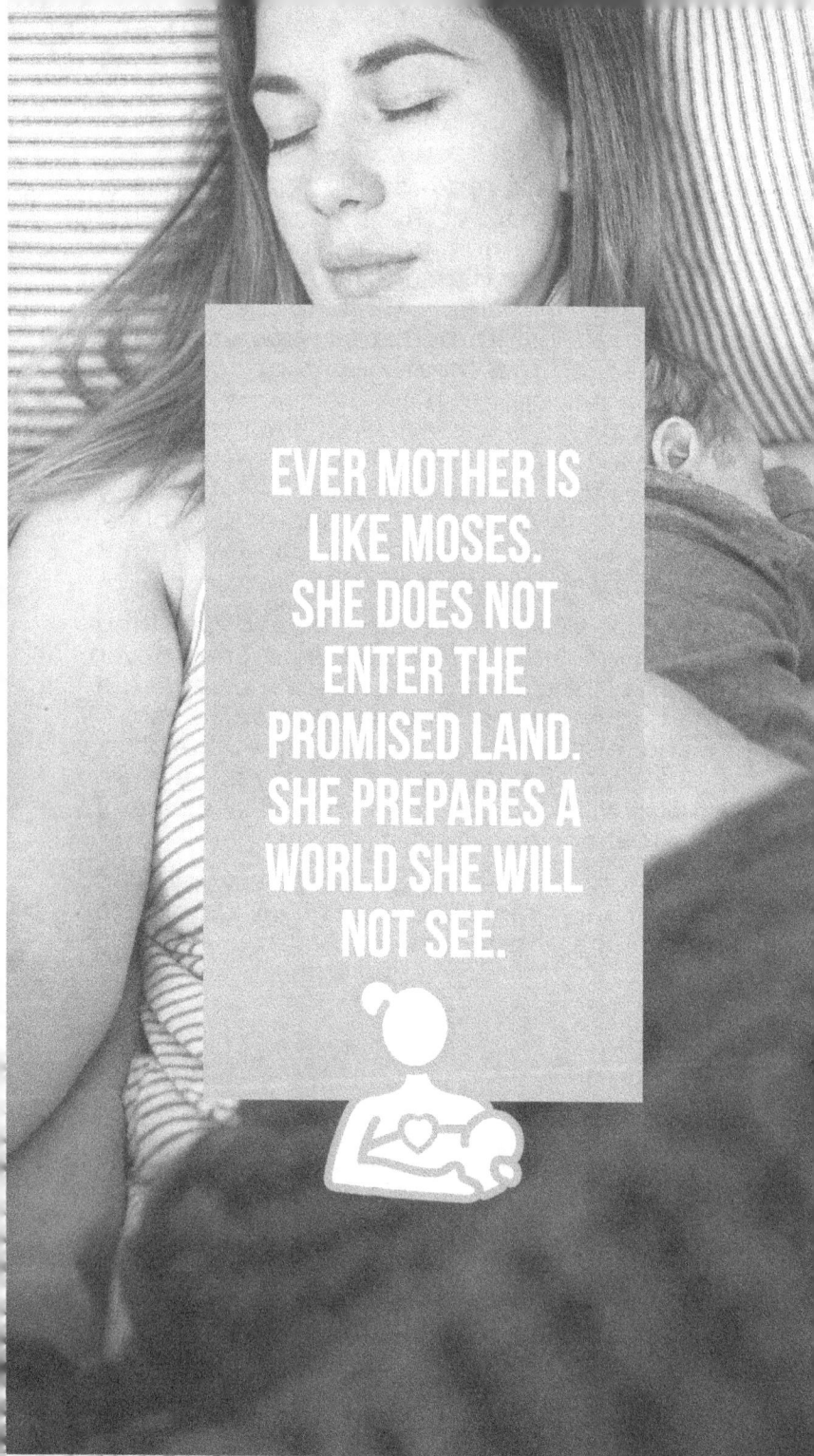

EVER MOTHER IS
LIKE MOSES.
SHE DOES NOT
ENTER THE
PROMISED LAND.
SHE PREPARES A
WORLD SHE WILL
NOT SEE.

When W. P. L. Mackay was seventeen, he left his humble Scottish home to attend college. His mother gave him a Bible in which she wrote his name and a verse of Scripture. Unfortunately, college was only the beginning of a downhill lifestyle for him. At one point he pawned the Bible to get money for whiskey. His mother, however, prayed for him until she died.

Eventually, Mackay became a doctor. While working in a hospital, he encountered a dying patient who asked repeatedly for his "book." After the man died, Mackay searched the hospital room to find what book it was that had been so important to him. He was surprised to find the very Bible he had once pawned!

Mackay went to his office and stared again at the familiar writing of his mother. He thumbed through the pages, reading the many verses his mother had underscored in hopes her son might heed them in his life. After many hours of reading and reflection, Mackay prayed to God for mercy. The physician later became a minister. And the Book he once had treated so lightly became his most precious possession.

You may not live to see how your children will "turn out." But you can trust that nothing you do for their spiritual wholeness will have been in vain!

Then the Lord said to him, "This is the land I promised on oath to Abraham, Isaac, and Jacob . . . I have let you see it with your eyes, but you will not cross over into it."

DEUTERONOMY 34:3 NIV

A FOOD IS NOT NECESSARILY ESSENTIAL JUST BECAUSE YOUR CHILD HATES IT.

I n *Family—The Ties That Bind and Gag!* Erma Bombeck writes: "In retrospect, it was only a matter of time before the Family Dinner Hour passed into history and fast foods took over . . . My pot roast gave way to pizza . . . My burgers couldn't compete with the changing numbers under the Golden Arches. I couldn't even do chicken . . . right!

"The old rules for eating at home—sit up straight, chew your food, and don't laugh with cottage cheese in your mouth—didn't fit the new ambiance. A new set of rules emerged." Bombeck suggests these among the new rules:

When ordering from the back seat of the car, do not cup your mouth over Daddy's ear and shout.

Never order more than you can balance between your knees.

Front-of-the-car seating is better than back seat if you have a choice. The dashboard offers space for holding beverages.

Afterward, each person should be responsible for his/her trash and should contain it in a bag. Two-week-old onion rings in the ashtray are not a pretty sight.

There is a right time for everything: a time to laugh.

ECCLESIASTES 3:1,4 TLB

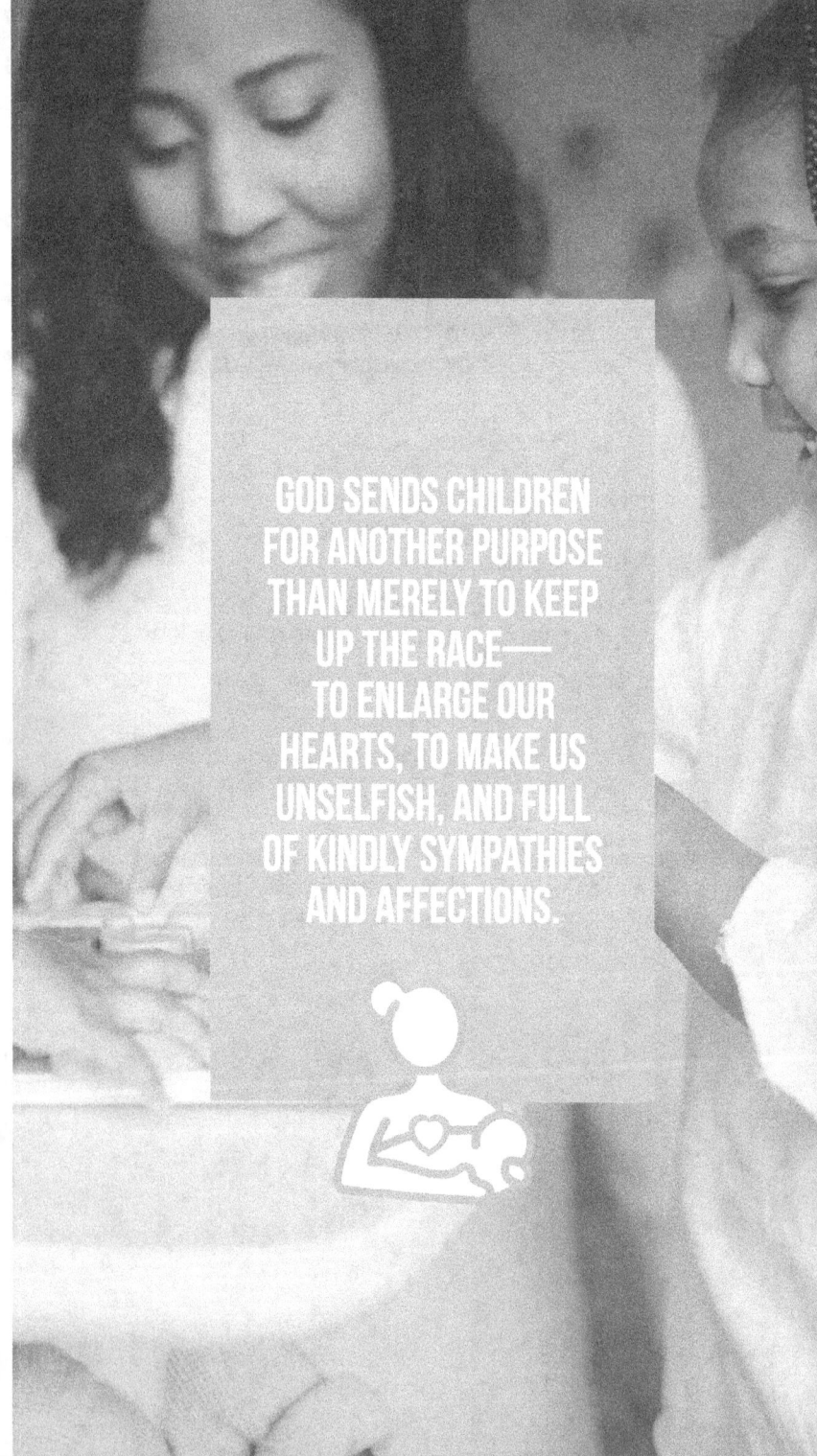

GOD SENDS CHILDREN FOR ANOTHER PURPOSE THAN MERELY TO KEEP UP THE RACE— TO ENLARGE OUR HEARTS, TO MAKE US UNSELFISH, AND FULL OF KINDLY SYMPATHIES AND AFFECTIONS.

In 1981, Elizabeth Glaser gave birth to a girl, Ariel. But moments after Ari was born, Elizabeth began to hemorrhage. She remembers watching silently as she received a transfusion of seven pints of blood . . . blood contaminated by HIV. Four years later, Ariel began to suffer baffling stomach pains and draining fatigue. She underwent a battery of tests, one of which gave a name to her illness: AIDS.

After Ariel's death, Elizabeth became a leading AIDS activist, co-founding the Pediatric AIDS Foundation. Many consider her to be the most effective AIDS lobbyist in the nation. She says of Ariel: "It was Ari who taught me to love when all I wanted to do was hate. She taught me to be brave when all I felt was fear. And she taught me to help others when all I wanted to do was help myself. I am active in fighting AIDS because I want to be a person she would be proud of; I was so proud of her . . . I think about her courage and I am able to go on."

About living with HIV, Elizabeth said, "Everything—from making peanut butter sandwiches and watching Jake [her son] play ball to planting the garden—has significance to me."

Children add another dimension to our lives—one that focuses on someone else besides ourselves.

My little children, let us not love in word, neither in tongue; but in deed and in truth.

1 JOHN 3:18

EVERY MOTHER HAS THE BREATHING PRIVILEGE OF SHARING WITH GOD IN THE CREATION OF NEW LIFE. SHE HELPS BRING INTO EXISTENCE A SOUL THAT WILL ENDURE FOR ALL ETERNITY.

A professor in a world-acclaimed medical school once posed this medical situation —and ethical problem—to his students: "Here's the family history: The father has syphilis. The mother has TB. They already have had four children. The first is blind. The second had died. The third is deaf. The fourth has TB. Now the mother is pregnant again. The parents come to you for advice. They are willing to have an abortion, if you decide they should. What do you say?"

The students gave various individual opinions, and then the professor asked them to break into small groups for "consultation." All of the groups came back to report that they would recommend abortion.

"Congratulations," the professor said. "You just took the life of Beethoven!"

A woman helps create the body of her child, and as her child grows, she nurtures its emotions and mind. Only God, however, can create the child's eternal soul. A soul must have a body on this earth. A body has a soul. Both God and mother are part-ners in the creation of a baby from the moment of conception.

No privilege is greater than the privilege of creating another human being. And no act requires greater faith!

For thou didst form my inward parts; thou didst weave me in my mother's womb.

PSALM 139:13 NASB

WE NEED TO BE PATIENT WITH OUR CHILDREN IN THE SAME WAY GOD IS PATIENT WITH US.

One of the most beautiful descriptions of patience in all of classic literature is this from Bishop Horne:

"Patience is the guardian of faith, the preserver of peace, the cherisher of love, the teacher of humility. Patience governs the flesh, strengthens the spirit, sweetens the temper, stifles anger, extinguishes envy, subdues pride: she bridles the tongue, restrains the hand, tramples upon temptations, endures persecutions, consummates martyrdom.

"Patience produces unity in the church, loyalty in the state, harmony in families and societies: she comforts the poor, and moderates the rich; she makes us humble in prosperity, cheerful in adversity, unmoved by calumny and reproach; she teaches us to forgive those who have injured us, and to be the first in asking forgiveness of those whom we have injured; she delights the faithful, and invites the unbelieving; she adorns the woman, and approves the man; she is beautiful in either sex and every age . . .

"She rides not in the whirlwind and stormy tempest of passion, but her throne is the humble and contrite heart, and her kingdom is the kingdom of peace."

Remember, when the opportunity arises to be patient with your child, consider how you would want God to respond to you in a similar circumstance.

The discretion of a man deferreth his anger; and it is his glory to pass over a transgression.

PROVERBS 19:11

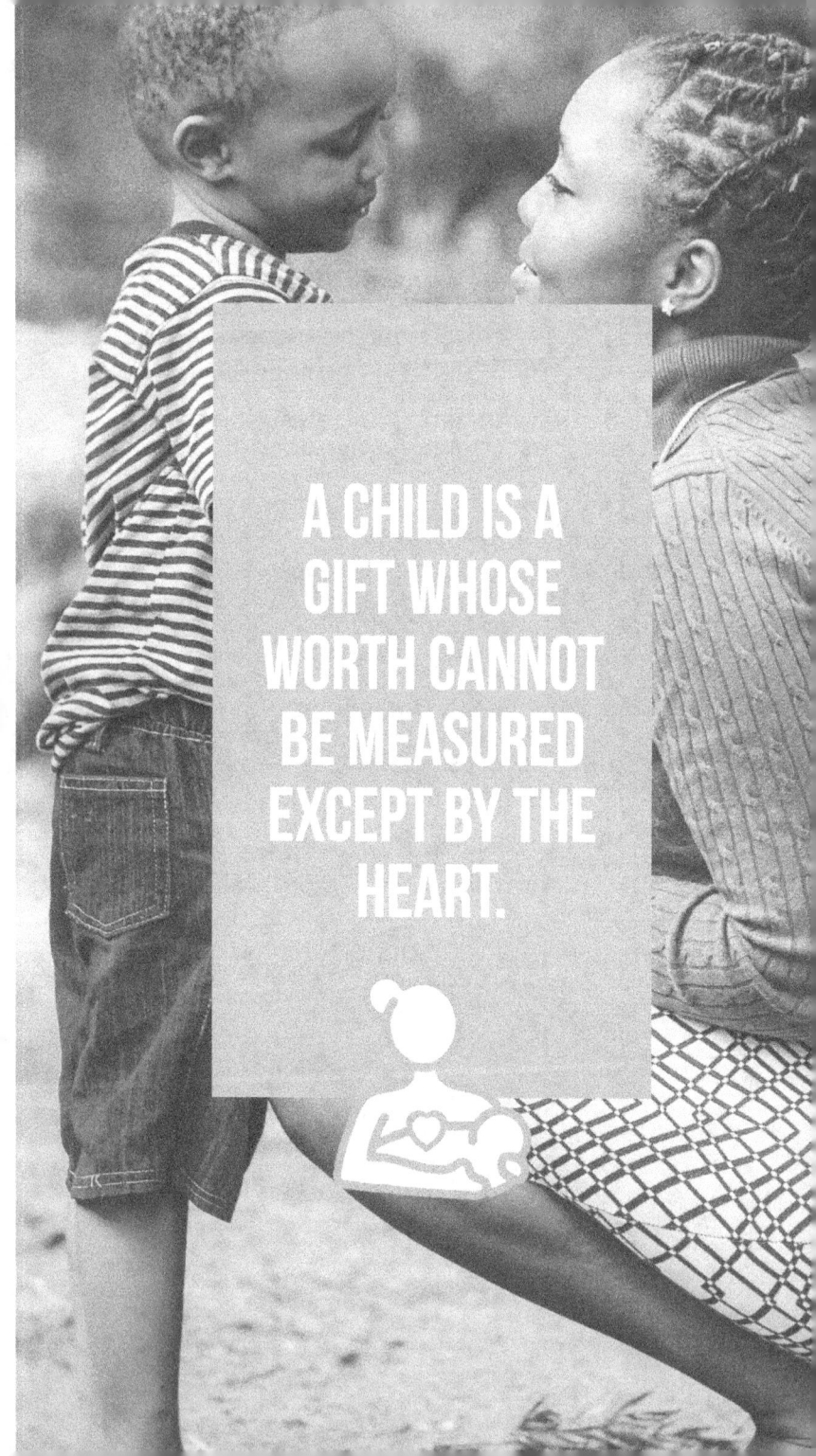

Margaret Bourke-White, one of the innovators of the photo essay in the field of photojournalism, was one of the first four staff photographers of *Life* magazine when it began in 1936. She was also the first woman photographer ever attached to U. S. armed forces in World War II. From early years, Margaret knew that she was counted as a "gift" to her parents. She recalls her mother telling her, "Margaret, you can always be proud that you were invited into the world."

In her autobiography, aptly titled *Portrait of Myself* she writes: "I don't know where she got this fine philosophy that children should come because they were wanted and should not be the result of accidents . . . When each of her own three children was on the way, Mother would say to those closest to her, 'I don't know whether this will be a boy or girl and I don't care. But this child was invited into the world and it will be a wonderful child.' She was explicit about the invitation and believed the child should be the welcomed result of a known and definite act of love between man and woman."

Have you told your child today that he or she is a gift—a child you wanted and "invited" into the world?

What good news that is to a child's ears!

Behold, children are a gift of the Lord; the fruit of the womb is a reward.

PSALM 127:3 NASB

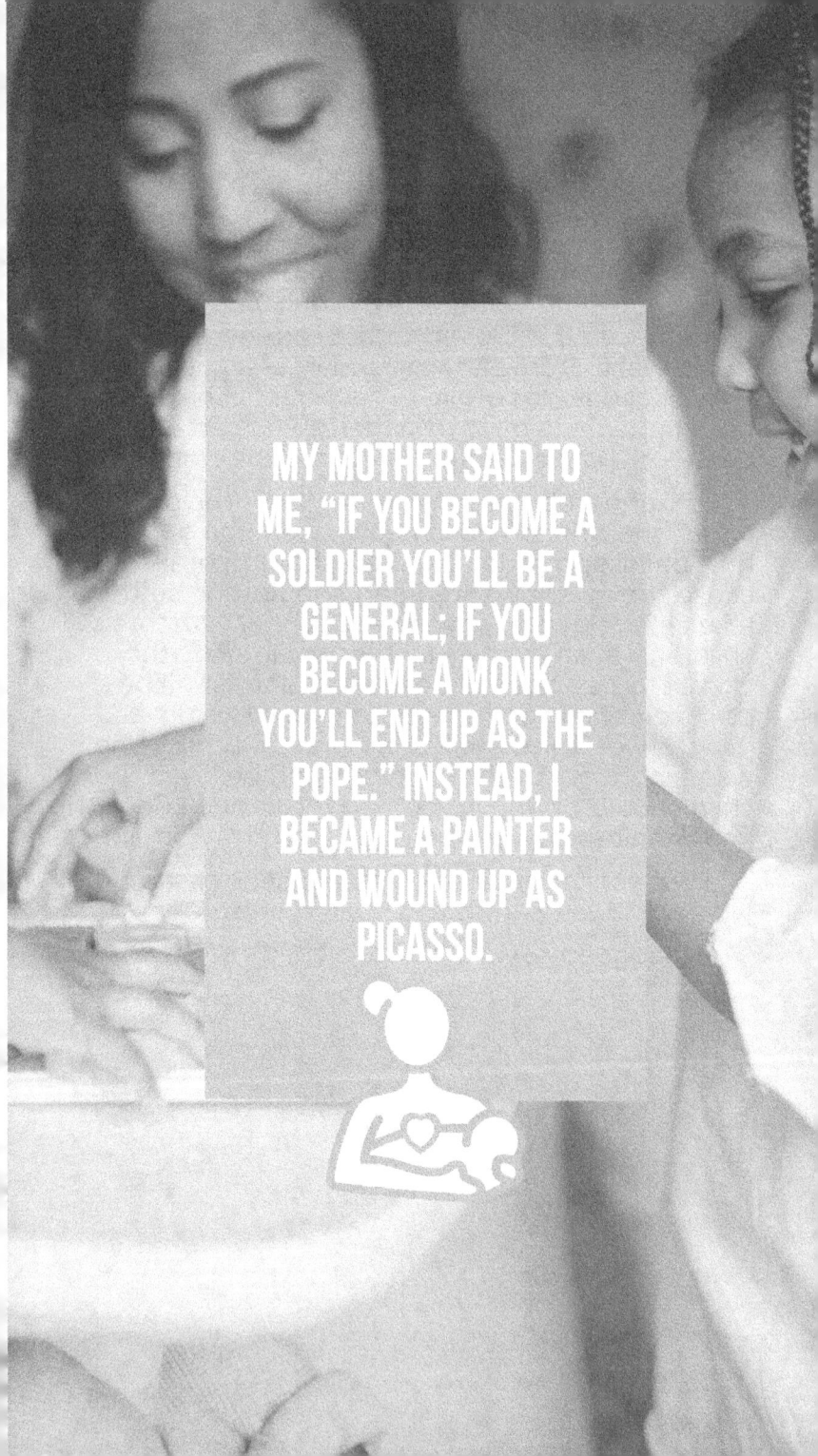

MY MOTHER SAID TO ME, "IF YOU BECOME A SOLDIER YOU'LL BE A GENERAL; IF YOU BECOME A MONK YOU'LL END UP AS THE POPE." INSTEAD, I BECAME A PAINTER AND WOUND UP AS PICASSO.

Shortly after arriving in the major leagues, pitcher Orel Hershiser was called to the office of Dodgers General Manager Tommy Lasorda. Orel knew the news wasn't going to be good. He had had a disappointing start as a relief pitcher. Lasorda, however, didn't focus on his record. He said instead, "You don't believe in yourself! You're scared to pitch in the big leagues! Who do you think these hitters are, Babe Ruth? Ruth's dead! You've got good stuff. If you didn't, I wouldn't have brought you up. I've seen guys come and go, son, and you've got it! You gotta go out there and do it on the mound. Be a bulldog out there. That's gonna be your new name: Bulldog. Bulldog Hershiser. I want you, starting today, to believe you are the best pitcher in baseball. I want you to look at that hitter and say, 'There's no way you can ever hit me.'"

Hershiser writes in his autobiography, *Out of the Blue*, "I couldn't get over that Tommy Lasorda felt I was worth this much time and effort . . . He believed I had more potential. He believed I had big league stuff." The next game, Hershiser pitched for three innings, and gave up only one hit.

Talk more to your child about his potential than his track record. He has more potential than history!

(Love) . . . believeth all things, hopeth all things, endureth all things.

1 CORINTHIANS 13:7

CHILDREN CERTAINLY BRIGHTEN UP A HOME. DID YOU EVER SEE A CHILD UNDER 12 TURN OFF AN ELECTRIC LIGHT?

Parents have a few habits that children never seem to understand, or to copy—such as flipping off lights in rooms with no one in them and turning off faucets in a bathroom. *In Family: The Ties That Bind—and Gag!* author Erma Bombeck offers these "Commandments for the Utilities:"

1. Thou shalt flush. Especially if thou is fifteen years old and has the use of both arms.

2. Thou shalt not stand in front of the refrigerator door waiting for something to dance.

3. Thou shalt not covet the rest of the family's hot water.

4. Thou shalt honor thy father's and mother's thermostat and keep it on normal.

5. Thou shalt remember last month's electricity bill and rejoice in darkness.

Unfortunately, notes Bombeck, these commandments generally lay in a family like broken stone tablets amidst wet towels and melting soap!

There is a right time for everything: a time to laugh.

ECCLESIASTES 3:1,4 TLB

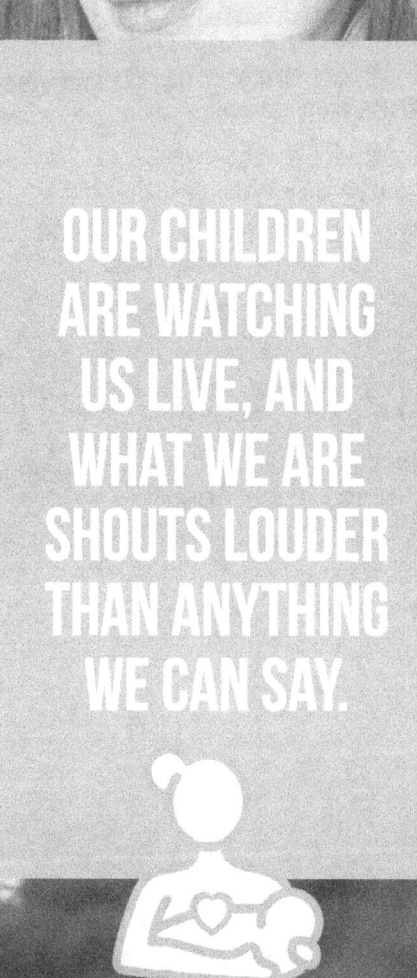

OUR CHILDREN
ARE WATCHING
US LIVE, AND
WHAT WE ARE
SHOUTS LOUDER
THAN ANYTHING
WE CAN SAY.

According to an old legend, there once was a man who had an only son, to whom he gave everything he owned. When his son grew up, he was unkind to his father, refused to support him, and turned him out of his own house.

As the old man prepared to leave his home, he turned to his young grandson and said, "Go and fetch the covering from my bed, that I may go and sit by the wayside and wrap myself in it and beg for alms."

The child burst into tears and ran for the covering. But rather than take it to his grandfather, he ran to his father and said, "Oh father, grandfather has asked for this so he can keep himself warm as he sits by the road and begs. Please cut it into two pieces. Half of it will be large enough for grandfather. And you may want the other half when I am grown to be a man and turn you out of doors."

The child's words struck to the very core of the uncaring son and he ran to his father, asked his forgiveness, and took care of him until his death.

What we *do* always comes across to our children as the loudest and clearest of messages.

In everything set them an example by doing what is good.

TITUS 2:7A NIV

HAPPY IS THE CHILD . . . WHO SEES MOTHER AND FATHER RISING EARLY, OR GOING ASIDE REGULARLY, TO KEEP TIMES WITH THE LORD.

Parents today often use dozens of excuses to justify not taking their children to church or having a family devotional time, but if that urge strikes you, remember the family of Lydia Murphy. She moved with her parents to Shawnee, Kansas, in 1859, and she writes of their first night in their new home, "The family Bible rested in the center of the room. We gathered around the table, seated on boxes and improvised chairs while the usual evening family prayers were held after the reading of a chapter of the Scriptures. During the fifty years of his Kansas citizenship, this morning and evening scripture reading and prayer was not once omitted in my father's house."

The Murphys had been devout Methodists but the nearest Methodist church was ten miles away. They therefore secured the services of a circuit-riding Methodist minister and opened their own home for worship, welcoming neighbors of all denominations. Within months, their home had become the center of both the social and religious life of the community. Services were held every two weeks on Saturdays. At other times, neighbors took turns reading Scriptures, leading prayers, and teaching Sunday school!

A child who sees his parents spend time with God has a sense of security that little else can ever establish.

...let the heart of them rejoice that seek the Lord. Seek the Lord, and his strength: seek his face evermore.

PSALM 105:3-4

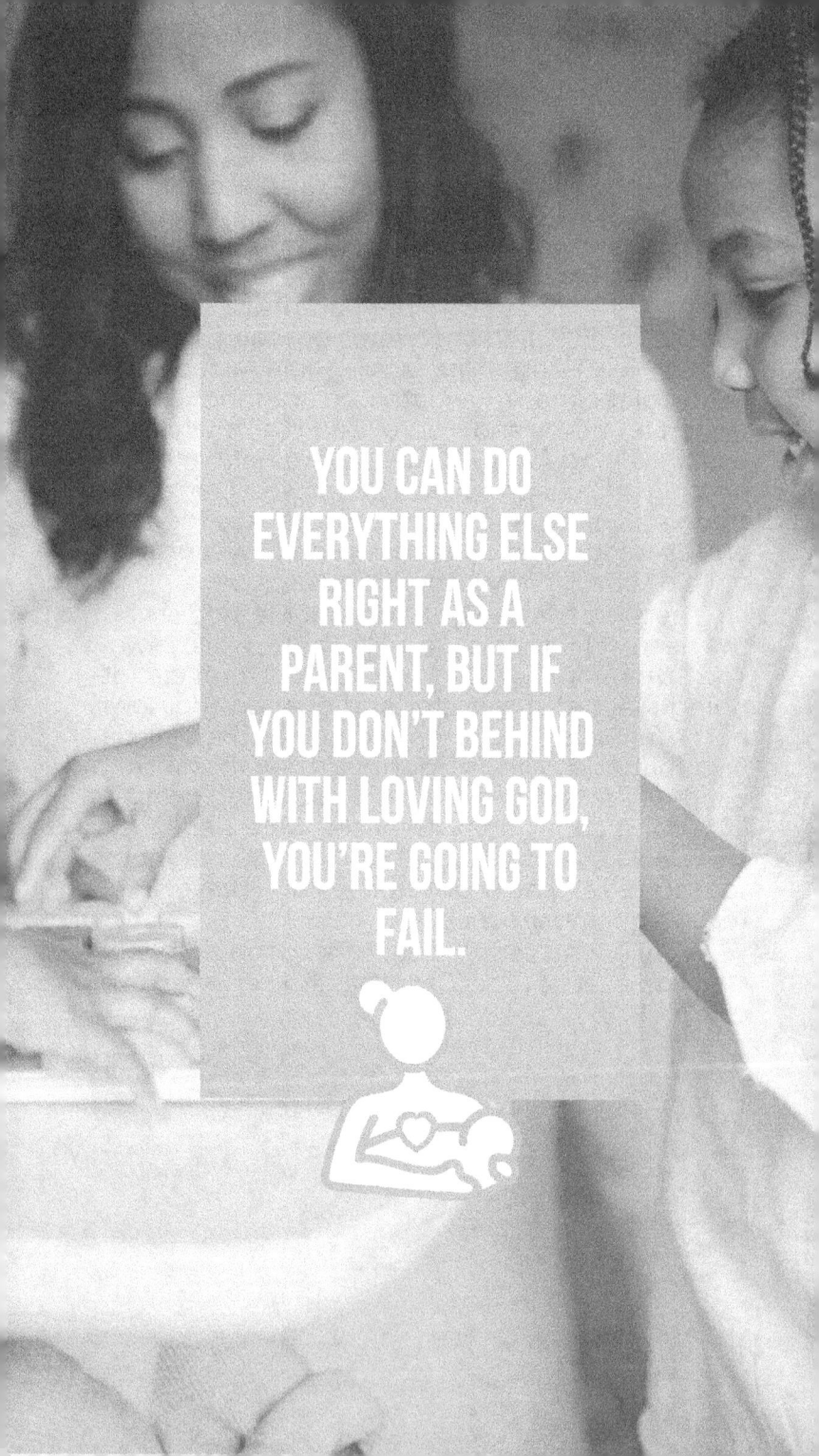

YOU CAN DO EVERYTHING ELSE RIGHT AS A PARENT, BUT IF YOU DON'T BEHIND WITH LOVING GOD, YOU'RE GOING TO FAIL.

Sarah Edwards, wife of revivalist and theologian Jonathan Edwards, bore eleven children. At her death, Samuel Hopkins eulogized her in this way:

"She had an excellent way of governing her children. She knew how to make them regard and obey her cheerfully, without loud, angry words, much less heavy blows . . . If any correction was necessary, she did not administer it in a passion . . . In her directions in matters of importance, she would address herself to the reason of her children, that they might not only know her will, but at the same time be convinced of the reasonableness of it . . . Her system of discipline was begun at a very early age and it was her rule to resist the first as well as every subsequent exhibition of temper or disobedience in the child . . . wisely reflecting that until a child will obey his parents, he can never be brought to obey God."

At the close of each day, after all in the family were in bed, Sarah and her husband shared a devotional time together in his study. With eleven children to "tuck into bed," Sarah did not allow any of them leeway in keeping her from this cherished time with her husband!

The Lord our God is one Lord: and thou shalt love the Lord thy God with all thine heart, and with all thy soul, and with all thy might.

DEUTERONOMY 6:4-5

BEAUTIFUL AS SEEMED MAMA'S FACE, IT BECAME INCOMPARABLY MORE LOVELY WHEN SHE SMILED, AND SEEMED TO ENLIVEN EVERYTHING ABOUT HER.

For more than a century, the majestic statue titled "Liberty Enlightening the World" has towered near the entrance to New York Harbor as a symbol of America's freedom.

The famous sculptor of the statue, Bartholdi, spent twenty years supervising the construction of his masterpiece. He personally helped raise the four million dollars needed to pay for the statue, which was presented by France as a gift to the United States. When the fund-raising program for the statue lagged, Bartholdi pledged his own private fortune to keep the project funded, and practically impoverished himself in the process.

At the start, when Bartholdi was seeking for a model on whom to pattern "Liberty," he received a great deal of advice from art experts. Most of the leading authorities advised him to find a grand heroic figure as his pattern. After examining countless heroes, however, Bartholdi chose as his model . . . his own mother. Just as no other statue in the world so eloquently lights the way to freedom, so no other woman so beautifully lighted Bartholdi's own world.

Remember, your children are watching even the very expressions of your face—be sure a fair amount of the time it wears a smile.

For the joy of the Lord is your strength.

NEHEMIAH 8:10

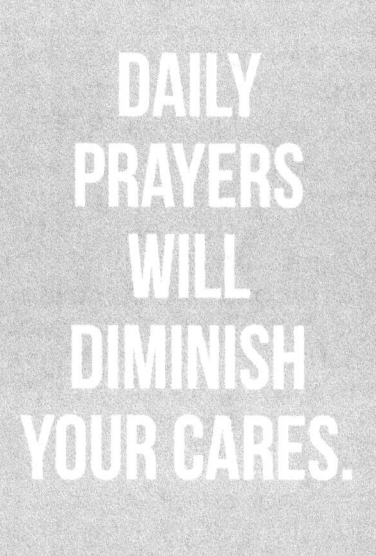

DAILY
PRAYERS
WILL
DIMINISH
YOUR CARES.

Like many women, Carol found herself routinely emptying her husband's pockets before doing his laundry. She often pulled "lists" from his pockets, including prayer lists. Her husband rarely listed people's names, only what he was praying that the Lord would do in their lives.

One Monday a woman named Betty, a delivery woman who picked up and delivered her husband's uniforms, came to Carol's door. Carol had never seen Betty smile before, but this day, she glowed. She said, "I want to thank you for the prayers." Then she explained, "Every week I clean out the cargo pockets of your husband's fatigues. I thought that God had given up on me, but He has been speaking to me through the prayers that I find in your husband's pockets. I was starving for God and for His Word. Those scraps of paper with prayers were like food. I couldn't wait until Monday to see if I would find another message. I claimed each one as my own. Yesterday I accepted Jesus as my Savior. My new church has a group who minister to people like me."

Only God knows the final outcome of all your prayer requests. He alone is the "Finisher" and the great "Amen" of what you request before His throne.

Evening, and morning, and at noon, will I pray, and cry aloud: and he shall hear my voice.

PSALM 55:17

CLEANING YOUR HOUSE WHILE YOUR KIDS ARE STILL GROWING IS LIKE SHOVELING THE WALK BEFORE IT STOPS SNOWING.

Elinor Goulding Smith offers this analysis of a child's room:

"The child's room is a sight to make strong men faint, and induces in mothers a condition characterized by trembling, pallor, dysphasia, weakness . . . The room is characterized by litter to a depth of two to three feet, except under the bed where it is perhaps only six inches deep. You can see no article of furniture, each being buried completely, and emerging as simply a higher mound of rubbish. You once, many years before, saw an occasional bureau top (let me see, was it maple?) or a desk top (birch—I think) but alas, they are only a memory now. A few bits of furniture stick up above the level of the rubbish—the very top of a desk lamp protrudes above a mountain of papers, books, crayons, hedge shears, gym sneakers, the remains of a tongue sandwich, two peach pits, a camera, a microscope, some jars of extremely aromatic pond water, a deck of marked cards, coping saw, overdue library books, bicycle tire pumps, a Siamese fighting fish no longer in the prime of life who lives in the bottom half of a cider jug, and so on . . . right up to the top of the desk lamp. You look at the top of the lamp happily. 'At last,' you say, as you totter across the room, 'a landmark!'"

A merry heart doeth good like a medicine.

PROVERBS 17:22

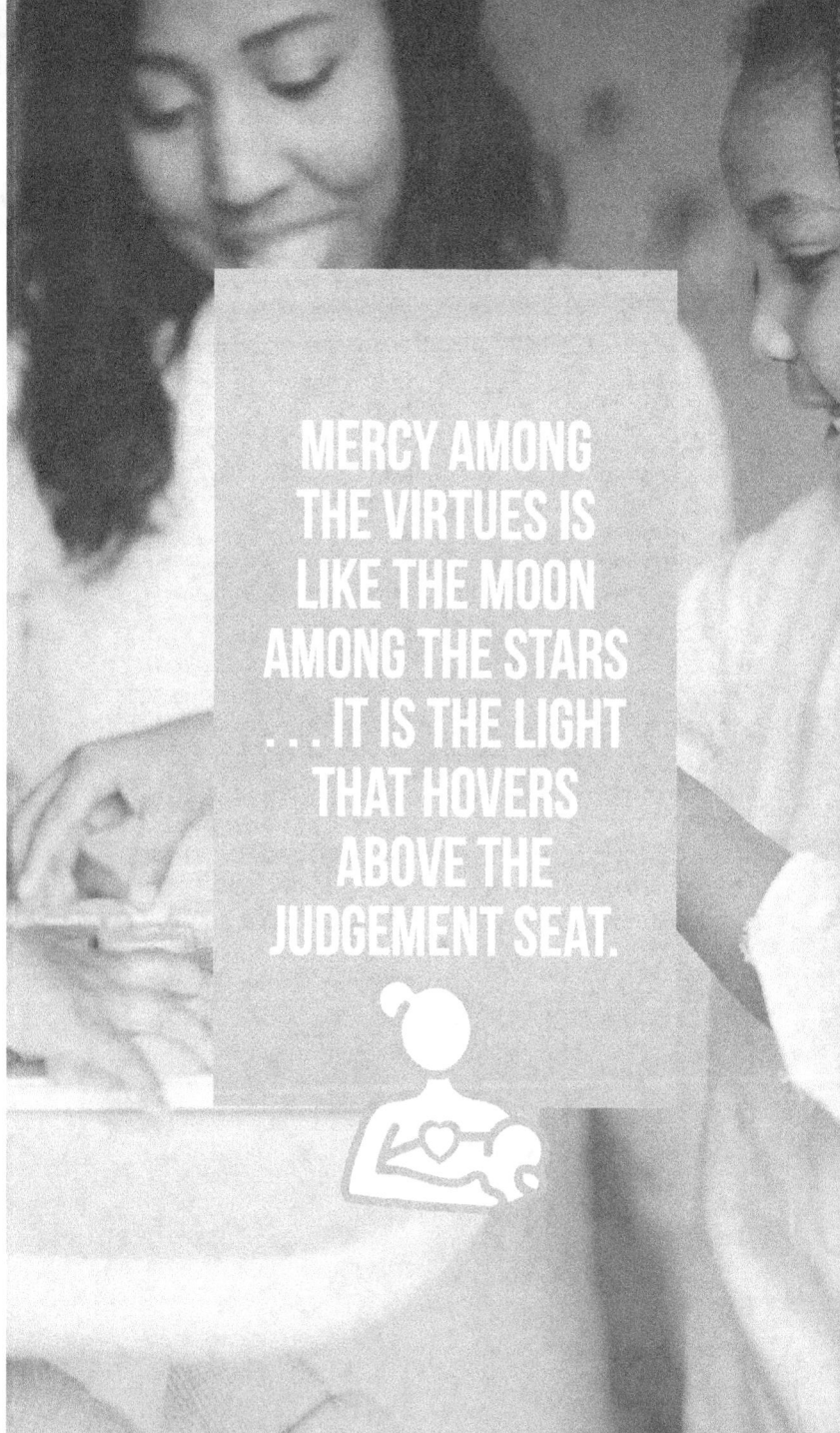

MERCY AMONG THE VIRTUES IS LIKE THE MOON AMONG THE STARS . . . IT IS THE LIGHT THAT HOVERS ABOVE THE JUDGEMENT SEAT.

According to a traditional Hebrew story, Abraham was sitting by his tent one evening when he saw an old man walking toward him. He could tell long before the man arrived that he was weary from age and his journey. Abraham rushed out to greet him, and then invited him into his tent. He washed the old man's feet and gave him something to drink and eat.

The old man immediately began eating without saying a prayer or invoking a blessing. Abraham asked him, "Don't you worship God?"

The old traveler replied, "I worship fire only and reverence no other god."

Upon hearing this, Abraham grabbed the old man by the shoulders and with indignation, threw him out of his tent into the cold night air.

The old man walked off into the night and after he had gone, God called to His friend Abraham and asked where the stranger was. Abraham replied, "I forced him out of my tent because he did not worship You."

The Lord responded, "I have suffered him these eighty years although he dishonors Me. Could you not endure him one night?"

Who today may need to experience your mercy as a tangible expression of the mercy God is extending to him or her?

Mercy triumphs over judgment!

JAMES 2:13 NASB

NOTHING HAS
A BETTER
EFFECT UPON
CHILDREN
THAN PRAISE.

A mother once left her children with her single sister in order to work for three weeks overseas. Although she missed her children tremendously, she was also glad for a break. She was feeling worn out as a single parent, struggling to juggle her job and her role as a mother. The demands of constant discipline sometimes seemed too much. As she prepared to return to her family, she thought, *I wonder how sis coped. I hope she heeded my parting words not to let them get away with murder.* The last thing she looked forward to was a round of arguing and reprimanding.

To her great surprise, she arrived at her sister's home to find her children playing quietly, eager to see her but quick to obey her sister's slightest request. "What did you do?" she whispered to her sister. "They're never this well behaved!"

Her sister replied, "Nothing, really. Before you left, I read a little article about parenting and I just did what it said."

The woman said, "What was it? Give me the formula!"

The sister picked up the article and read, "Tell children what to do, far more than you tell them what not to do. And then praise them for what they do —instead of criticizing them for what they don't do." Smiling at her sister, she added, "It seemed to work!"

Anxiety in the heart of a man weighs it down, but a good word makes it glad.

PROVERBS 12:25 NASB

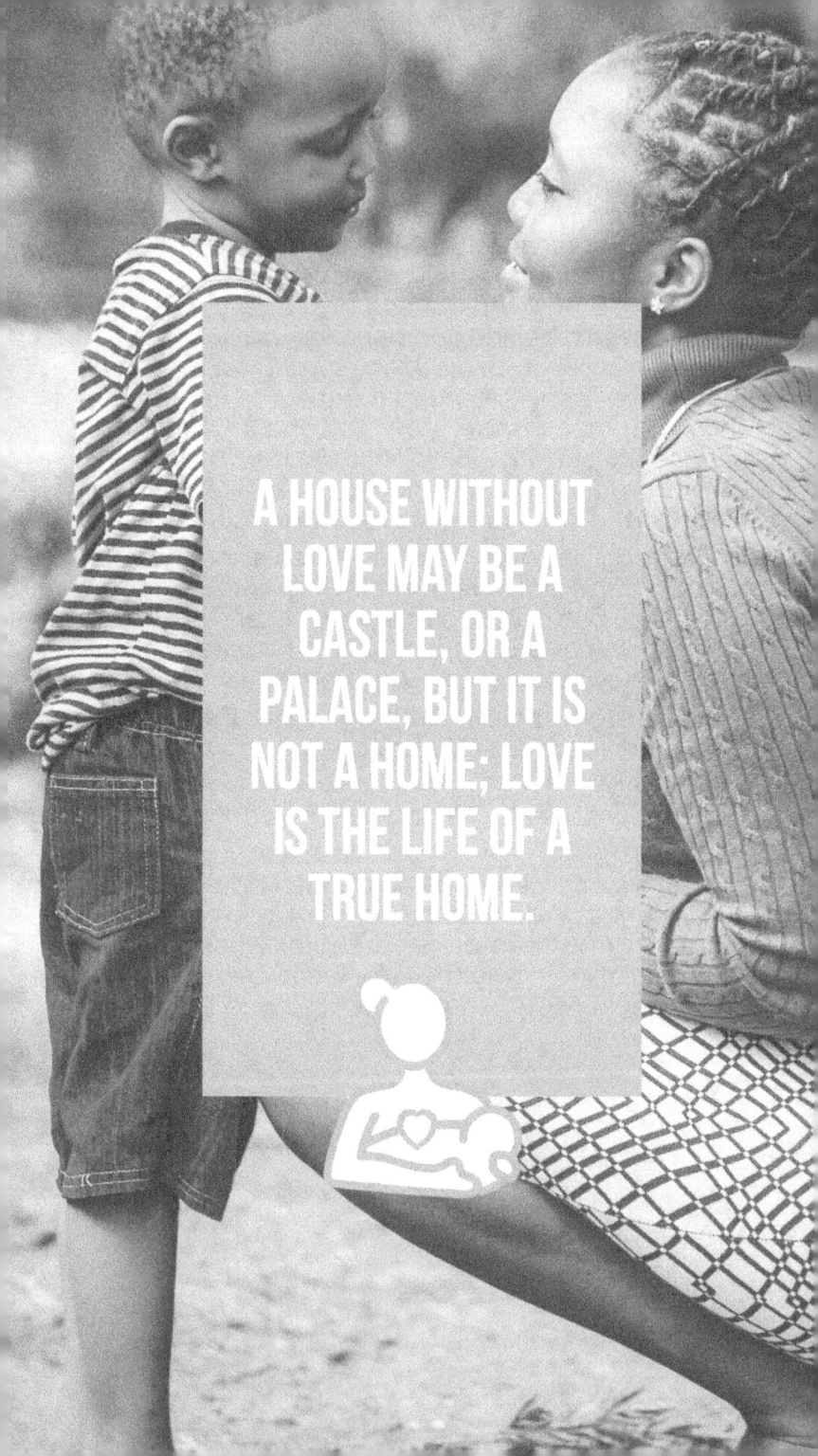

A HOUSE WITHOUT LOVE MAY BE A CASTLE, OR A PALACE, BUT IT IS NOT A HOME; LOVE IS THE LIFE OF A TRUE HOME.

Women are often tempted to think that their homemaking skills—such as cooking, decorating, cleaning—are what turn a house into home. But consider how one of the most famous cooks of all time, Julia Child, recalls her own childhood:

"I know I'm happy. I was very fortunate in my family background because I had a very loving, supportive family. We had no conflict. My sister was five years younger and we had a brother halfway between, so we never had any sibling rivalry. My parents were happy; we were not rich, but comfortably well-off. My mother thought everything we did was absolutely marvelous. I think your background makes an awful lot of difference. I don't know what you do if you've been abused, or haven't been praised enough so that you don't feel that you're okay. I was very fortunate in having such a happy background. I was never brilliant in school, but I never had any problems either, so I didn't feel inferior. I did have the problem of being twice as tall as anyone else, but that didn't seem to make any difference because my mother always said we were so wonderful, no matter what."

Notice . . . Julia didn't make one mention of her mother's cooking skills or food . . . only of praise!

Better a dry crust with peace and quiet than a house full of feasting with strife.

PROVERBS 17:1 NIV

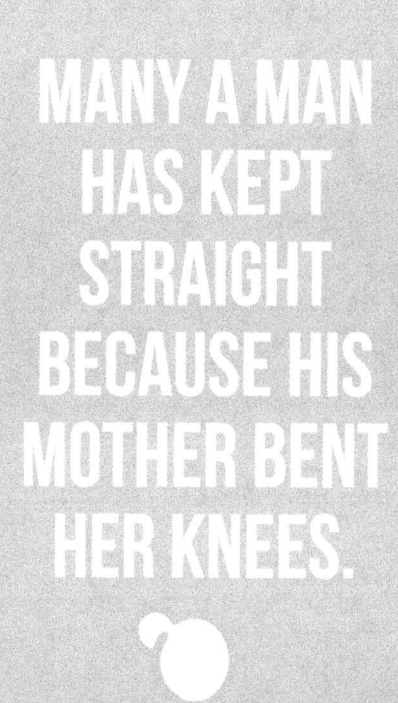

MANY A MAN HAS KEPT STRAIGHT BECAUSE HIS MOTHER BENT HER KNEES.

*A*n old woman with a halo of silvered hair—the hot tears flowing down her furrowed cheeks—her worn hands busy over a washboard in a room of poverty—praying—for her son John—John who ran away from home in his teens to become a sailor—John of whom it was now reported that he had become a very wicked man—praying, praying always, that her son might be of service to God. The mother believed in two things, the power of prayer and the reformation of her son. God answered the prayer by working a miracle in the heart of John Newton. John Newton, the drunken sailor became John Newton, the sailor-preacher [who wrote the words to "Amazing Grace."] Among the thousands of men and women he brought to Christ was Thomas Scott. . . [who] used both his pen and voice to lead thousands of unbelieving hearts to Christ, among them William Couper . . . [who] in a moment of inspiration wrote "There Is a Fountain Filled with Blood." And this song has brought countless thousands to the Man Who died on Calvary. All this resulted because a mother took God at His word and prayed that her son's heart might become as white as the soapsuds in the washtub.

SPRING IN THE VALLEY
MRS. CHARLES E. COWMAN

The earnest prayer of righteous man has great power and wonderful results.

JAMES 5:16 TLB

THE MORE A CHILD
BECOMES AWARE
OF A MOTHER'S
WILLINGNESS TO
LISTEN, THE MORE
A MOTHER WILL
BEGIN TO HEAR.

A busy mother of four children found her job as wife and mom a careful balancing act. Each day was filled to the brim with a part-time job, home chores, and chauffeur duty. She had found the most efficient way for her to handle the weekly grocery shopping was to go alone, unhampered by "help" that usually inflated her grocery bill and strained her patience.

On one shopping day, her 13-year-old son asked, "Where ya goin', Mom?"

She replied, "To the grocery store. I'll be back soon."

Her son asked, "Can I go with you?"

She almost had the words "some other time" out of her mouth when something inside checked her and she heard herself say, "OK."

Once in the car, she braced herself for the struggle she anticipated over the use of the radio. Instead, her son began to talk. "When I grow up, I'm going to be rich," he announced.

"Oh?" she said.

"Yeah," he said. "Then I can give my kids everything they want."

She asked, "Do you know any kid who gets everything he wants?" Her son gave her the name of such a child. "Do you like him?" Mom asked.

After a long pause, he grinned and said, "Naw, he's the meanest, most unhappy kid I know. His dad's never around and his mom's always too busy."

If you want to know—really know—your child, take time to listen to him.

A wise man will hear, and will increase learning; an da man of understanding shall attain unto wise counsels.

PROVERBS 1:5

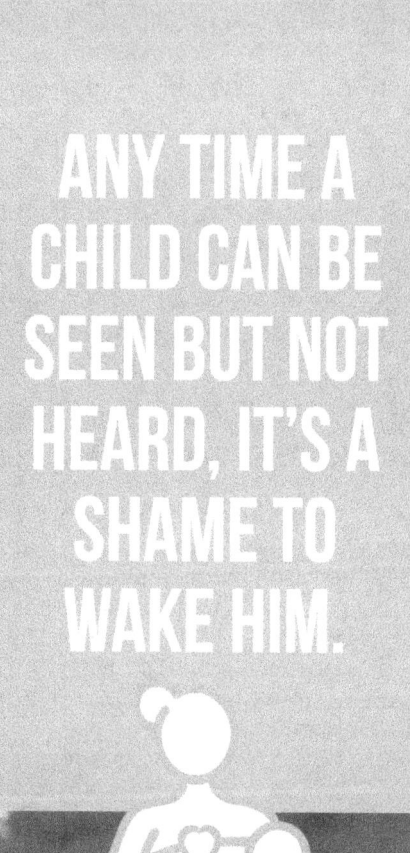

ANY TIME A CHILD CAN BE SEEN BUT NOT HEARD, IT'S A SHAME TO WAKE HIM.

A salesman telephoned a household and a 4-year-old boy answered. He said, "May I speak to your mother, please?"

The little boy replied, "She's in the shower right now and can't come to the phone."

The salesman asked, "Well, is anyone else at home?"

"Yes," the boy said, "my sister is here."

"Well, OK," the salesman continued. "May I speak to her, please?"

"I guess so," the boy said. "I'll go get her."

At this point the salesman heard a clunk as the boy laid down the receiver. This was followed by a very long silence on the phone.

Finally the little boy came back on the line and said, "Are you still there?"

"Yes," the salesman said, trying hard to sound patient, "I thought you were going to put your sister on the phone."

The boy replied, "I tried, mister. But she's sound asleep and I couldn't lift her out of her crib."

A merry heart doeth good like a medicine.

PROVERBS 17:22

M any a woman has felt "alone" during and after childbirth, but consider the true story of Martha Martin, wife of an Alaskan prospector in the 1920s.

While she was pregnant, her husband left her at their camp to run an errand to a neighboring island. A series of disasters struck almost immediately. First, an avalanche pinned her unconscious under a rock on the mountainside for several days. She managed to crawl back to their cabin and reset the broken bones she had suffered, making a splint for her leg and a cast for her arm. Then, a storm prevented her husband's return. Stranded, injured, alone, and with supplies almost gone, she quickly learned to be self-sufficient—killing animals for food and using their fur to make coverings for the coming baby. Bit by bit, she began burning portions of the cabin for heat.

Martha had never seen a child born before she went into two hard days of labor. But she kept her head and helped herself after her daughter finally arrived. She later baptized the infant Dannas. Several weeks later, some Indians appeared and she finally had help until her husband, who had been caught on the other island, arrived. Her published diary was appropriately titled, *O Rugged Land of Gold*.

Babies aren't so hard to figure out. A little common sense and lots of love can cover just about everything.

If any of you lack wisdom, let him ask of God, that giveth to all men liberally, and upbraideth not; and it shall be given him.

JAMES 1:5

A SWEATER IS A GARMENT WORN BY A CHILD WHEN HIS MOTHER FEELS CHILLY.

Eight-year-old William was appreciative but not enthusiastic when he found skis under the Christmas tree. They had not been high on his wish list, but his father knew he would need them for an upcoming family trip.

As it turned out, the skis were the best gift he ever received. William took to the sport his first day on the slopes and he joined the resort's junior racer program. For the next ten years, William skied every winter weekend, sometimes getting up in subzero cold to be at the mountain early. The skis taught him self-discipline and persistence. He learned to get up after falling hard. At home, he learned to budget his time to allow for homework. William became a hard-working focused young adult willing to dare because he wasn't afraid to fail. The skis did for William what the long-gone record player and toy train could not.

Just as you give your child nutritious food and make your child wear warm clothing *ultimately for his benefit*, so, too, choose gifts wisely for your child. Provide what is most beneficial, not necessarily what is desired. Give gifts that are challenging, bring out your child's talents, and broaden your child's creativity and horizons. Such gifts last far beyond one season!

She has no fear of winter for her household, for she has made warm clothes for all of them.

PROVERBS 31:21 TLB

FINGERPRINTING CHILDREN IS A GOOD IDEA. IT WILL SETTLE THE QUESTION AS TO WHO USED THE GUEST TOWEL IN THE BATHROOM.

A group of four-year-olds were gathered in a Sunday school class one spring. Their teacher asked them, "Does anyone know what today is?"

A little girl held up her hand and said, "It's *Palm* Sunday."

"Wonderful!" exclaimed the teacher. "Now does anyone know what next Sunday is?" No answer.

Finally, as if a light had just come on, the same little girl shouted, "I do! Next Sunday is Easter."

The teacher responded, "That's fantastic!" Ready to drive her point home, she asked, "Now, does anyone know what makes next Sunday Easter?"

At this the little girl jumped up and said, "Yes! Next Sunday is Easter because Jesus rose from the grave." Before the teacher could congratulate her on yet another correct answer, the little girl continued, "But if He sees His shadow, He has to go back in for seven weeks."

Listen closely to what others tell you. Weigh it against what you know to be God's truth. Information is different from truth. It comes in varying degrees of accuracy, whereas truth comes only in one package, labeled: the whole truth and nothing but the truth.

But test everything that is said to be sure it is true, and if it is, then accept it.

1 THESSALONIANS 5:21 TLB

ANY MOTHER
COULD PERFORM
THE JOBS OF
SEVERAL AIR-
TRAFFIC
CONTROLLERS
WITH EASE.

Lillian took an active role in Sunday school work. She didn't teach a class, but she served on a number of committees. Once she called on a woman who had just moved to town to ask her to serve on a fund-raising committee. "I'd be glad to if I had the time," the woman said, "but I have three young sons and they keep me on the run. I'm sure if you have a boy of your own, you'll understand how much trouble three can be."

Lillian replied, "Of course, that's quite all right. And I do understand."

"Have you any children, Mrs. Gilbreth?" the woman asked.

Lillian replied, "Oh, yes."

The woman pursued the line, "Any boys?"

Lillian said, "Yes, indeed."

The woman persisted, "May I ask how many?"

Lillian graciously replied, "Certainly. I have six boys."

The woman gulped, "Six boys? Imagine a family of six!"

Lillian added, "Oh, there are more in the family than that. I have six girls, too."

As Frank B. Gilbreth, Jr., and Ernestine Gilbreth Carey tell in their book, *Cheaper by the Dozen*, the newcomer then whispered, "I surrender. When is the next meeting of the committee? I'll be there, Mrs. Gilbreth. I'll be there."

She looketh well to the ways of her household, and eateth not the bread of idleness.

PROVERBS 31:27

PARENTS MUST GET ACROSS THE IDEA THAT, "I LOVE YOU ALWAYS, BUT SOMETIMES I DO NOT LOVE YOUR BEHAVIOR."

Little Edward misbehaved during dinner one evening. His father, a strict but fair disciplinarian, reprimanded him. Still, Eddy didn't change his ways. The father finally said, "Eddy, if you do not behave, you will be sent to your room and there will be no more food for you tonight."

Eddy didn't listen, but continued to misbehave. At that, he was ordered to march to his bedroom, change into his nightclothes, and climb into bed.

As he lay in bed, Eddy's every thought turned to food. He couldn't remember ever having felt more hungry, or more alone or alienated from the family. He began to cry. Then he heard a noise on the stairs, and footsteps walking closer and closer to his room. The door opened and in came his father.

Closing the door behind him, he came over to Eddy's bed and said, "I love you, Eddy, and Eve come to spend the night with you."

Not all *behavior* is worthy of applause. But every moment of a child's life and every ounce of a child's *being* is worthy of love.

Those whom I love, I reprove and discipline; be zealous therefore, and repent.

REVELATION 3:19 NASB

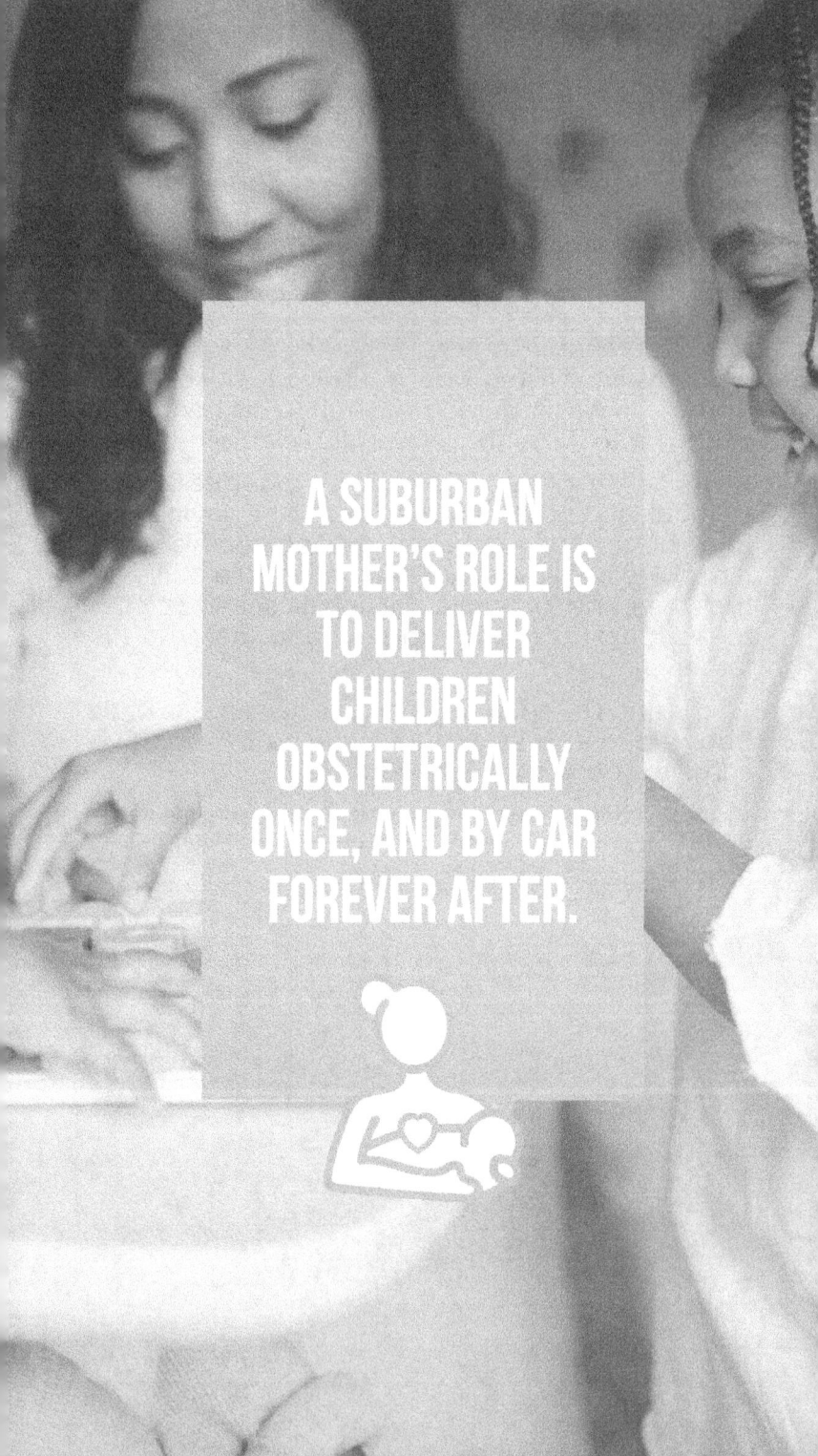

A SUBURBAN MOTHER'S ROLE IS TO DELIVER CHILDREN OBSTETRICALLY ONCE, AND BY CAR FOREVER AFTER.

A mother once faced the prospect of sixteen trips to church! Various combinations of her children were serving in various roles for three different Sunday services. The one serving the seven o'clock service had to be there fifteen minutes early to robe and light the candles.

So Mom doubled back for the kids who were going to attend that service since they weren't ready when he left the first time. And so it went for each service—two trips . . . and the same coming home. In all, three services, Sunday school, and two different youth group meetings, and the total number of trips was sixteen! Since the church was six miles from their home, she drove ninety-six miles that morning, all before lunch. She moaned to herself more than once, "This is the last time my husband goes out of town on business over a weekend!"

To her dismay, she found a police car in their driveway upon her final trip home. An officer had been sent to check on a fairly large number of past-due parking tickets acquired by her husband. "Been busy this morning?" the officer asked. The woman recounted the litany of her morning. And then the officer asked the worst possible question, "May I see your license?" It had been expired for two months!

There is a right time for everything; a time to laugh.

ECCLESIASTES 3:1,4 TLB

LEVEL WITH YOUR CHILD BY BEING HONEST. NOBODY SPOTS A PHONY QUICKER THAN A CHILD.

A little girl shouted with glee at the unexpected appearance of her grandmother in her nursery. "I've come to tuck you into bed and give you a goodnight kiss," the grandmother explained.

"Will you read me a story first?" the little girl asked.

Grandma, dressed elegantly for the impending dinner party downstairs, couldn't resist the soulful plea in her granddaughter's eyes. "All right," she replied, "but just one."

At the close of the story, the little girl snuggled into her bed, ready for sleep, but not before she said, "Thank you, Grandma. You look pretty tonight."

The grandmother smiled and replied, "Yes, I have to be pretty for the dinner party your parents are hosting."

"I know," the little girl said. "Mommy and Daddy are entertaining some very important people downstairs."

"Why, yes," said the grandmother. "But how did you know that? Was it because I surprised you by coming upstairs tonight? Was it my dress that gave it away?" Each time her granddaughter shook her head with a vigorous "no." Finally, the grandmother asked, "Was it that I only read one story to you?"

"No," the little girl giggled. "Just listen! Mommy is laughing at all of Daddy's jokes."

In all things willing to live honestly.

HEBREWS 13:18

AS PARENTS, WE NEVER STAND SO TALL AS WHEN WE STOOP TO HELP OUR CHILDREN.

In her book, *American Girl*, Mary Cantwell tells of her great embarrassment and agony at not being able to do math like the other children in her class at school. She writes:

"It was agony to me to be so stupid. The more Miss Fritzi tried to show me how to translate the marks into symbols, the more cotton seemed to be stuffing the corners of my head. The cotton seemed even thicker on the nights Papa sat beside me at the desk in the living room, pencil points breaking under his fierce attack. I snuffled and shook and his voice took on a steel edge, and when at last my mother shyly volunteered, the suffering eyes we turned on her were identical.

"For several nights she sat at the desk ... and summoned up her old schoolteacher's skills. Sniffling at her left, I bent over a scratch pad watching while her small, shapely hand (a hand that could trace a line of gold leaf as fine as a hair) traced swoops and curlicues. Suddenly they assembled themselves into sense and the cotton fled my head, leaving it as clear and clean as a tide- rinsed seashell ... I knew a triumph second only to that I'd known on the morning I finally succeeded in tying my shoelaces into bows. I could add!"

Taking the time to help your child—no matter what the task—can change their world and yours.

Be humble, thinking of others as better than yourself. Don't think about your own affairs, but be interested in others, too, and in what they are doing. Your attitude should be the kind that was shown us by Jesus Christ.

PHILIPPIANS 2:3B-5 TLB

A GOOD
LAUGH IS
SUNSHINE IN
A HOUSE.

Business consultant C. W. Metcalf tells how he once signed up for a hospice training program to work with terminally ill patients. He was assigned to Roy, an elderly man with colon cancer. Offering to assist Roy one day, Metcalf said, "Maybe you want me to help you out of those Mickey Mouse pajamas and into something more respectable."

Roy whispered back, even in his great pain, "I like these pj's. Mickey reminds me that I can still laugh a little, which is more than the doctor has ever done. Maybe you should get some pj's with Goofy on them." Roy laughed, but Metcalf didn't. "Young man," he continued, "you're one of the most depressing people I've ever met. I'm sure you're a nice person, but if you're here to help, it ain't working."

Metcalf was angered to hear the truth put so bluntly.

On the last day of his training, Metcalf learned that Roy had died. His instructor handed him a paper bag that Roy had left for him. Inside, he found a T-shirt with the grinning face of Goofy. A note read: "Put on this shirt at the first sign you're taking yourself too seriously. In other words, wear it all the time." Metcalf laughed! Roy had taught him one of the best lessons he ever learned: humor isn't an occasional joke. It's a basic survival tool for living life to the fullest!

The light in the eyes [of him whose heart is joyful] rejoices the hearts of others.

PROVERBS 15:30 AMP

EACH LOVING ACT SAYS LOUD AND CLEAR. "I LOVE YOU, GOD LOVES YOU. I CARE, GOD CARES."

When Rose Kennedy died at age 104, the world lost one of the most dedicated and famous mothers of this century. She was mother to nine children, among them a former United States President and Attorney General, and a current United States Senator.

In spite of her own marital challenges, the birth of a mentally challenged child, and the early deaths of four of her children, Rose Kennedy lived a life of faith and strength before her children and grandchildren. At her funeral, her son Ted put into perspective the considerable impact that she had on the lives of her family members—with actions both great and small—conveying to her children her love and care, and God's love and care:

"She sustained us in the saddest times.

. . . Her faith in God was the greatest gift she gave us.

. . . She was ambitious not only for our success but for our souls. From our youth we remember how, with effortless ease, she could bandage a cut, dry a tear, recite from memory 'The Midnight Ride of Paul Revere,' and spot a hole in a sock from a hundred yards away."

Great mothers don't always bear children who achieve greatness in the eyes of the world, but great mothers always do convey great love.

Beloved, let us love one another: for love is of God; and every one that liveth is born of God . . . for God is love.

1 JOHN 4:7-8

CHILDREN HAVE MORE NEED OF MODELS THAN OF CRITICS.

The daughter of missionaries to India, Wendy resented being put into a "box" and as a teenager in boarding school, she rebelled against what was expected of her. Her parents returned to Canada so the family might be together, but Wendy continued to rebel. Her mother and father, however, didn't judge or condemn her. She says, "They just kept on loving me. I discovered that I could fight rules and people who criticized me, but I couldn't put up walls against love. Because of my parents' patient love for me, I stopped rebelling, and . . . I recommitted my life to Christ."

As a young adult, Wendy is now a missionary to India! One of her students, Anne, had a very negative attitude toward Christianity. Wendy said, "I prayed diligently for Anne, and decided that I would treat her with the same loving-kindness with which my parents had treated me. I accepted Anne as she was, without placing spiritual expectations on her. When Anne realized that I didn't intend to judge her . . . she began opening up to me." In March, Anne accepted Christ into her life. Wendy concludes, "A 'close family' has little to do with geography and being together physically. But [it] has everything to do with loving . . . supporting . . . and communicating with each other."

Be their ideal; let them follow the way you teach and live; be a pattern for them in your love your faith, and your clean thoughts.

1 TIMOTHY 4:12 TLB

INSOMNIA:
A CONTAGIOUS
DISEASE OFTEN
TRANSMITTED
FROM BABIES
TO PARENTS.

n *Murphy Must Have Been a Mother*, Teresa Bloomingdale recalls a conversation she had with her husband, who said, "I love new babies."

"Since when?" I joked. "You were the one who always wished they could be born housebroken and able to play baseball! You had no patience at all with the squalling infants who leaked from both ends and spit up on every shirt you owned. It wasn't until they got into their terrible twos that you thought the kids were worth keeping!"

"That's not true and you know it," he said with a sigh. "I truly loved those infants, even the ones who couldn't tell time and kept us up all night . . . Don't tell me you wouldn't just love to start all over again!"

"True, I loved having a new baby every year . . . when I was young and lively and had not yet become addicted to sleep. But at our age? No, thank you."

In planning to help her son and daughter-in-law, Bloomingdale was determined to be the model grandmother—up at night, folding diapers, making formula. But then she discovered she was out of a job. The baby's *great*-grandmother had arrived to help out!

Is it true that the elderly need less sleep? If so, great-grandmas truly may be best suited for newborns!

There is a high time for everything: a time to laugh.

ECCLESIASTES 3:1,4 TLB

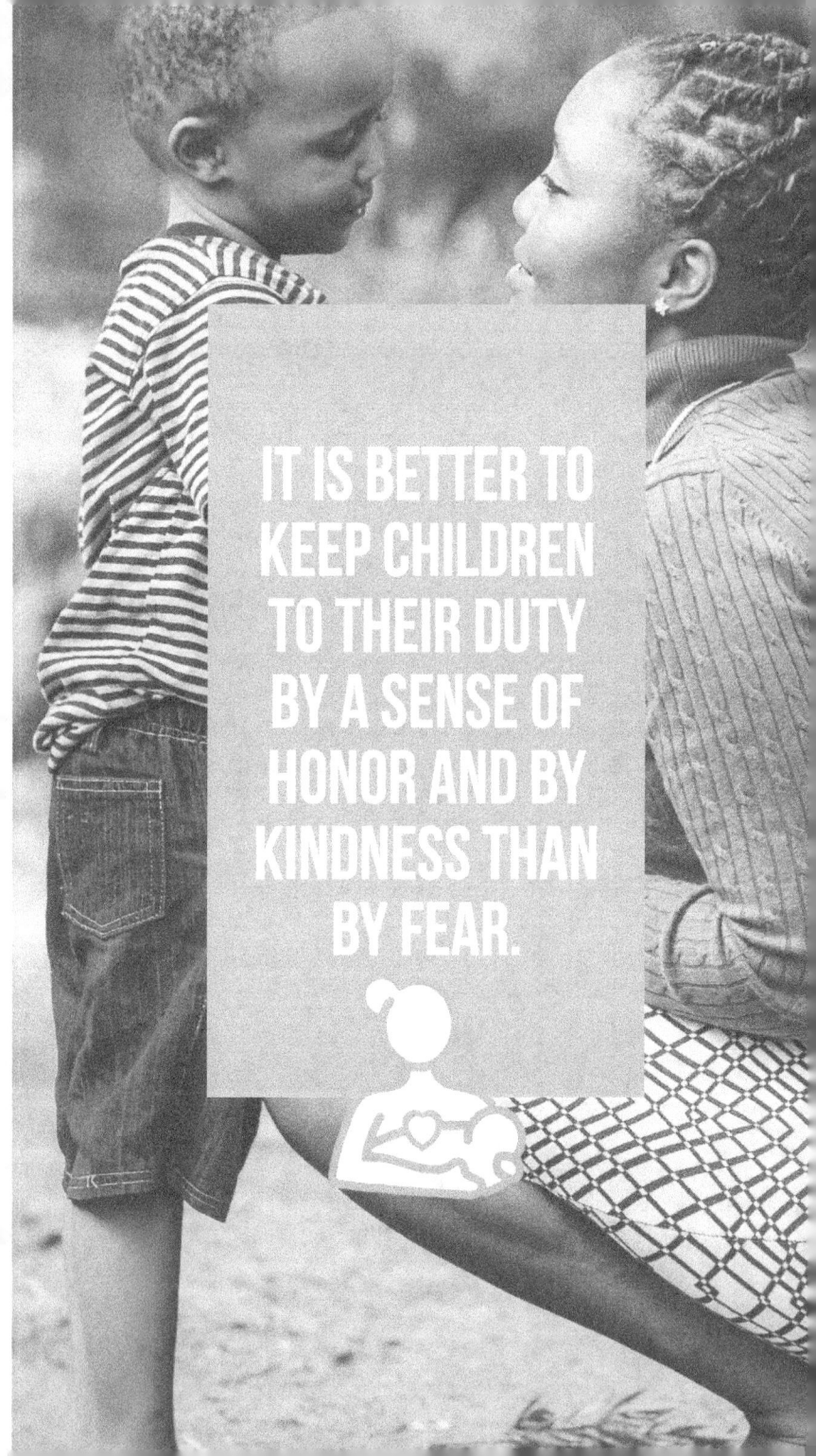

IT IS BETTER TO KEEP CHILDREN TO THEIR DUTY BY A SENSE OF HONOR AND BY KINDNESS THAN BY FEAR.

A little girl once paid a visit to relatives who lived in the country. While walking along a country road, she found a land terrapin also walking on the warmed pavement. As she moved closer to examine it, the terrapin closed its shell like a vice. When she tried to pry him open with a stick, her uncle intervened, "No, no. That is not the way. I'll show you what we need to do."

The uncle picked up the small creature and carried it into the house. There he set it on the hearth. In a few minutes the terrapin began to get warm, he stuck out his head and feet, and calmly crawled toward the girl.

"People are sort of like terrapins, too," her uncle said. "If you try to force a person to do anything, they'll usually close up tightly. But if you warm them up with a little kindness, they'll more than likely open up and come your way."

If you had to pick only one trait around which to live all the time, what would it he? Order . . . honors . . . knowledge . . . passion . . . fame? Probably not. The most livable of all traits is one every person can show: kindness.

. . . do not irritate and provoke your children to anger—do not exasperate them to resentment—but rear them [tenderly] in the training an discipline and the counsel and admonition of the Lord.

EPHESIANS 6:4 AMP

(ENCOURAGEMENT) IS THE ART OF "TURNING YOUR CHILDREN ON," HELPING THEM TO DO FOR THEMSELVES, NOT DOING FOR THEM.

Once upon a time there was a little boy who was given everything he wanted. As an infant, he was given a bottle at the first little whimper. He was picked up and held whenever he fussed. His parents said . . . he'll think we don't love him if we let him cry.

He was never disciplined for leaving the yard, even after being told not to. He suffered no conse-quence for breaking windows or tearing up flower beds. His parents said . . . he'll think we don't love him if we stifle his will.

His mother picked up after him, made his bed, and cleaned up all his messes. His parents said . . . he'll think we don't love him if we give him chores.

Nobody ever stopped him from using bad words or telling dirty jokes. He was never reprimanded for scribbling on his bedroom wall. His parents said . . . he'll think we don't love him if we stifle his cre-ativity.

He never was required to go to Sunday school. His parents said . . . he'll think we don't love him if we force religion down his throat.

One day the parents received news that their son was in jail on a felony charge. They cried to each other, "All we ever did was love him and do for him." Unfortunately, that is, indeed, all they did.

> And thou shalt teach them ordinances and laws, and shalt shew them the way wherein they must walk, and the work that they must do.
>
> EXODUS 18:20

HOME, SWEET HOME—
WHERE EACH
LIVES FOR THE
FOR THE OTHER,
AND ALL LIVE
FOR GOD.

Joni Eareckson Tada writes a wonderful tribute in *Secret Strength* to a genuine "home, sweet home":

"Not long ago I entered a friend's home and immediately sensed the glory of God. No, that impression was not based on some hee-bie-jeebie feeling or super-spiritual instinct. And it had nothing to do with several Christian plaques I spotted hanging in the hallway. Yet there was a peace and orderliness that pervaded that home. Joy and music hung in the air. Although the kids were normal, active youngsters, everyone's activity seemed to dovetail together, creating the impression that the home had direction, that the kids really cared about each other, that the parents put love into action.

"We didn't even spend that much time 'fellowshipping' in the usual sense of the word —talking about the Bible or praying together. Yet we laughed. And really heard each other. And opened our hearts like family members. After dinner I left that home refreshed. It was a place where God's essential being was on display. His kindness, His love, His justice. It was filled with God's glory."

The sweetness of the Lord makes any home sweet!

For none of us lives to himself alone and none of us dies to himself alone. If we live, we live to the Lord; and if we die, we die to the Lord. So, whether we live or die, we belong to the Lord.

ROMANS 17:7-8 NIV

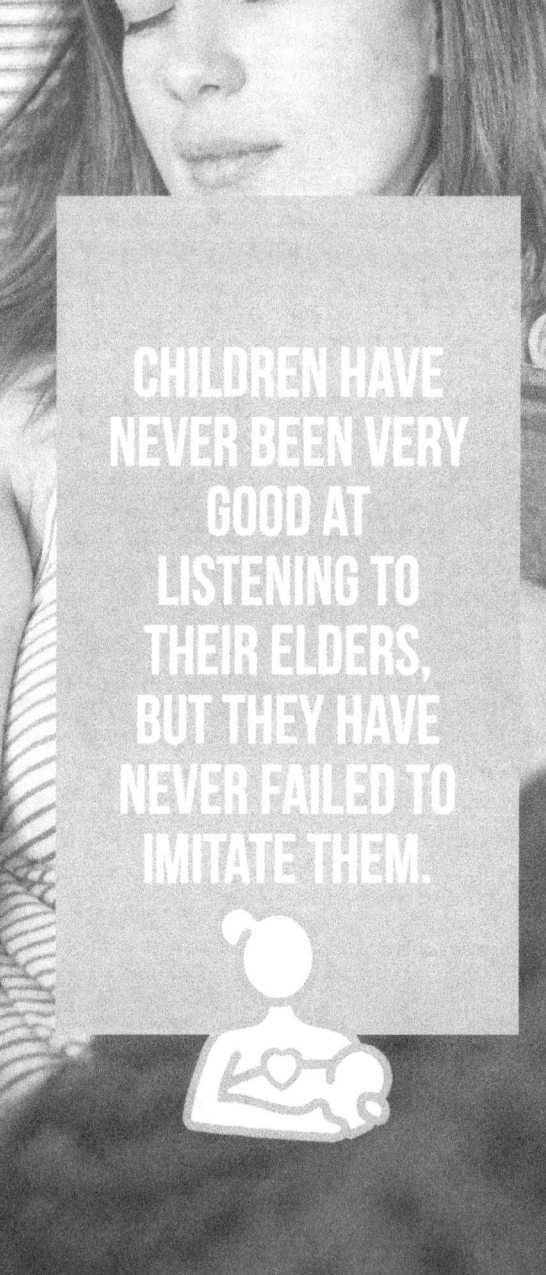

CHILDREN HAVE NEVER BEEN VERY GOOD AT LISTENING TO THEIR ELDERS, BUT THEY HAVE NEVER FAILED TO IMITATE THEM.

The story is told of a devout Christian who was faithful in his daily devotions. He read portions of Scripture and a devotional book, meditated silently for awhile, and then prayed. As time went by, his prayers became longer and more intense. He came to cherish this quiet time in his bedroom. His cat liked it, too! She would snuggle against him, purring loudly. This interrupted the man so he put a collar around the cat's neck and tied her to the bedpost whenever he wanted undisturbed devotional time.

The daughter of this man noticed how much his devotional time meant to him, and she adopted the practice. She dutifully tied her cat to the bedpost and proceeded to read and pray. Her prayer time was shorter, however. The day came when her son grew up. He desired also to keep some of the family traditions, but by his generation, the pace of life had quickened greatly. He felt he had no time for elaborate devotions, so he eliminated the time for meditation, Bible reading, and prayer. Still, in order to carry on the religious tradition, while dressing each morning, he tied his cat to the bedpost!

Explain to your children *why* you keep certain rituals, lest they follow them blindly, without meaning.

As ye know what manner of men we were among you for your sake. And ye became followers of us.

1 THESSALONIANS 1:5-6

A BABY IS GOD'S OPINION THAT THE WORLD SHOULD GO ON.

When ancient men and women witnessed great manifestations of nature's power —such as volcanic eruptions, giant waterfalls, hurricanes, great earthquakes, lightning bolts— they referred to them as "God's deeds," because they knew that no matter how strong they might be as individual people or collective bands of people, they could not do anything as powerful. Even today, great natural catastrophes are termed "acts of God" by insurance companies.

Unfortunately, these displays of nature were often devastating to people, and thus "deeds of God" became equated in the minds of many as "punishments by God." The thinking developed that when God intervenes in the affairs of mankind, it is generally for the purpose of reprimand.

How unfair to God! The truth is, when God chooses to intervene in the affairs of men and to set history on a new course, He does not send a lightning bolt, tidal wave, or tornado— rather. He causes a baby to be born.

The conception of a baby may not be regarded as earthshaking news to anyone other than the baby's family, but from God's perspective, it is the most powerful "deed" He performs!

And God blessed them, and God said unto them, "Be fruitful, and multiply, and replenish the earth, and subdue it."

GENESIS 1:28

FAMILIARITY
BREEDS
CONTEMPT
—AND
CHILDREN.

A couple in their mid-thirties were deeply in love and eager to be married. They went to their pastor for the premarital counseling required before their wedding. He probed various questions about their personal faith, ability to communicate openly and honestly, their commitment to each other, their understanding of church service, their views on money, and so on. Finally, he said, half asking and half commenting, "I'm sure you are eager to get started on a family?"

"Oh, yes, we want children," the young woman said. Her fiancé nodded in agreement.

"Then I hope you have a dozen," the pastor responded enthusiastically.

The man laughed and said, "If that's God's will, I'm willing to do my part."

The young woman, however, gulped and remained silent. "Well, actually, sir," she finally said. "I discussed that with the Lord on my thirty-fifth birthday and we decided that His will is for no more than two."

A merry heart doeth good like a medicine.

PROVERBS 17:22

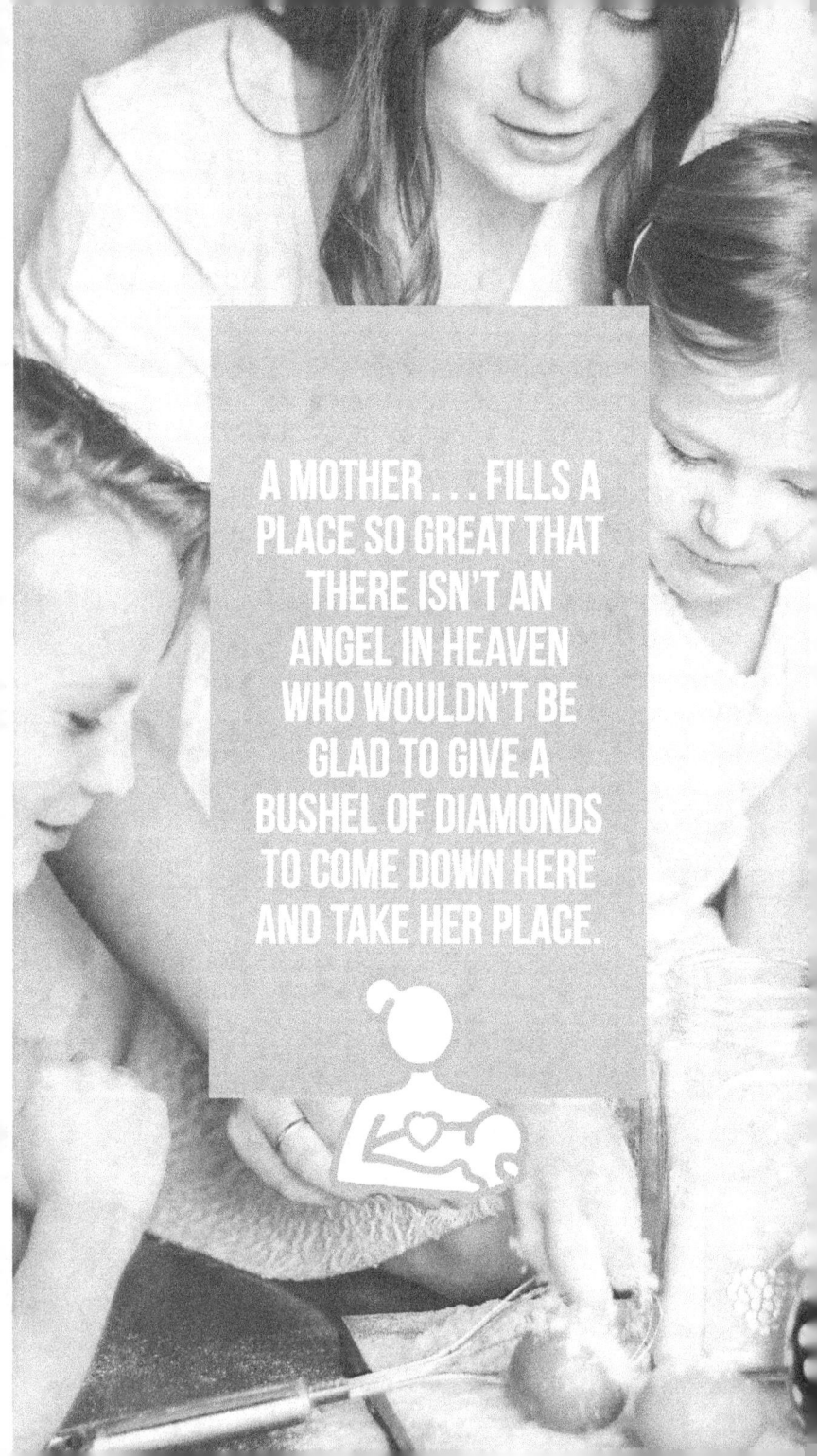

A MOTHER . . . FILLS A PLACE SO GREAT THAT THERE ISN'T AN ANGEL IN HEAVEN WHO WOULDN'T BE GLAD TO GIVE A BUSHEL OF DIAMONDS TO COME DOWN HERE AND TAKE HER PLACE.

A thirteen-year-old girl named Amy was not only struggling with growing into womanhood, but also with discovering her "identity." She had been adopted from South Korea and had no information about or remembrance of her birth mother. As much as she loved her adoptive parents, she began to speak frequently about what her "real mother" might be like.

During this time, Amy's dentist determined that Amy needed braces. On the day her braces were fitted, Amy went home from the dentist's office in pain. As the day wore on, her discomfort grew and by bedtime she was miserable. Her mother gave her medication and then invited her to snuggle up in her lap in the rocking chair, just as she had done when she was a little girl. As the mother rocked and stroked Amy, she began to relax in comfort. She was nearly asleep when she said to her mother in a drowsy voice, "I know who my real mom is."

"You do?" her mother asked gently.

"Yes," she replied. "She's the one who takes away the hurting."

Mothers may not always be able to "kiss it and make it well," but the love they give their children goes a long way toward making their children "whole."

And the angel came in unto her, and said, "Hail, thou that art highly favoured, the Lord is with thee: blessed art thou among women."

LUKE 1:28

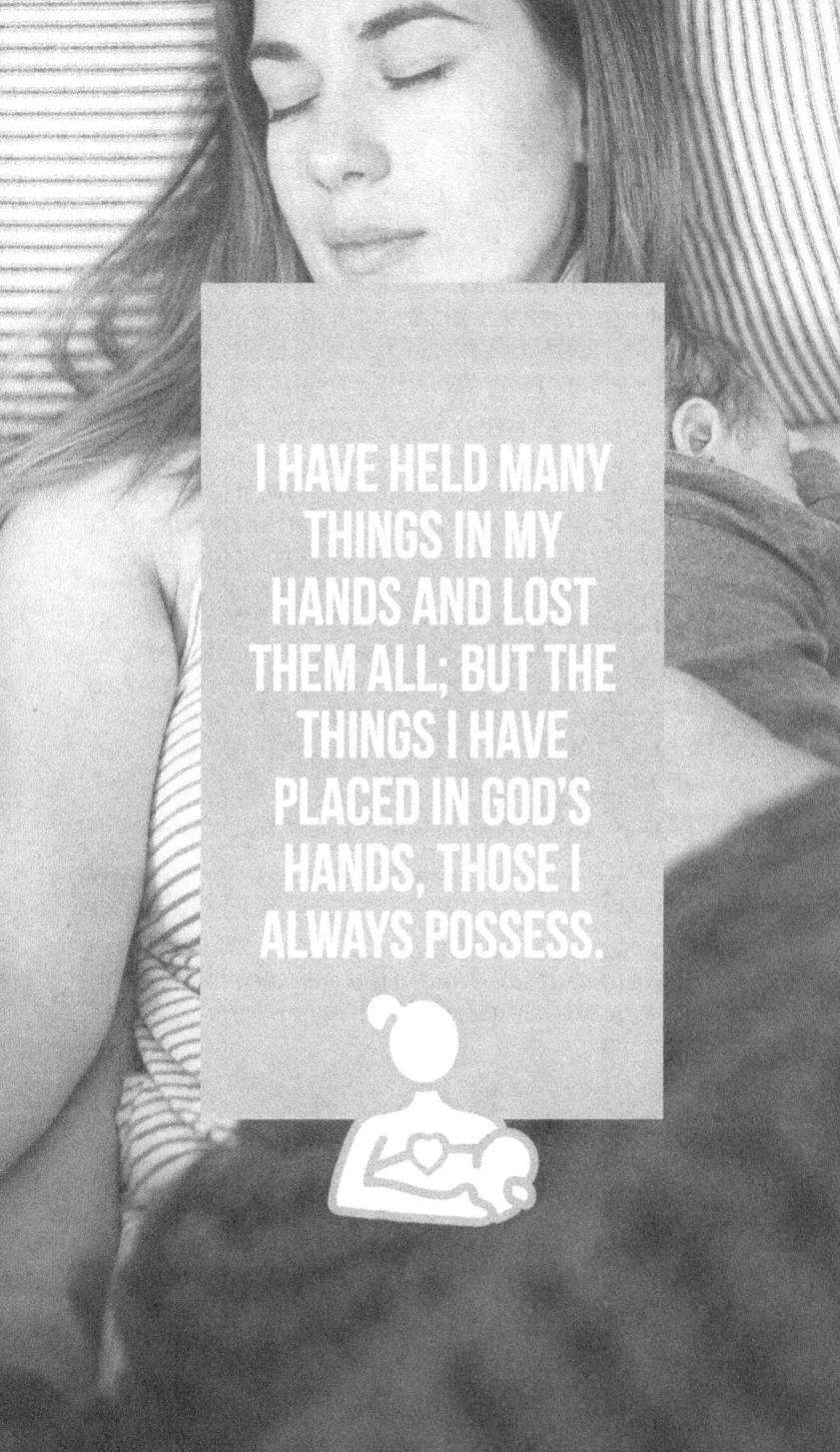

I HAVE HELD MANY THINGS IN MY HANDS AND LOST THEM ALL; BUT THE THINGS I HAVE PLACED IN GOD'S HANDS, THOSE I ALWAYS POSSESS.

*T*ime magazine ran in its January 25, 1988, issue an article about the introduction of the videocassette recorder in the marketplace. The article said: "The company had made a crucial mistake. While at first Sony kept its Beta technology mostly to itself, JVC, the Japanese inventor of the VHS [format], shared its secret with a raft of other firms. As a result, the market was overwhelmed by the sheer volume of the VHS machines being produced."

The result was a drastic undercutting of Sony's market share of VCRs. The first year, Sony lost forty percent of the market and by 1987, it controlled only ten percent of the market with its Beta format. In the end, Sony jumped on the VHS bandwagon. While it continued for many years to make Beta-format video equipment and tapes, Sony's switch to VHS ultimately sent Beta machines to the consumer-electronics graveyard.

Even in a cutthroat business, sharing has its rewards. How much deeper, broader, and richer are the rewards of sharing those things that are spiritual and eternal in nature.

For I know whom I have believed, and am persuaded that he is able to keep that which I have committed unto him against that day.

2 TIMOTHY 1:12

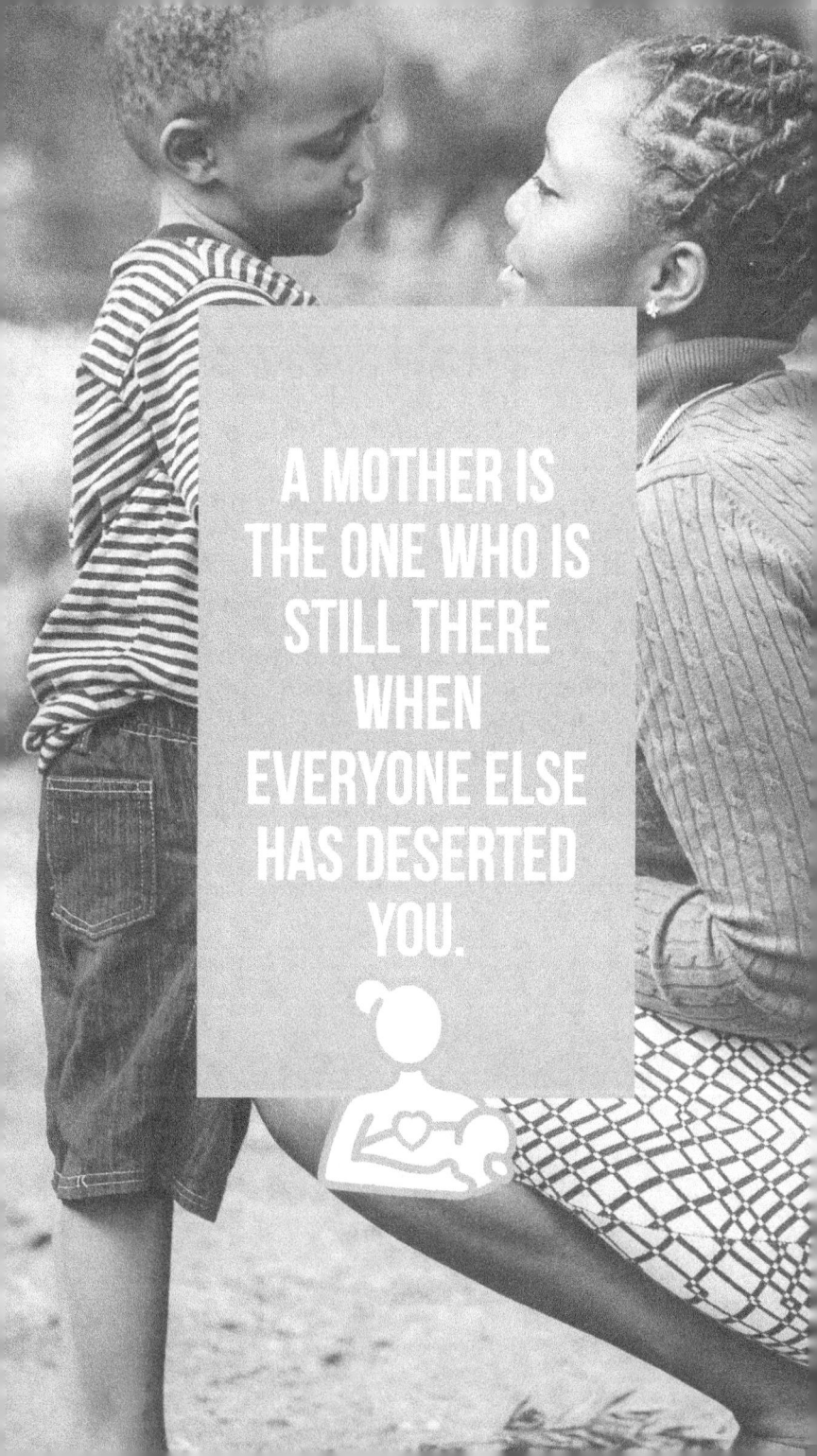

A MOTHER IS THE ONE WHO IS STILL THERE WHEN EVERYONE ELSE HAS DESERTED YOU.

A number of years ago a popular Mother's Day card summed up what many adult women feel. The cover of the card read, "Now that we have a mature, adult relationship, there's something I'd like to tell you." On the inside were these words: "You're still the first person I think of when I fall down and go boom."

None of us ever get beyond feeling a "need" for our mothers—the one person who has nurtured us, comforted us, and cared for us as no other person ever has or ever will. It is only when we are mothers ourselves, however, that we tend to realize how important our own mothers were to us. As Victoria Farnsworth has written:

Not until I became a mother did I understand how much my mother had sacrificed for me.

Not until I became a mother did I feel how hurt my mother was when I disobeyed.

Not until I became a mother did I know how proud my mother was when I achieved.

Not until I became a mother did I realize how much my mother loves me.

Why not call your mother today and tell her how much you love her?

If you love someone you will be loyal to him no matter what the cost.

1 CORINTHIANS 13:7 TLB

A GOOD DEED IS NEVER LOST; HE WHO SOWS COURTESY REAPS FRIENDSHIP, AND HE WHO PLANTS KINDNESS GATHERS LOVE.

I n the late nineteenth century, a Member of Parliament traveled to Scotland to make a speech. He traveled to Edinburgh by train, and then took a carriage southward to his destination. The carriage, however, became mired in mud. A Scottish farm boy came to the rescue with a team of horses and pulled the carriage loose. The politician asked the boy how much he owed him.

"Nothing," the lad replied.

"Are you sure?" the politician pressed, but the boy declined payment. "Well, is there anything I can do for you? What do you want to be when you grow up?"

The boy responded, "A doctor." The aristocratic Englishman offered to help the young Scot go to the university, and he followed through on his pledge.

More than half a century later, Winston Churchill lay dangerously ill with pneumonia—stricken while attending a wartime conference in Morocco. A new "wonder drug" was administered to him, a drug called penicillin that had been discovered by Sir Alexander Fleming. Fleming was the young Scottish lad once befriended. His benefactor? Randolph Churchill, Winston's father!

Sometimes the good that you do may very well come back to you in the form of the miracle you need.

For whatsoever a man soweth, that shall he also reap. And let us not be weary in well-doing; for in due season we shall read, if we faint not.

GALATIANS 6:7,9

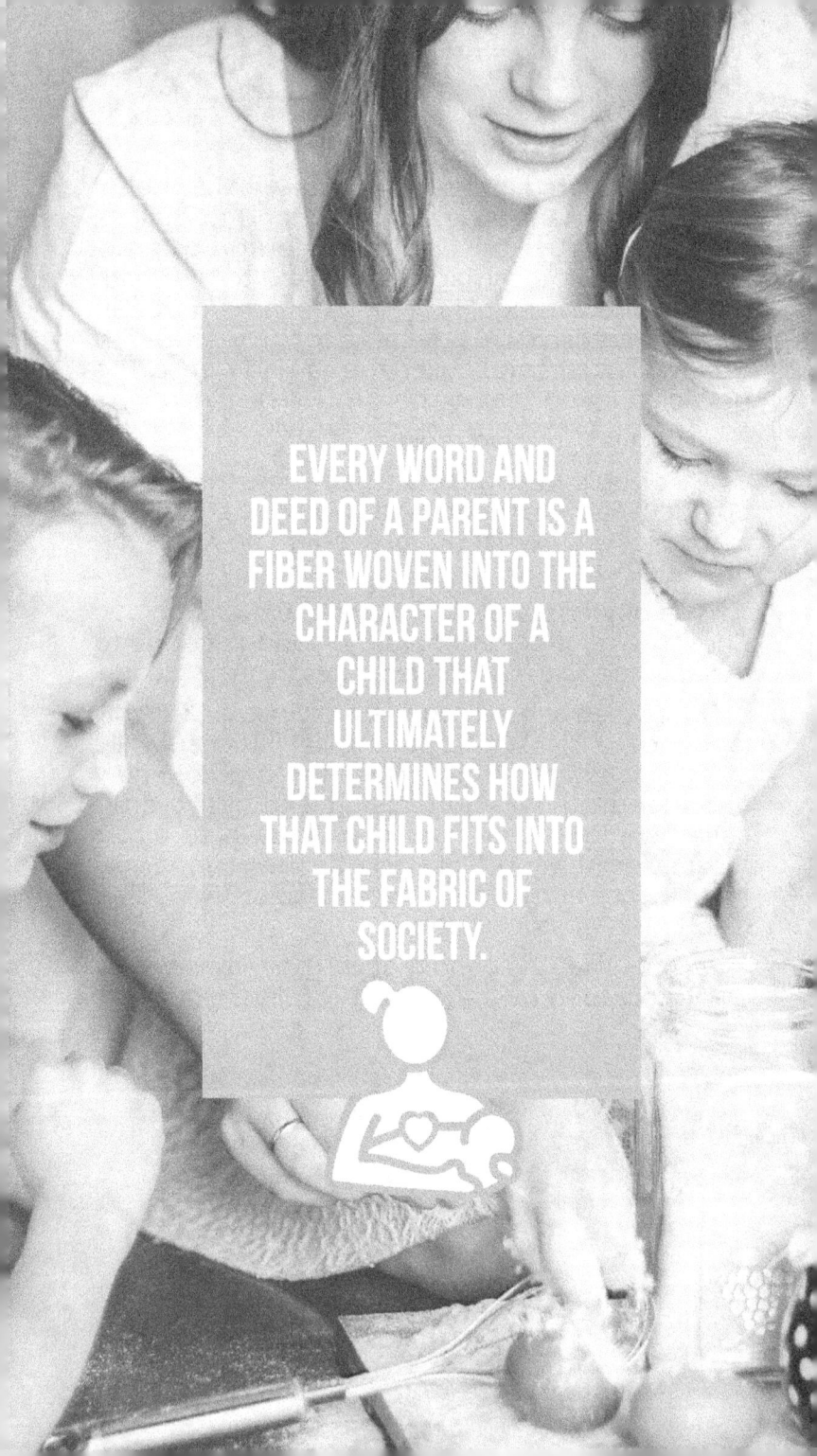

EVERY WORD AND DEED OF A PARENT IS A FIBER WOVEN INTO THE CHARACTER OF A CHILD THAT ULTIMATELY DETERMINES HOW THAT CHILD FITS INTO THE FABRIC OF SOCIETY.

The Lazy B Ranch—all 260 square miles of it—lies on the New Mexico and Arizona border. Most of it scrub brush, it has been in the Day family since 1881. When Harry and Ada Mae Day had their first child, they traveled 200 miles to El Paso for the delivery. Ada Mae brought her baby girl home to a difficult life. The four-room adobe house had no running water and no electricity. There was no school within driving distance. One would think that with such limited resources, a little girl's intellectual future might be in question. But Harry and Ada Mae were determined to "stitch learning" into their children.

Ada Mae subscribed to metropolitan newspapers and magazines. She read to her child hour after hour. When her daughter was four years old, she began her on the Calvert method of home schooling and she later saw that her daughter went to the best boarding schools possible. One summer, the parents took their children on a car trip to visit all the state capitols west of the Mississippi River. When young Sandra was ready for college, she went to Stanford, then on to law school . . . and eventually, she became the first woman justice to sit on the Supreme Court of the United States of America.

Every day you make an investment into the character of your child. Make BIG investments!

You will be judged on whether or not you are doing what Christ wants you to. So watch what you do and what you think.

JAMES 2:12 TLB

CHILDREN OFTEN HOLD A MARRIAGE TOGETHER—BY KEEPING THEIR PARENTS TOO BUSY TO QUARREL WITH EACH OTHER.

A little boy sat on the curb in front of his house one day, his head cradled in his hands. A friend walked by and said, "Hey, watcha worried about?"

The boy said, "I've been thinking. Dad slaves away at his job so I'll have lots of cool toys and plenty of food and a nice house with a room all my own. He told me last night he's working hard so I can go to college someday if I want to."

"That's causing you to worry?" asked the friend.

"Well, that's not all," said the boy. "Mom works hard every day cooking and doing the laundry and taking me places and helping me when I get sick."

"I don't get it," said the friend. "What do you have to worry about? It sounds like your life is just fine!"

The little boy said, "I'm worried they might try to escape!"

There is a right time for everything: a time to laugh.

ECCLESIASTES 3:1,4 TLB

Popular writer and speaker Tony Campolo tells a story about his wife. When he was on the faculty of the University of Pennsylvania, his wife was often invited to faculty gatherings and inevitably a woman lawyer or sociologist would confront her with the question, often framed in a condescending tone of voice, "And what is it that you do, my dear?"

Mrs. Campolo gave this as her response: "I am socializing two Homosapiens in the dominant values of the Judeo-Christian tradition in order that they might be instruments for the transformation of the social order into the teleologically prescribed utopia inherent in the eschaton." Then she would politely and kindly ask the other person, "And what is it that you do?"

The other person's response was rarely as overpowering!

Too often women feel as if they should apologize for being mothers or wives who "work at home" for the betterment of their families and husbands. In reality, these roles can be noble callings—ones with far-reaching impact and eternal consequences!

Many women do noble things, but you surpass them all.

PROVERBS 31:29 NIV

I THINK THAT SAVING A LITTLE CHILD AND BRINGING HIM TO HIS OWN, IS A DARNED SIGHT BETTER THAN LOAFING AROUND THE THRONE.

A little girl, only three years old, had just learned she was adopted, but she had failed to react one way or the other to that news. Her mother was at a loss as to how to explain the adoption any further.

The next day at church the little girl watched as a number of people came forward at the close of the service to accept Jesus Christ as their Savior and Lord. She asked her mother, "What are they doing?"

Her mother was quick to reply. "God has offered to adopt all of them as His children and they are taking Him up on His offer so they can live with Him forever in Heaven and always know that He loves them with all His heart." The little girl nodded and watched in awe as the pastor prayed with each person.

The next day, the mother overheard her little girl speak into her cocker spaniel's silky ear, "I just wanted you to know I'm adopting you 'cause God and Mommy and Daddy have adopted me. And that way we can live together forever."

Never assume that a child is too young to follow Christ. As much as a child is able, let him accept and follow. Give approval and full acceptance to his decision. Eventually, "following" will seem to be the only desirable choice for the child to make!

The fruit of the righteous is a tree of life;
and he that winneth souls is wise.

PROVERBS 11:30

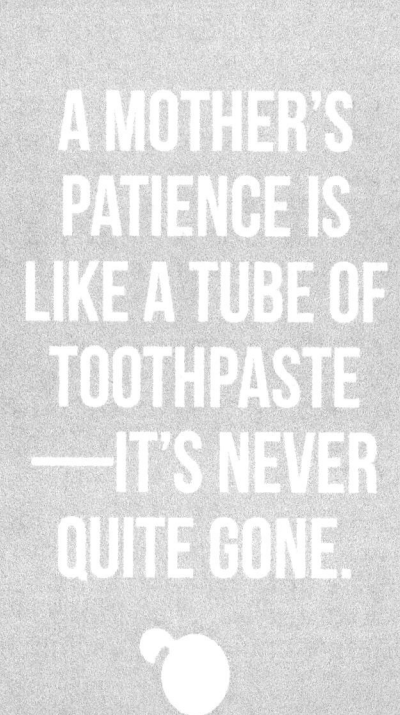

A MOTHER'S PATIENCE IS LIKE A TUBE OF TOOTHPASTE —IT'S NEVER QUITE GONE.

Accarding to a fable, a woman showed up one snowy morning at 5 AM at the home of an "examiner" of "suitable mother" candidates. Ushered in, she was asked to sit for three hours past her appointment time before she was interviewed. The first question given to her in the interview was, "Can you spell?" Yes, she said. "Then spell 'cook.'"

The woman responded, "C-O-O-K."

The examiner then asked, "Do you know anything about numbers?"

The woman replied, "Yes, sir, some things."

The examiner said, "Please add two plus two."

The candidate replied, "Four."

"Fine," announced the examiner. "We'll be in touch." At the board meeting of examiners held the next day, the examiner reported that the woman had all the qualifications to be a fine mother. He said, "First I tested her on self-denial, making her arrive at five in the morning on a snowy day. Then I tested her on patience. She waited three hours without complaint. Third, I tested her on temper, asking her questions a child could answer. She never showed indignation or anger. She'll make a fine mother." And all on the board agreed.

Being strengthened with all power according to his glorious might so that you may have great endurance and patience.

COLOSSIANS 1:11 NIV

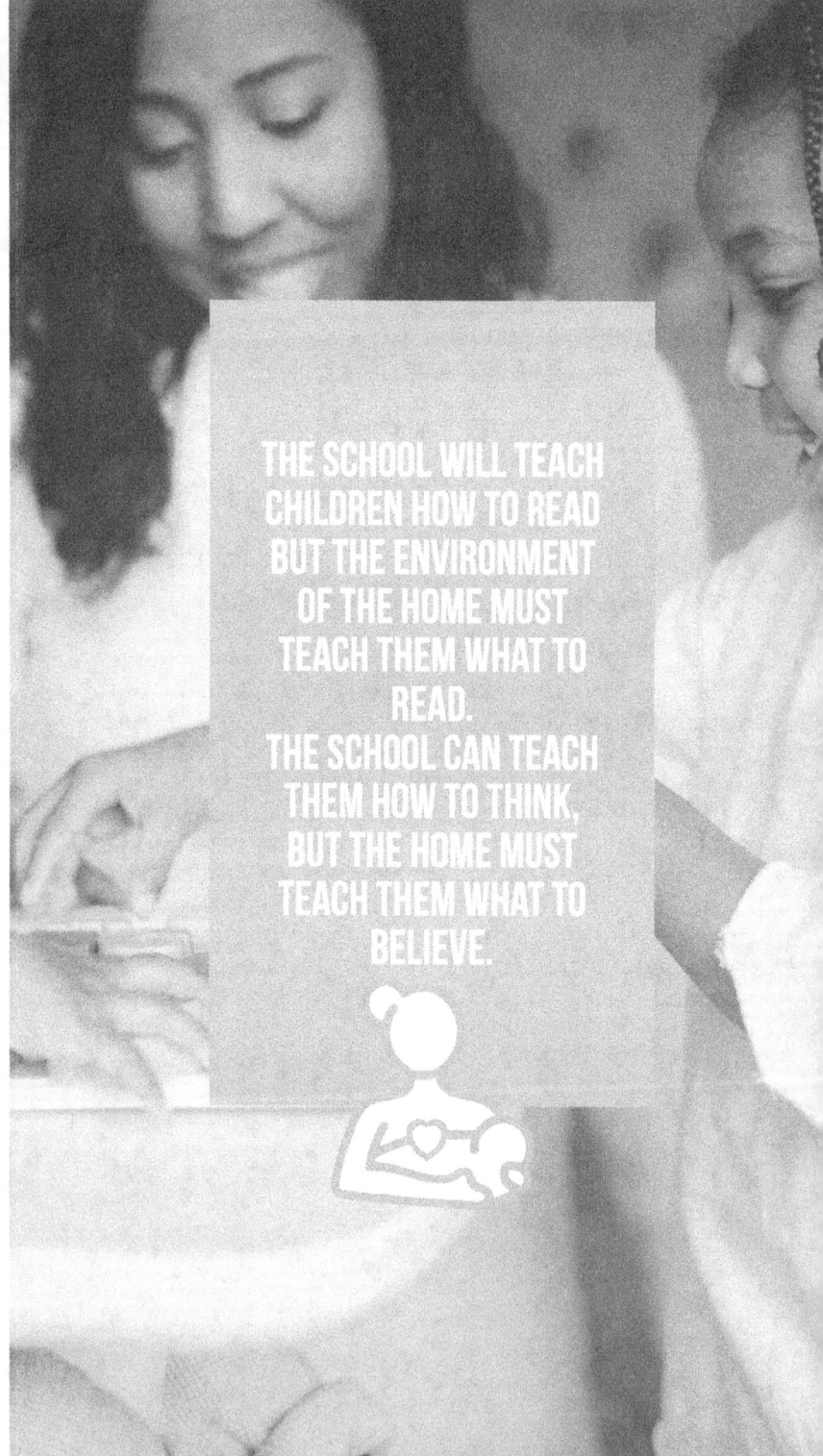

THE SCHOOL WILL TEACH CHILDREN HOW TO READ BUT THE ENVIRONMENT OF THE HOME MUST TEACH THEM WHAT TO READ.
THE SCHOOL CAN TEACH THEM HOW TO THINK, BUT THE HOME MUST TEACH THEM WHAT TO BELIEVE.

L ewis Smedes of Fuller Theological Seminary, has written a wonderful tribute to the impact a godly home can have upon a child's faith:

"May I share with you some reasons why I believe? All good reasons, none of them the really real reason. There's my family. I believe because I was brought up in a believing family. I don't make any bones about that. I don't know what would have happened to me if I had been born in the depths of Manchuria of a Chinese family. I just don't know. I do know that I was led to believe in the love of God as soon as I learned I should eat my oatmeal. We did a lot of believing in our house. We didn't have much else to do, as a matter of fact. Other kids sang 'Jesus loves me this I know 'cause the Bible tells me so.' I sang, 'Jesus loves me this I know, 'cause my ma told me so.'

"I wasn't alone. You probably heard about a reporter asking the great German theologian, Karl Barth, toward the end of his career: 'Sir, you've written these great volumes about God, great learned tomes about all the difficult problems of God. How do you know they're all true?' And the great theologian smiled and said, "Cause my mother said so!"'

Families are God's primary missionary society.

Teach a child to choose the right path, and when he is older he will remain upon it.

PROVERBS 22:6 TLB

THINK OF THE SACRIFICE YOUR MOTHER HAS TO MAKE IN ORDER THAT YOU MIGHT LIVE. THINK OF THE SACRIFICE GOD HAD TO MAKE THAT YOU AND YOUR MOTHER MIGHT LIVE.

In *My Mother Worked and I Turned Out Okay*, Katherine Wyse Goldman tells about Margaret, one of five children in a family during the 1930s and 1940s.

Margaret's mother left her alcoholic husband and took her children to live in a three-room apartment, which was all she could afford. Even at that, she had to work two jobs. Her night job was editing the company newspaper for the Pennsylvania Railroad from 10 PM to 7:30 AM. The children would greet their mother by the curb when her trolley pulled up in the morning, and she'd get them ready for school. After only a couple of hours of sleep, she'd go to her day job from 10 AM to 4 PM, at which time her children would greet her at the same curb. After a light supper, the children did their homework as quietly as possible so their mother could get a few more hours of sleep. Margaret said of her mother: "Mother never had a day off both jobs at the same time. My grandmother wanted to put us in foster homes, but my mother said no, that she could do it. She'd tell us the way we lived was temporary."

What wonderful wisdom to remember about any of the hardships we experience as mothers—this, too, is only temporary!

This is love: not that we loved God, but that he loved us and sent his Son as an atoning sacrifice for our sins.

1 JOHN 4:10 NIV

A BABY IS AN ANGEL WHOSE WINGS DECREASE AS HIS LEGS INCREASE.

A mother once told this story about her young son who wouldn't go to kindergarten:

"I can't go to school!" he would cry, his big blue eyes filling up with tears. "There's a gorilla up on the corner waiting to gobble me up! You can't see him, but he's there! He hides when grownups come around. Do you want me to be gobbled up by a gorilla?"

By the time the first ten days of school had passed, this mother had tried everything: bribery, pleading, threatening. She even locked him out of the house only to find him sitting under the neighbor's bushes, waiting for the time to come home.

Then one day as he dawdled on the porch steps pleading with his mother not to send him to sure death, one of his classmates, Tommy, came walking up the street and talked him into going to school. Her son met Tommy every day for the rest of the year.

This mother writes, "Wherever you are today. Tommy, know' that you have my undying gratitude, though I do have one request. Your kindergarten pal has been in school for eighteen years and is still playing eeny-meeny-miney-mo with his college majors. Would you mind dropping in and cajoling this kid into graduating?"

A merry heart doeth good like a medicine.

PROVERBS 17:22

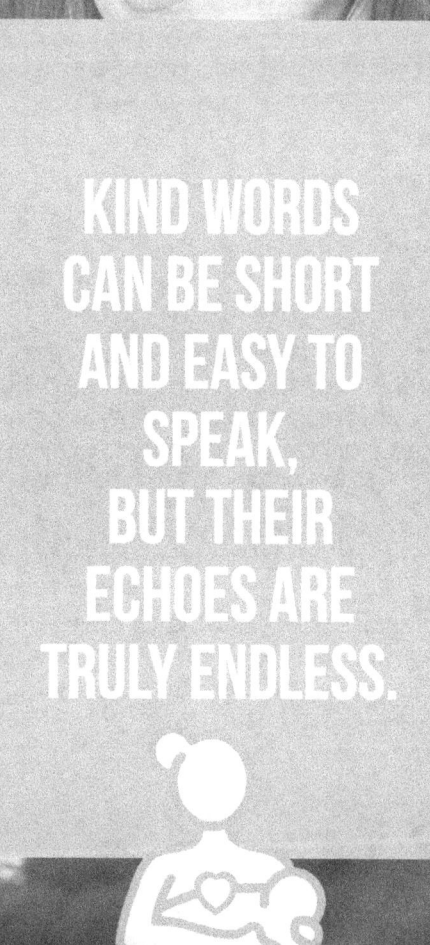

KIND WORDS
CAN BE SHORT
AND EASY TO
SPEAK,
BUT THEIR
ECHOES ARE
TRULY ENDLESS.

When the American poet and writer Edgar Guest was a young man, his first child died. He wrote about this experience: "There came a tragic night when our first baby was taken from us. I was lonely and defeated. There didn't seem to be anything in life ahead of me that mattered very much.

"I had to go to my neighbor's drugstore the next morning for something, and he motioned for me to step behind the counter with him. I followed him into his little office at the back of the store. He put both hands on my shoulders and said, 'Eddie, I can't really express what I want to say, the sympathy I have in my heart for you. All I can say is that I'm sorry, and I want you to know that if you need anything at all, come to me. What is mine is yours.'"

Guest recalls that this man was "just a neighbor across the way—a passing acquaintance." He says of the druggist that he "may long since have forgotten that moment when he gave me his hand and his sympathy, but I shall never forget it—never in all my life. To me it stands out like the silhouette of a lonely tree against a crimson sunset."

Is there someone who needs to hear your kind word today?

She opens her mouth in skillful and godly Wisdom, and on her tongue is the law of kindness—giving counsel and instruction.

PROVERBS 31:26 AMP

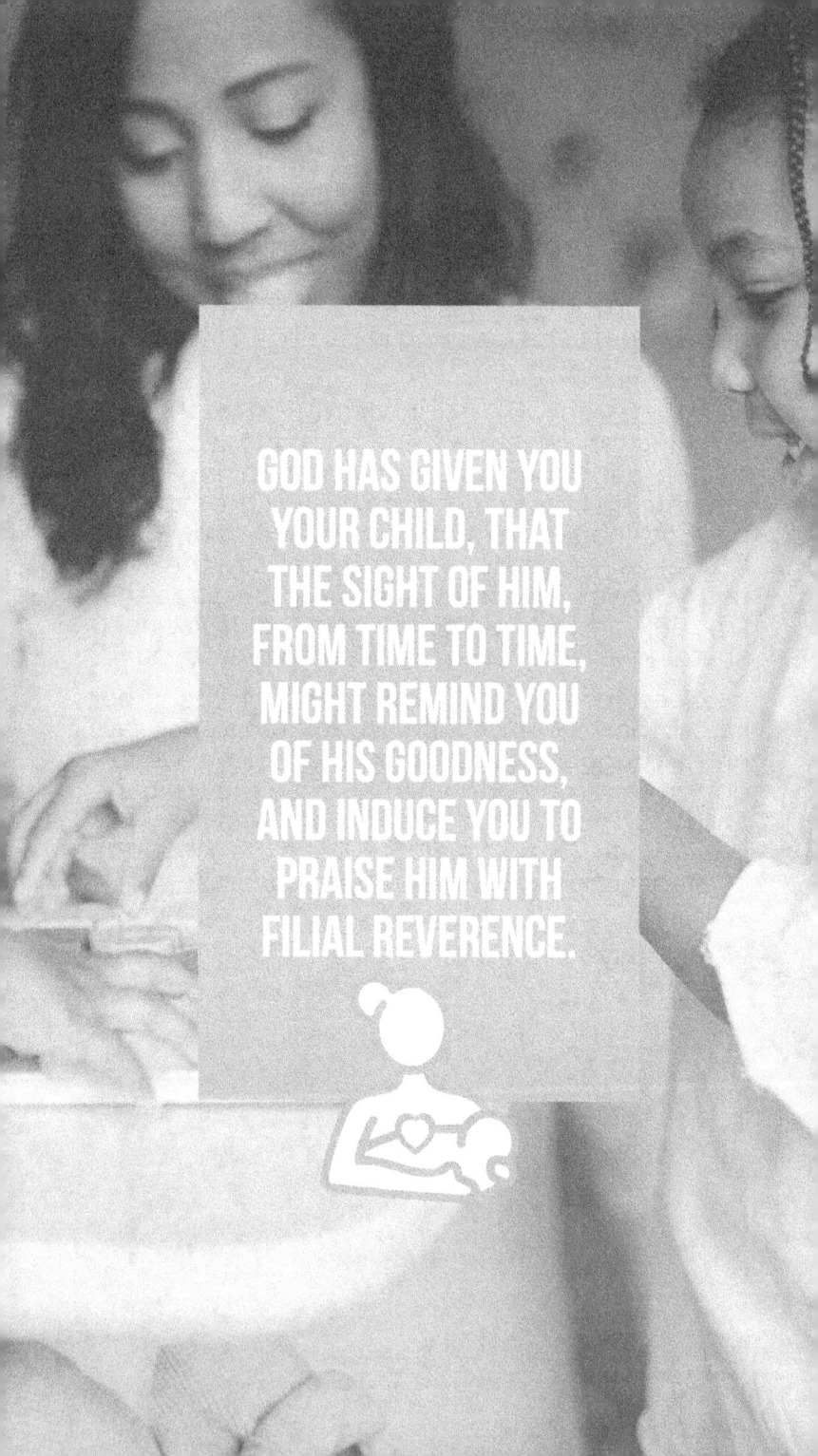

GOD HAS GIVEN YOU YOUR CHILD, THAT THE SIGHT OF HIM, FROM TIME TO TIME, MIGHT REMIND YOU OF HIS GOODNESS, AND INDUCE YOU TO PRAISE HIM WITH FILIAL REVERENCE.

While driving along a freeway on a cold, rainy night, the adults in the front seat of a car were talking when suddenly, they heard the horrifying sound of a car door opening, then the whistle of wind, and a sickening muffled sound. They quickly turned and saw that the three-year-old child riding in the backseat had fallen out of the car and was tumbling along the freeway. The driver screeched to a stop, and then raced back toward her motionless child. To her surprise, she found all the traffic stopped just feet away from her child. Her daughter had not been hit.

A truck driver offered his assistance and drove the girl to a nearby hospital. The doctors there rushed her into the emergency room, and soon came back with the good news: other than being unconscious and bruised and skinned from her tumble, the girl was fine. No broken bones. No apparent internal damage.

As the mother rushed to her child, the little girl opened her eyes and said, "Mommy, you know I wasn't afraid."

The mother asked, "What do you mean?"

The little girl explained, "While I was lying on the road waiting for you to get back to me, I looked up and right there I saw Jesus holding back the traffic with His arms outstretched."

See how very much our heavenly Father loves us, for he allows us to be called his children—think of it—and we really are!

1 JOHN 3:1 TLB

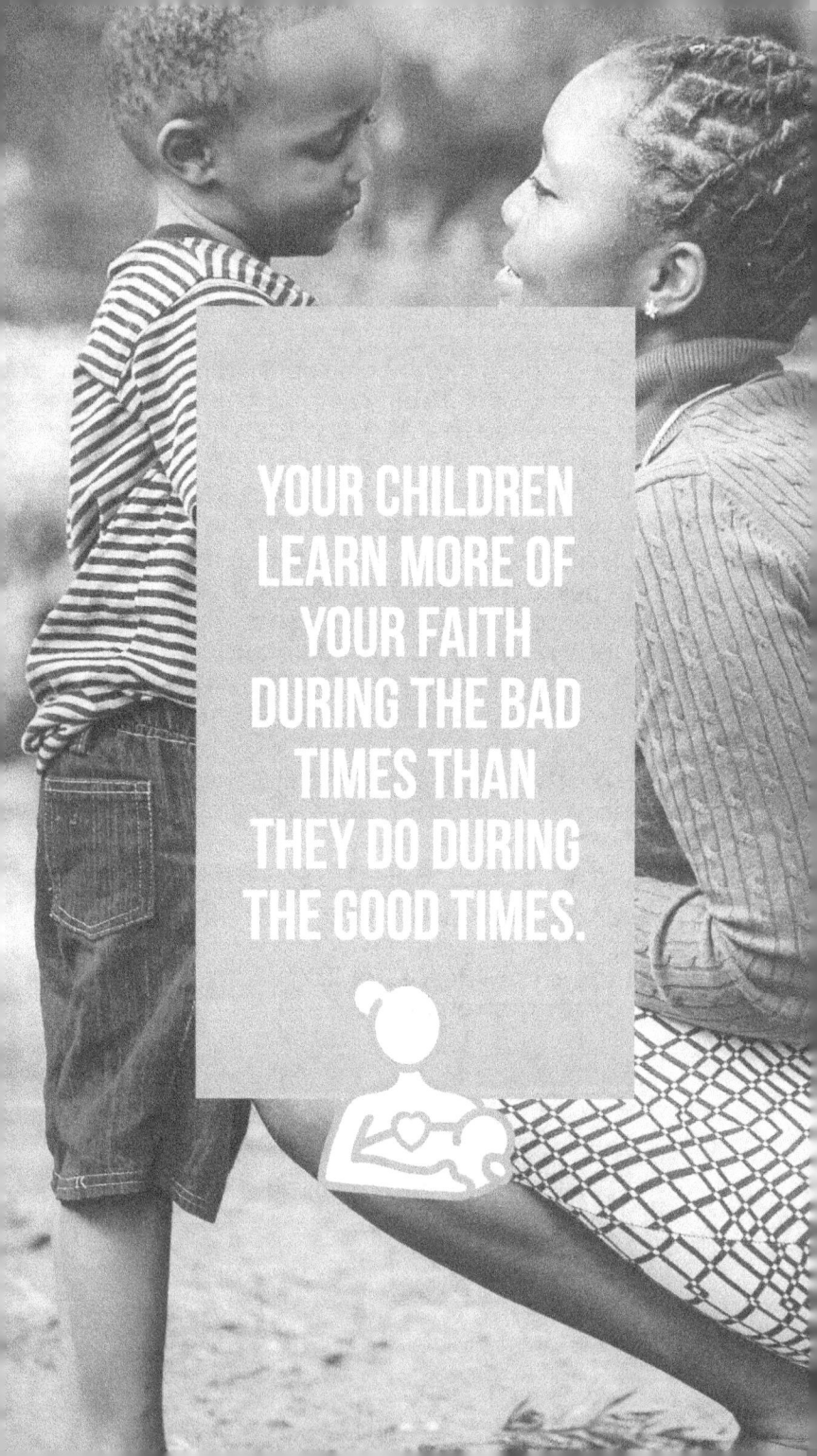

YOUR CHILDREN
LEARN MORE OF
YOUR FAITH
DURING THE BAD
TIMES THAN
THEY DO DURING
THE GOOD TIMES.

When Eleanor Sass was a child, she was hospitalized for appendicitis. Her roommate was a young girl named Mollie, who was injured when an automobile hit the bicycle she was riding. Mollie's legs had been badly broken and though the doctors performed several surgeries, Mollie faced a strong possibility that she would never walk again. She became depressed, uncooperative, and cried a great deal. She only seemed to perk up when the morning mail arrived. Most of her gifts were books, games, stuffed animals—all appropriate gifts for a bedridden child.

Then one day a different sort of gift came, this one from an aunt far away. When Mollie tore open the package, she found a pair of shiny, black-patent-leather shoes. The nurses in the room mumbled something about "people who don't use their heads," but Mollie didn't seem to hear them. She was too busy putting her hands in the shoes and "walking" them up and down her blanket. From that day, her attitude changed. She began cooperating with the nursing staff and soon, she was in therapy. One day Eleanor heard that her friend had left the hospital . . . and the best news of all, she had walked out, wearing her shiny new shoes!

Consider it all joy, my brethren, when you encounter various trials.

JAMES 1:2 NASB

During a dinner party, the hosts' two young children entered the dining room totally nude and began to walk slowly on tiptoe around the table. The parents were at first so astonished, and then so embarrassed, that they pretended nothing unusual was happening. They kept the conversation going, and the guests cooperated in the charade, also pretending as if nothing extraordinary was happening in the room.

After completely encircling the table, the children tiptoed from the room. There was a moment of silence at the table as everyone exhaled, and stifled their giggles. Then one of the children was overheard saying to the other in the adjacent hallway, "You see, Mommy was right. It is vanishing cream!"

While their rambunctious energy and inexhaustible curiosity can be tiring to adults, toddlers don't mean to misbehave nearly as much as they mean to make sense of the world in which they find themselves. Your discipline, patience, and encouragement are like red, yellow, and green lights governing their "tear" through the exploration process.

When your children try your patience, try to respond in such a way that you can hear a verdict of "not guilty."

The Lord is on my side; I will not fear: what can man do unto me?

PSALM 118:6

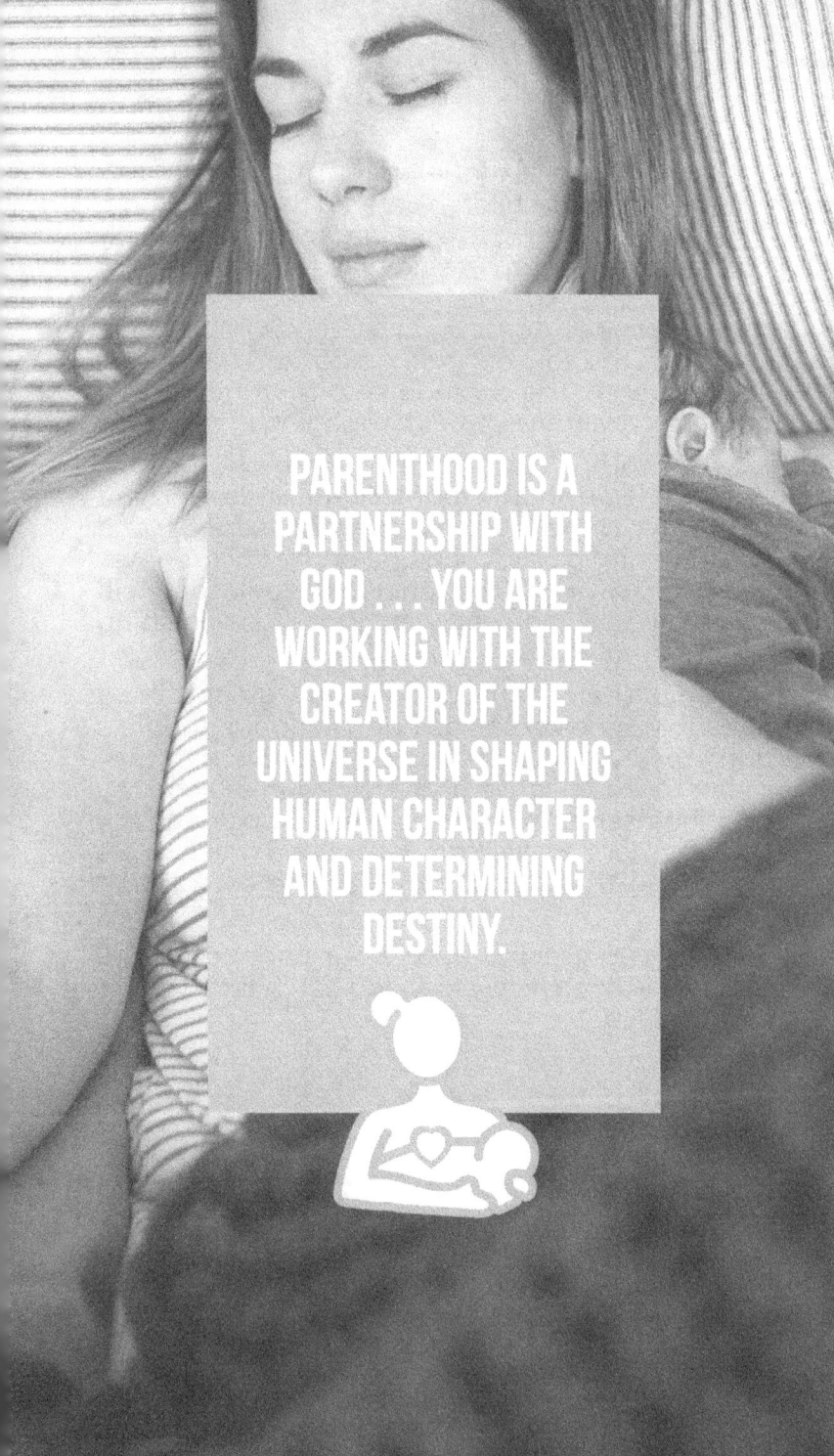

PARENTHOOD IS A PARTNERSHIP WITH GOD . . . YOU ARE WORKING WITH THE CREATOR OF THE UNIVERSE IN SHAPING HUMAN CHARACTER AND DETERMINING DESTINY.

Columnist Abigail Van Buren published a Parent's Prayer in her "Dear Abby" column. It read, in part:

"Oh, heavenly Father, make me a better parent. Teach me to understand my children, to listen patiently to what they have to say, and to answer all their questions kindly. Keep me from interrupting them or contradicting them. Make me as courteous to them as I would have them be to me. Forbid that I should ever laugh at their mistakes, or resort to shame or ridicule when they displease me. May I never punish them for my own selfish satisfaction or to show my power.

"Let me not tempt my child to lie or steal. And guide me hour by hour that I may demonstrate by all I say and do that honesty produces happiness. Reduce, I pray, the meanness in me. And when I am out of sorts, help me, O Lord, to hold my tongue. May I ever be mindful that my children are children and I should not expect of them the judgment of adults.

"Let me not rob them of the opportunity to wait on themselves and to make decisions. Bless me with the bigness to give them all their reasonable requests, and the courage to deny them privileges I know will do them harm . . . And fit me, Oh Lord, to be loved and respected and imitated by my children. Amen."

We are labourers together with God.

1 CORINTHIANS 3:9

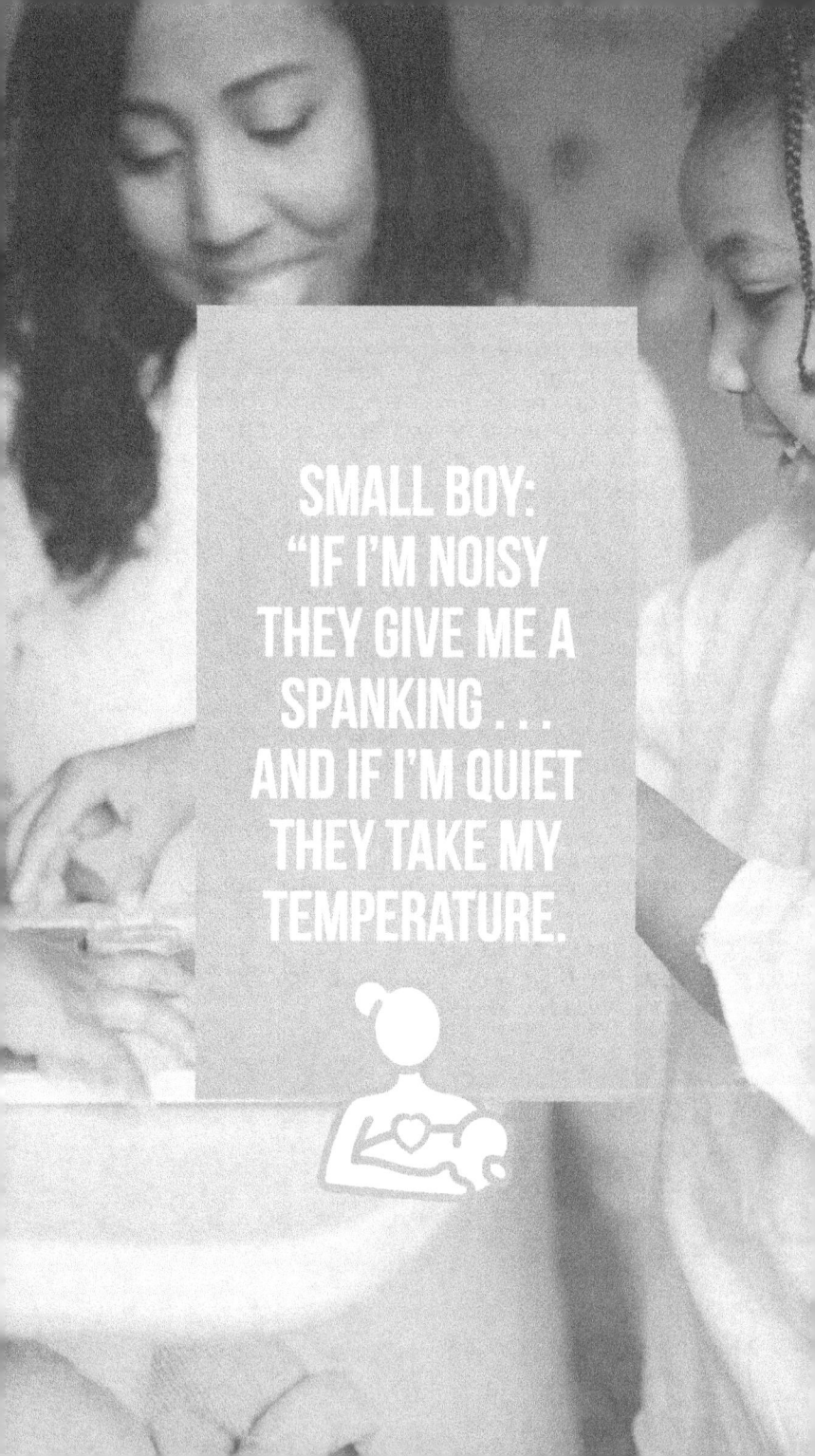

Kais Rayes writes that he and his wife found their whole life turned upside down when their first child was born. Every night, the baby seemed to be fussy, and many nights, it seemed to the young couple that their baby cried far more than he slept. Says Rayes, "My wife would wake me up, saying, 'Get up, honey! Go see why the baby is crying!'" As a result, Rayes found himself suffering from severe sleep deprivation.

While complaining to his co-workers about his problem one day, one of his colleagues suggested a book on infant massage. He immediately went in search of the book and that night, he tried the technique, gently rubbing his baby's back, arms, head, and legs until the baby was completely relaxed and obviously had fallen into a deep sleep. Quietly tiptoeing from the darkened room so as not to disturb the rhythmic breathing of the baby, he made his way directly to his own bed in hopes of enjoying a well-deserved full night of sleep.

But . . . in the middle of the night . . . his wife awoke him in a panic. "Get up, honey!" she said as she jostled him awake. "Go see why the baby is not crying!"

A merry heart doeth good like a medicine.

PROVERBS 17:22

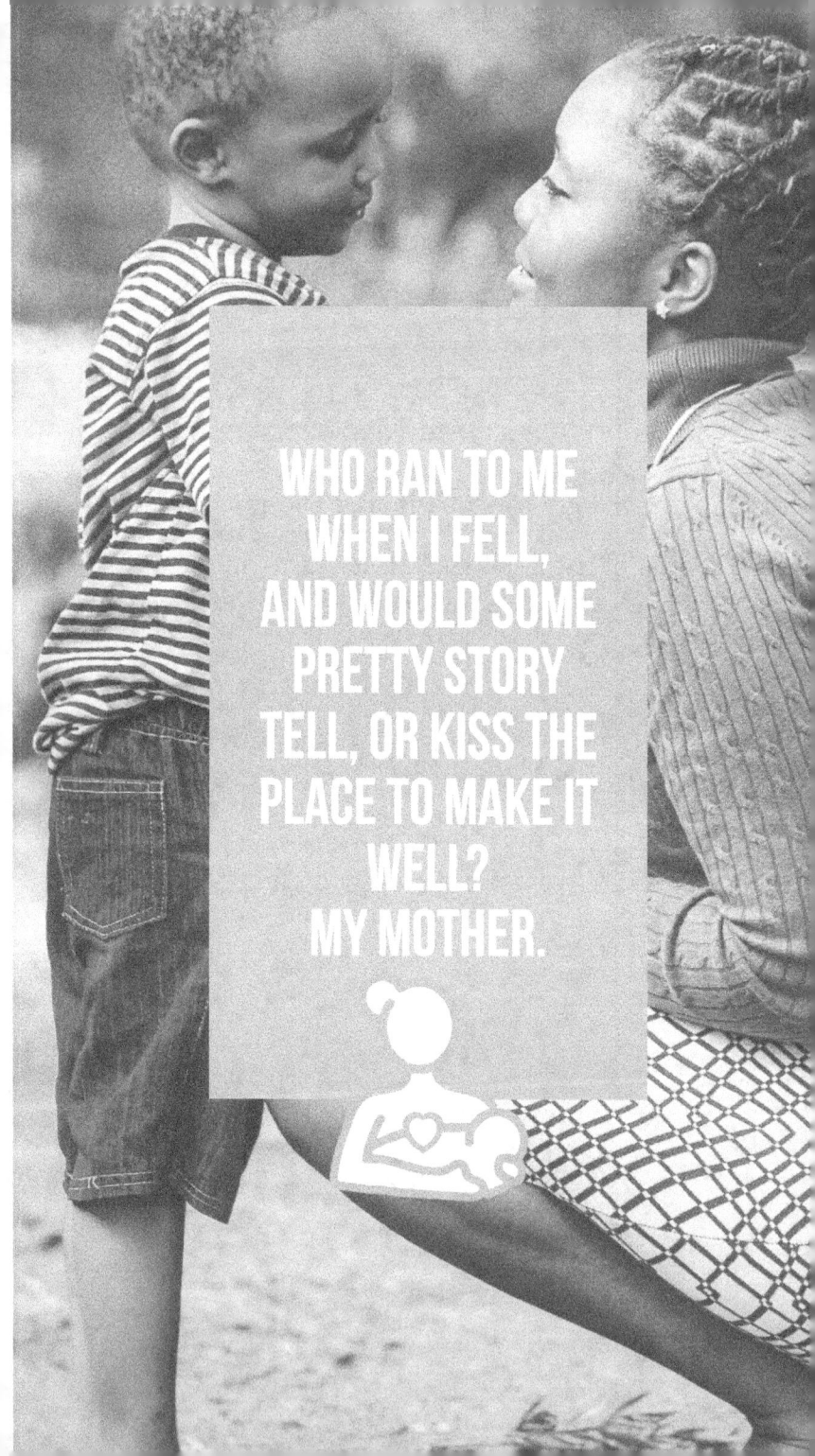

A young girl was very late in coming home from school. Her mother watched the clock nervously and with growing concern. Finally she arrived. Her mother, nearly frantic at that point, hugged her daughter, and after giving her a thorough appraisal and realizing nothing appeared to be wrong, demanded, "Where were you? What took you so long? Haven't I told you to be home by 4 o'clock?"

The girl answered her mother's first question, "I was at Mary's house."

"And what was so important that you couldn't get home on time?" her mother scolded.

Her daughter replied, "Her favorite doll got broken."

"Did you break it?" the mother asked. When her daughter shook her head, she then asked, "Could the doll be fixed?" Again, the girl replied with a "no." Both bewildered and frustrated, the mother asked a third time, "So what was the point of staying so long?"

Tears began to well up in the little girl's eyes and stream down her face under her mother's inquisition. "I helped her cry," she said softly.

The Scriptures tell us to "rejoice with them that do rejoice, and weep with them that weep" (Romans 12:15). Mothers may not be able to do everything for their children, but they all can do that!

As one whom his mother comforters, so
will I comfort you.

ISAIAH 66:13

A mother was at her wit's end. Her baby had screamed all day, nonstop. She knew he was in the throes of teething, but what could she do? She had tried rocking him, giving him pieces of ice, carrying him, and every other remedy suggested by her mother and friends. Nothing had worked. Finally, in great frustration, she laid her child in his crib, took a shower, washed her hair, set it, and went to sit under her hair dryer. She thought, *If I can't stop my baby's crying, at least I can stop myself from bearing his cries.* To her surprise, when she came out from under the hair dryer to get a drink of water, she found her baby asleep. The next day when he began to cry, she turned on the hair dryer and within minutes, he was calm. She discovered the vacuum cleaner also had this effect, as well as the sound of the tumbling dryer. She said, "I got more housework done than I ever dreamed possible, all in an attempt to calm my child."

Sometimes tantrums are the result of overstim-ulation. A child is too tired, surrounded by too many sights and sounds, feeling too many conflicting feelings … and yes, even receiving too much reaction from parents! In removing some of the stimula-tion, a child is given just what he needs: calm.

And every man that striveth for the mastery is temperate in all things.

1 CORINTHIANS 9:25A

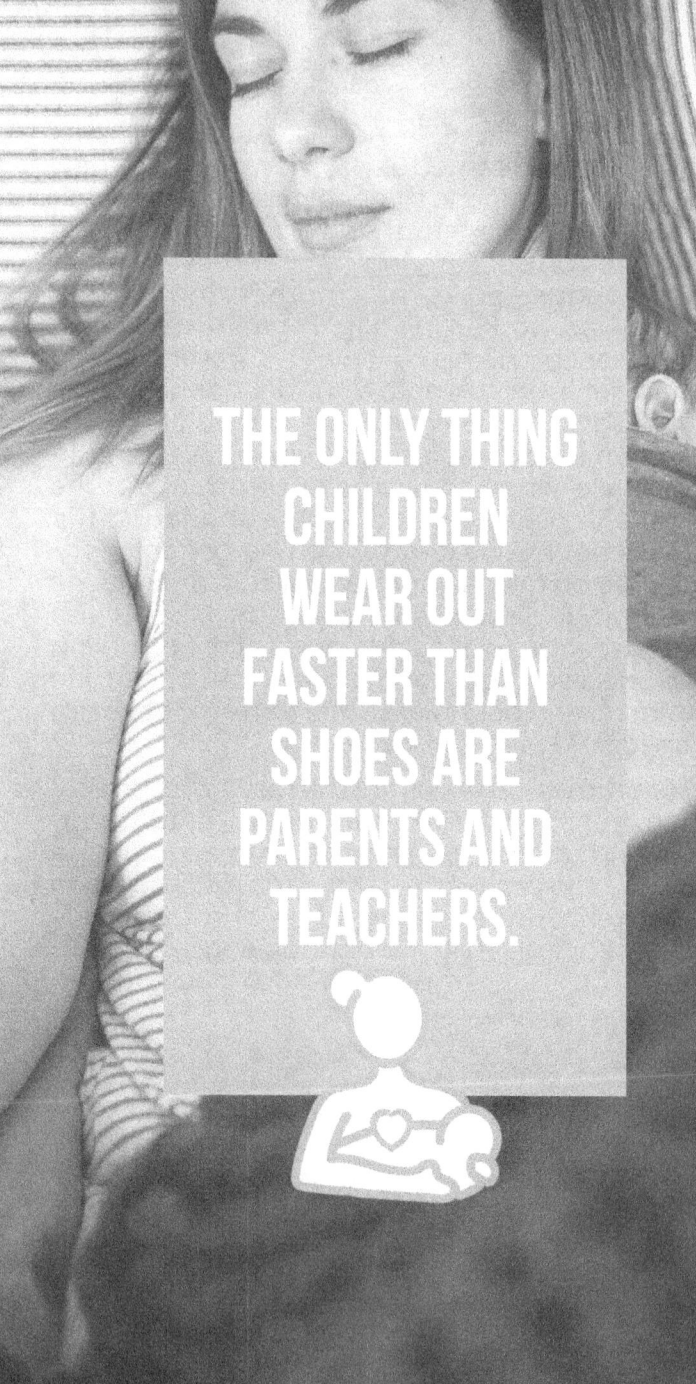

THE ONLY THING CHILDREN WEAR OUT FASTER THAN SHOES ARE PARENTS AND TEACHERS.

In her book *Murphy Must Have Been A Mother*, Teresa Bloomingdale tells about her daughter's preparing for high school. "I don't have anything to wear," the daughter complained.

Mother agreed, "I know that, honey, and I told you we'd go on a shopping spree next Saturday."

"I can't buy clothes now!" the daughter said.

"Why not? School starts next week," asked Mom.

The daughter said, "I can't get clothes for school until I go to school and see what clothes I should get. What if I showed up in jeans and all the other girls were in skirts? I'd die!"

"Then wear a skirt," the mother suggested.

"And find everyone else in jeans?" the daughter asked. When Mom suggested she call a friend and find out what she was going to wear, the daughter said, "Are you kidding? She'd think I don't have a mind of my own!"

Another friend finally called and the two girls decided on their first-day-of-the-year outfits: blue jeans, white knit shirts, white bobby socks, and topsider shoes. The author wrote, "And these are the girls who spent eight years complaining because they had to wear look-alike uniforms!"

He gives power to the tired and worn out, and strength to the weak.

ISAIAH 40:29 TLB

A woman was preparing to leave her child with a babysitter while she joined her husband for the weekend. He had been out of town for several weeks and she was looking forward to their time together, even as she felt a little fear and doubt about leaving her four-year-old daughter. She watched from a window as her daughter churned down the driveway on her tricycle, making a right turn at the tree. Her "driving" over the tree roots, however, ended in the tricycle tipping over. She came running into the house with a wail and lifted her skinned knee for her mother to kiss it.

"Who will kiss my knee while you're away?" her daughter asked, her chin quivering. The mother was about to mention the babysitter when she heard herself saying, "I know! God will do it." Her daughter beamed, well satisfied with that answer, and immediately headed back to her tricycle.

The mother found her answer reviving her own faith, and she left for her weekend feeling much more positive about leaving her daughter in the Heavenly Father's hands!

I prayed for this child, and the Lord has granted me what I asked of him. So now I give him to the Lord. For his whole life he will be given over to the Lord.

1 SAMUEL 1:27-28 NIV

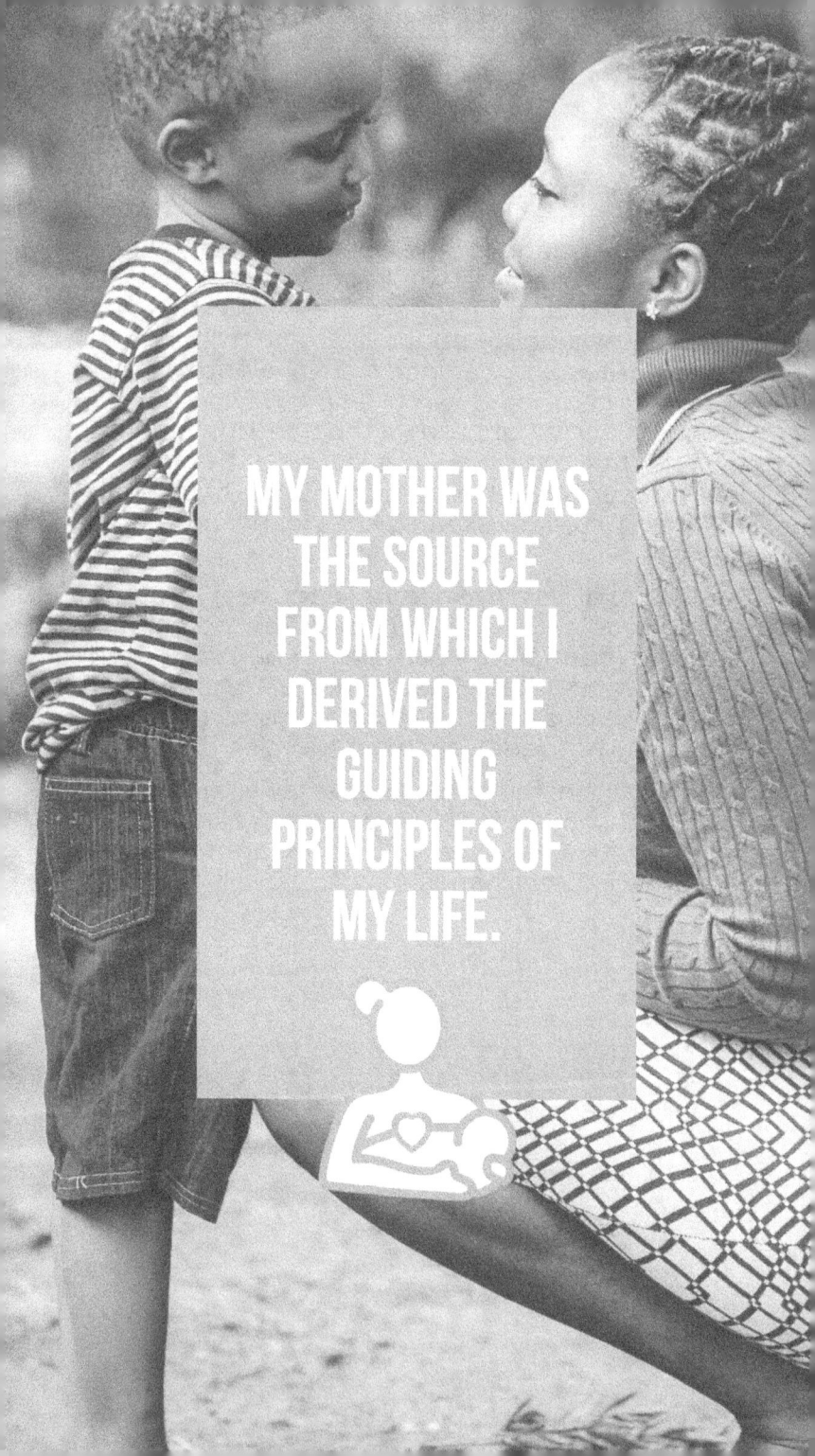

MY MOTHER WAS THE SOURCE FROM WHICH I DERIVED THE GUIDING PRINCIPLES OF MY LIFE.

During a special program at church, a little girl was to recite the Scripture she had been assigned for the occasion. When she got in front of the crowd, however, the sight of hundreds of eyes peering at her caused her to have a bout of stage fright. She completely forgot her verse and was unable to utter a single word.

Her mother, sitting in the front row, leaned forward, and after several attempts, finally got her daughter's attention. She moved her lips and gestured but her daughter didn't seem to comprehend what she was doing. Finally, the mother whispered the opening phrase of the verse she was to recite, "I am the light of the world."

The little girl's face lit up and she smiled with confidence. "My mother is the light of the world!" she announced boldly.

Her words brought a smile to the face of each audience member, of course, and yet upon reflection, most had to admit that she had declared an eloquent truth. A mother is the light of her child's world.

Let your light shine brightly today on your child's behalf!

Be ye followers of me, even as I also am of Christ.

1 CORINTHIANS 11:1

ACKNOWLEDGMENTS

We acknowledge and thank the following people for the quotes used in this book:

C.H. Spurgeon
Ruth Bell Graham
Thomas Fessenden
Madeline Cox
Elbert Hubbard
V. Gilbert Beers
Hazel Scot
Dorothy Law Nolte
A.W. Thorold
Henry Ward Beecher
John A. Shedd
Whately
Penelope Leach
Imogene Fey
James Dobson
Wilferd A. Peterson
Mary Cholmondeley
Earl Riney
Dr. Anthony P. Witham
Lowell
Erma Bombeck
Mary Lamb
Mary Kay Blakely
Jean Hodges

Milwaukee Journal
Sydney J. Harris
George M. Adams
Dorothy Parker
John J. Plomb
Jessamyn West
T.L. Cuyler
Abraham Lincoln
James Russell Lowell
Paul Swets
Charles Meigs
Henry Wadsworth Longfellow
Leo J. Burke
Dorothy Canfield Fisher
Lin Yutang
Henry Home
Franklin Roosevelt
Ed Dussault
Don Herold
Helen Pearson
Lionel M. Kaufman
Joseph Addison
Syrus

Lady Bird Johnson
Raymond Duncan
Shannon Fife
Mildred B. Vermont
Fran Lebowitz
Peter Marshall
Oliver Wendell Holmes
Barbara Bush
C.G. Jung
Anna B. Mow
Lane Olinhouse
Helen Steiner Rice
Dr. William Mitchell
Dr. Charles Paul Conn
G.W.C. Thomas
Pope Paul VI
Katherine Whitehouse
Mary Howitt
James Keller
Renee Jordan
Theresa Ann Hunt
Pablo Picasso
Larry Christenson
Alvin Vander Griend
Leo Tolstoy
Betty Mills
Phyllis Diller
Edwin Hubbel Chapin
Sir P. Sidney
John Lubbock
Anne Tyler
Barbara Johnson

Lisa Alther
Amy Vanderbilt
Peter DeVries
M. MacCracken
Thackeray
Joyce Heinrich
Annette LaPlaca
Joseph Joubert
Terence
T.J. Bach
James Baldwin
Carl Sandburg
Mark Twain
Billy Sunday
Earline Steelburg
St. Basil
David Wilkerson
The Saturday Evening Post
Jacqueline Jackson
John Hay
Charles A. Wells
Mother Teresa
Christian Scriver
Beverly LaHaye
Judity Clabes
Ruth Vaughn
Coronet
Ann Taylor
Dr. J. Kuriansky
John Wesley

Additional copies of this book and other titles in the
God's Little Devotional Book series are available online.

If you have enjoyed this book, or if it has impacted
your life, we would like to hear from you.
Please contact us at:
info@honorbooks.com

Visit www.honorbooks.com for more.

www.ingramcontent.com/pod-product-compliance
Lightning Source LLC
Chambersburg PA
CBHW071139130626
46553CB00004B/1446